Neil Ducoff's
FAST
FORWARD®
SECOND EDITION

The Definitive Guide to Salon, Spa & Medspa Management

D1614668

Published by Strategies
40 Main Street, Suite 7
Centerbrook, Connecticut 06409
www.strategies.com

Co-written by Mara Dresner
Cover design by Eric Ducoff
Page layout by Cameron Taylor
Proofreading by Victoria Kelsey

Book set in Baskerville and DIN

Library of Congress Control Number: 2012949212
Ducoff, Neil
Dresner, Mara.
    FAST FORWARD: The Definitive Guide to Salon, Spa & Medspa
    Management / Neil Ducoff & Mara Dresner. – 2nd ed.
        413p. | 18.4cm.
    ISBN 978-1-932520-11-8
    1. Business Management.   2. Leadership.   3. Entrepreneurship.
    4. Creative Thinking.   I. Title.

Second Strategies Press Edition
10 9 8 7 6 5 4 3
Printed in the United States of America

Neil Ducoff's
FAST FORWARD®
SECOND EDITION

The Definitive Guide to Salon, Spa & Medspa Management

co-written by Mara Dresner

strategies™

LEADERSHIP • PERFORMANCE • GROWTH

CENTERBROOK • CONNECTICUT

This book is dedicated to the
Professional Beauty Industry that
I have served for over 40 years.

Acknowledgements

Fast Forward is the culmination of over 40 years of work in the professional beauty industry. Therefore, it's only fitting to begin by thanking my mother, Esther Ducoff, for suggesting that I become a hairdresser, and my father, Harry Ducoff, for helping me open my first salon in 1973. Although both are gone, they were entrepreneurs and inspired me to turn my visions into reality. Thanks Mom and Dad, I hope I made you proud.

Behind every man is a great lady. For over 42 years, my wife Joanne has supported me through both the good and bad times. Travel is a part of my work and that means countless trips and time spent on the road. As vice president of administration for Strategies, Joanne keeps us all in line, protects our cash and takes care of our customers like no one else.

Eric Ducoff has been vice president of Strategies for over 17 years. Without Eric, Strategies wouldn't have anyone to obsess over our branding, marketing, website and message. Eric may be a "behind the scenes" guy, but you see and experience his work in everything that is Strategies.

Cameron Taylor has been our graphic designer for many years; he's the guy who makes us look great in print and on the web. Next to the writing, Cameron spent more time working on *Fast Forward* than anyone else. Thank you Cameron.

Mara Dresner is the co-author of *Fast Forward*. Mara has been my editor for many years and has mentored me on my writing skills and voice. Mara labored over every word in *Fast Forward* to make sure it delivered on its promise to be a true business resource. Mara, I know we will find new projects to work on together – and I look forward to that day.

Bruce Hourigan is not only the president of Strategies, but also my friend. Bruce championed the publishing of *Fast Forward* Second Edition because he knows the value it will bring to our customers. He made sure this project made it across the finish line.

I want to extend special thanks to Paula Kent Meehan, founder of Redken Laboratories. Paula gave me my first shot at public speaking and teaching business. Paula, you knew the value of teaching leadership and business long before everyone else. Thank you.

Lastly, I want to thank my incredible team of Certified Strategies Coaches that help spread Strategies business systems and methodologies around the world: Daryl Jenkins, Bonnie Conte, Mary Walker, Michael Yost, Lisa (Miss Miss) Cochran, Chris Murphy, Ronit Enos and Kristin Stutz. Each and every one of you makes me proud. It takes a team to carry the Strategies torch.

Contents

Introduction by Neil Ducoff

Growing a salon, spa or medspa today is akin to venturing through a minefield of historically inefficient business practices and beliefs. Times have changed. Yesterday's success strategies seem tired and rusty in today's rapid-fire, change-everything-now business climate.

We wrote *Fast Forward* to offer those in the salon/spa/medspa industry a comprehensive, friendly, useable book. It speaks the language of business in a style that all individuals, from those behind the chair, in the treatment room, behind the desk or in the office, can learn from.

Fast Forward addresses the business issues and problems confronting today's owners, managers, administrators and employees. Readers will discover the kind of exciting, nononsense and easy-to-follow approaches to business growth that Strategies is known for. Most importantly, this book will be a reference to which all industry professionals and business people can turn for fast answers, guidance and insight into today's real-life growth problems.

A little *Fast Forward* history

Work began on the first edition of *Fast Forward* in the fall of 1998. The idea of publishing a business reference book for the salon and spa industry was the brainchild of Nancy Flinn, a friend and one of the industry's most respected marketing consultants. What began with a meeting at Nancy's home in

Weston, Conn., evolved into a 485-page book that owners and managers quickly and passionately dubbed "my business bible."

The first edition of *Fast Forward* was published in the spring of 2000. It contained fifteen chapters on critical topics that touched on every conceivable business hot button that existed at the time. It took two years to complete *Fast Forward*. It was my first book and what a huge project it was. I labored over every aspect of the book, designed each and every page, as well as its cover. (I always hated the cover. It was supposed to be metallic inks of silver and cranberry. It ended up a blah gray and pink.) Nancy Flinn contributed the chapter on industry statistics. Friends and experts Andrew Finkelstein, Matthew Cross and Larry Oskin also contributed to *Fast Forward's* content.

It was personally fulfilling when owners would bring their books to Strategies seminars packed with so many sticky notes marking key pages that the books themselves were falling apart. For me, all of those books laden with sticky notes and dog-eared pages were visual proof that *Fast Forward* was one damn good business reference book.

Complete Rewrite

Although some content became dated over time, *Fast Forward* has remained powerful and relevant for twelve years since it was first published. In all, *Fast Forward* was reprinted three times. In 2010 the decision was made to begin a complete rewrite of *Fast Forward*. Along with my trusted editor, Mara Dresner, we began to identify what portions of the original *Fast Forward* had to go and what was heading for a rewrite. Not one page of the original *Fast Forward* would transition "as is" to the new Second Edition.

Why rewrite perfectly good content? The answer is simple and has everything to do with writing style. *Fast Forward* was my first book. (I'm on book number three now.) I've written volumes of work since 2000. My writing voice and style is more refined. Terminology has changed. Industry segments, such as the medspa, didn't exist when I first wrote *Fast Forward*. More importantly, my expertise and experience has grown. Strategies has grown and evolved, too. (In 2013, Strategies will celebrate 20 years in business.) A complete rewrite of *Fast Forward* was the no-compromise way to publish the Second Edition of a great book.

We pulled the Industry Statistics chapter simply because statistics can become dated by the time the book goes to press. Besides, there are plenty of industry statistics available through the Professional Beauty Association (PBA) at www.probeauty. org. We also pulled the Technology chapter that essentially provided a roadmap to selecting salon/spa software along with a list of the players at the time. It was dated content and we felt that ample resources exist for selecting software in the marketplace and through software providers. What is Strategies' software of choice? Here's a hint: www.harms-software.com. We use Harms software to run Strategies. We also deleted the chapter on Taxes. I'm sure you're OK with that decision.

The one chapter that necessitated a complete rewrite was the Marketing chapter. This little thing called "social media" didn't exist when the first book was written. Social media is a marketing animal unto itself and we wanted to deliver a working understanding of its power in business today.

We added a chapter on Stress Relief that focuses on finding a balance between work and everything else. What we thought was stressful over a decade ago is nothing compared to leading and growing a business today.

Lastly, we added a chapter on Exit Strategy. Unless you plan to live for eternity, you're gong to need a plan to exit your company some day. Too many owners have an exit strategy that sounds like, "Hey, when I die – they'll figure it out." You've worked too many years to trust your exit to luck. It's a good and essential read – and a fitting final chapter to the book.

Business is a voyage

Consider the exuberance and euphoria of opening day – the freshness of your new business with sparkling equipment and furnishings. As the voyage continues, progress is charted, and as the business and the crew mature, the voyage may stop at ports of call along the way.

Some businesses will settle in at certain stages of the voyage. Perhaps they're not physically or financially prepared to continue, or perhaps their initial provisions or leadership skills were inadequate. Perhaps they were unclear on their destination, or simply began questioning their ability to press on. It's easy to drop anchor and put the voyage on indefinite hold. Leadership gives way to abdication. The excitement and vision that once captured the crew's imagination fades – their focus shifts elsewhere, to other voyages offering fresh opportunities. As the business stalls, the grip of complacency tightens. Meanwhile, other brave explorers and competitors press forward to discover new opportunities and rewards.

The lessons of business success are based on a single tenet: Forward progress is not an option. A business cannot rest on its laurels, previous achievements or market status. Author and speaker Tom Peters says, "No longer is it the big eat the small – now the fast eat the slow." Your business is no exception. You must lead and drive your business forward or it will be rendered irrelevant. You must lead change to remain fast.

Shifting into Fast Forward

This book will be your map – a pathway through the fog and confusion of growing a business. It will be a collection of keys to open the doors of productivity, efficiency, performance and profit. You will discover how to raise the anchor that holds you fast to yesterday's achievements at the expense of tomorrow's adventures, opportunities and rewards. (Anchors prevent motion. Where there is no motion, there can be no progress.) *Fast Forward* will be the catalyst to create the energy and self-confidence to break through the chaos and confusion that are the ever-present partners of change and forward progress.

Where and how quickly your business voyage progresses depends on you. The necessary constant is knowledge followed by action. *Fast Forward* is a tool kit to navigating your business to the highest levels of achievement and success. This book covers a lot of ground on many different fronts, tackling old issues with fresh ideas and strategies. You must put it to work. Use it a little and you will make a little progress. Use it a lot and you will travel further and faster than you ever dreamed possible.

We push the envelope of traditional industry business thinking and practices. It's the best of the best.

Exploration and implementation

Your current reality will determine your pace in implementing the concepts and systems presented in *Fast Forward.* Just remember, you cannot do it all at once. As you progress, bookmark pages and sections that rank high on your "fix it" list. When finished, prioritize the list to develop your game plan.

Do you have to implement everything in this book? Of course you don't. *Fast Forward* is a resource guide designed to offer information, strategies and insight on a vast array of business issues. Use what you need. However, don't just gravitate to topics or strategies that get you excited. Put effort into topics and strategies that push you out of your comfort zone. For example, getting into numbers, financial reports and cash-flow planning may not be your thing – but they certainly are non-negotiable essentials to generating profit and financial success.

Think outside the box

I have always been entrepreneurial, and the inner workings of business persist as a constant source of intrigue for me. I grew up in my parents' dry cleaning business and have been involved in service-based businesses ever since. After college, I explored the opportunities in the beauty salon business and, in 1970, entered Franklin Beauty School. There was never a doubt that I would own a salon. I opened my first in 1973 and a second in 1975.

Those were great times, driven by the precision haircutting boom and the energy of the post-war baby boom generation. Salon retailing also came of age. In those days, if your salon offered great haircuts and styling, you made money. And in most cases, you should have. Rent and overhead expenses were incredibly low compared to today's costs of doing business. There was plenty of margin for error. We were having a ton of fun leading the charge and riding the crest of change.

But change is relentless. Read and explore this book as a forward thinker. Don't lock yourself into "what is" while unlimited opportunities are waiting to be seized. Don't hesitate. Don't fear the natural progression of business change. Shift your business thinking into fast forward. Absorb the knowledge, data and systems contained in these pages. Challenge yourself. Take your business, and your team, to that next level of success – both professionally and personally.

Now it's time to cast off the dock lines, and begin your business voyage.

Strategies is here to help you along the way.

About the authors

 During the last 40 years, **Neil Ducoff** has coached thousands of businesses, including Aveda, Gillette, Proctor & Gamble, Unilever, TIGI Haircare, Canmeng International Taiwan, Mana Products, Kerastase Paris, EvelineCharles Canada and L'Oreal, on how to achieve the highest levels of success and profitability by creating dynamic, no-compromise, company cultures. He has led countless seminars throughout North America, the United Kingdom, Taiwan, China, Spain and Mexico – as well as served as a presenter at major healthcare, computer, manufacturing and franchise conferences, including Jack Stack's National Gathering of Games, the 2011 Quality Conference, the inaugural Esthetics China Exhibition and Congress, and the 2012 Business Innovation Conference.

Neil is the founder and CEO of Strategies, the premier training and coaching company for small to medium sized businesses that he founded in 1993. Based in Centerbrook, Conn., Strategies' cutting-edge curriculum of business courses is led by a national network of certified coaches that have completed a rigorous training program.

Neil has gained international respect as the guru of team-based compensation. As well as the award-winning *No-Compromise Leadership: A Higher Standard of Leadership Thinking and Behavior,* he is the author of *Fast Forward,* the salon and spa industry's definitive business reference manual. His new book, *Wake Up!,* is a collection of powerful strategies that delivers the "wake up" that every leader needs in these crazy times.

Neil has been published in *The Journal of the American Management Association*. He has been honored with the 2005 Art of Business Award, named one of 12 business "Legends and Icons" by the annual Serious Business Conference in New Orleans in 2006, and invited by the B.E.S.T Foundation and the Anderson School of Business at UCLA to serve as a judge for both the 2006 and 2008 Global Salon Business Awards.

Mara Dresner is the author of *Super-Charge Your Staff Meetings: 52 ways to create fun, meaningful, memorable meetings that your employees will love,* a Grand Award winner from the 2012 Awards for Publication Excellence (APEX).

Mara's plays have been produced by theaters across the country, including the American Theatre of Actors in New York City; DeVry University in Illinois; Muscatine Country Arts Council in Iowa; Center Stage Players in West Virginia; Evansville (Wisc.) High School; and the Theatre Guild of Simsbury and Windsor Jesters in Connecticut. Her farce *An Impeccable Larceny* is published by Samuel French (www.samuelfrench.com). She is a member of the Dramatists Guild.

She has voiced countless radio commercials and corporate projects (including the Strategies voicemail system!) and has appeared in a number of commercials and films. An award-winning journalist, she teaches acting, public speaking and creative writing in adult education programs.

"Last night we had our pretax year-end meeting with our accountant, and received the amazing news that we had a 15% profit this year, versus 0% profit last year! And, we had 100% growth! The growth is proof positive – Strategies principles are the fundamental keys that turned this business around."

Rachel Aidan
Aidan James Salon
Nashua, N.H.

"In recent years the professional beauty industry has filled up with myriad salon/spa business 'experts' and coaches. Most bring 'bubble-up' enthusiasm to the salon/spa that quickly dissipates back to 'business as usual' with no noticeable improvements. Long-term change is Strategies' goal, and their track record of successful clients speaks for itself."

Alexander Irving
Esche & Alexander Public Relations
Oceanside, Calif.

"Neil Ducoff and his Strategies team do more than give your business a facelift; they give your business a complete makeover. That makeover includes behavior modification for management: Neil's voice becomes that of your conscience to practice no-compromise leadership. At times, that conscience feels like a boot in your butt. But stepping-up your game – even if it's with a push – is most rewarding."

Carolyn Severo
Radiance Salon & Medi-Spa
Ashburn & Leesburg, Va.

CHAPTER ONE

Leadership

No compromise is the only way to succeed.

*No compromise is the only
way to succeed.*

Leadership

S hakespeare once said, "Uneasy lies the head that wears a crown." Centuries later, it's still true. Being the leader is hard work. It's fun to be at the top of the heap in good times. Not so much when you're inundated with dozens of difficult choices.

Whether your company flourishes is squarely on your shoulders. Each action you take, every word you choose, the e-mails you send ripple throughout your organization. Yes, even on the day you stormed through your business because you got a parking ticket or there was a long line at the post office. Your staff may interpret that as trouble brewing in your business. If you don't greet your staff members as you walk by them, they may view that as your being displeased with their performance, rather than your being preoccupied with a meeting with a vendor. Or, if you dismiss a staff member's idea, she or he may believe that you are not open to input, when the reality is you're worried about a tax audit.

Your leadership team also takes its cues from you. They hear what you say, but like your front-line employees, they watch what you do – and how you do it. Everything you say and do is on the line for interpretation, evaluation and conclusion. And you may be sending a very different message than the one you think you are!

Strong leadership is the very essence of what it takes to move a business forward. Leaders help provide the mission, vision, values, objectives, standards and motivation to keep employees on task and working toward common goals. You may have a large staff or management team; you may just have a few people. The need for effective leadership is the same. That is, if you're serious about growing your business.

At Strategies, we call it "no-compromise leadership." It's not about being dictatorial and inflexible. Rather it's taking responsibility for the work that needs to be done and making sure that it gets done, every time, no matter what the task.

It's about not blaming or justifying. It's about being account-able – to your staff, your business, your customers and yourself. It's nothing short of a paradigm shift – and the results, when you stay the course, are remarkable. (For a detailed look at no-compromise leadership, including a game plan for implementation, check out Neil Ducoff's award-winning book, *No-Compromise Leadership: A Higher Standard of Leadership Thinking and Behavior.*)

Leadership 101

Leadership is hard work. Many people believe that if they have technical skills, leading the company will take care of itself. That couldn't be further from the truth! It's challenging, complicated work to be a leader. You need to be on your game all the time. You need to be an expert communicator, able to quickly adapt to changing circumstances, and have the ability to guide the people who trust you with their livelihoods into greater levels of achievement, all while taking care of day-to-day issues and planning for the long term.

Leadership starts in your head. Leaders – whether owners, managers or supervisors – must change their thinking to be effective. It's not enough to delegate; ultimately the company's success is in your hands. If a project fails or a sales goal isn't reached, you must evaluate your own participation and communication. Leaders who do well continually evaluate their own performances to see how they may improve what they do. This benefits your whole team, clients, vendors, and the business as a whole.

Leadership is about change. It's easier to keep the same old, same old than to bravely alter seemingly tried-and-true measures. In a highly competitive business environment, stagnation can equal death. Services must be added, retail kept fresh, customer experiences ever tweaked. If you're not moving forward, you're slipping back. Even in difficult economies, some businesses manage to thrive. When you examine these cases, you find leaders who are willing to let go of yesterday's ways of doing things. We live in a fast society; change is constant. Accept it. Leaders don't let their businesses get left behind.

You may by default have the title of owner or manager. That's not the same as being a leader. Titles are given; leadership is earned. Leadership is earned by actions. People may report to someone who has a title; they will follow someone who is a leader. Leader is not a default position. Leaders must work to gain respect; they earn authority by what they do. And it's a never-ending task.

Lack of leadership doesn't cause a vacuum; it causes chaos. In the absence of strong leadership, your business will spiral into disarray. If you have an extraordinary staff, it may not be obvious for a while. When an employee uprising is in the works, it's usually the result of poor leadership. When clients don't receive the level of service you'd like, check your leadership. When any process doesn't feel right, look in the mirror. You can't expect your staff to know where you want your business to go if you don't lead them.

Leadership is at the root of your company's culture. If you're not stepping up, don't expect your staff to. If you bend the rules, don't expect your staff to follow them. If you don't acknowledge great performances, don't expect them to continue. If you don't put your best self forth every day, don't expect your staff to go above and beyond. Culture is made up of small deeds and attitudes. It starts with leadership. Always.

Manager or leader?

It's possible to be both. It's crucial to understand the difference. In broad terms, managers "manage" resources or things, such as supplies and bills. Leaders, by definition, lead people. It may sound simple in theory, but it's an ongoing responsibility informed by the countless decisions you make every day. If your staff isn't on board with your goals for the company, then whom are you really leading?

Leaders:

- put themselves on the line.
- are willing to take well thought-out risks.
- commit to excellence.
- empower their followers.
- are not intimidated by the skills of others.
- encourage greatness.
- take responsibility for their actions.
- make tough decisions.
- motivate and reward their team members.
- continue their education.
- aren't afraid to say "no."
- aren't afraid to say "yes."

Do you have what it takes?

People become leaders when they demonstrate a strength, or combination of strengths, that attracts followers. One may be physically strong or knowledgeable or charismatic. Strength may emanate from an inner conviction or set of values. Strength may arise from a fully formed vision or the germ of an idea.

An effective leader:

• is flexible rather than rigid.

• is aware of the variables in any situation.

• knows his or her hot-button issues and works to control his or her response.

• is open to hearing other opinions.

• trusts his or her followers and gives them room to grow.

• lets their followers know their influence on a given issue and how leadership authority will be exercised.

• makes certain that expectations are clear and that staff has the necessary knowledge and skills to succeed.

• is quick to praise and isn't afraid to share credit.

Five typical leadership styles

There are five basic categories of how leaders make decisions. There are times when any of these will be effective; some are more empowering than others. The more you involve your staff, as a rule, the more invested they will feel in the process and desired outcomes. It's good to review these style descriptions from time to time to ensure that you are leading as effectively as possible in any given situation.

1. **Telling:** The leader identifies the problem, considers solutions, chooses one, and tells the followers what to do.

2. **Persuading:** Once again, the leader identifies the problem, considers solutions and chooses one. This time, instead of just announcing it, the leader tries to convince staff to accept it.

3. **Consulting:** The leader allows staff the opportunity to influence the decision by suggesting solutions. The leader then selects the most appropriate.

4. **Joining:** The leader participates as any other member of the team, and agrees to abide by the group's decision.

5. **Delegating:** The leader defines a problem and the boundaries within which it must be solved, then turns it over to the team (or selected staff members) and agrees to support their decision if it is within the stated boundaries.

Not every style is appropriate in every situation. In case of fire, for example, there would be no need (and detriment) to consult each team member before helping people safely exit the building! The trick is to find the best style for any situation.

Consider the following when choosing a style for any given situation. (These will become second nature and won't need a detailed analysis for each situation.)

1. **The leader:** Think about your values, your confidence in your team, how well you've communicated goals, and your personality.

2. **Your team:** Think about their knowledge and experience, their readiness for responsibility, and their understanding of the company values, vision and mission. Also consider who on the team is right for the decision. Not every decision requires input from the entire team.

3. **The situation:** Think about the nature of the problem, time constraints, precedent and who is best trained to deal with this type of issue.

A leader must take responsibility for the work of others, and learn to guide and coach rather than issue orders. This means giving up control and trusting. Know that even the best players on your team will stumble from time to time. After all, no one hits a home run every time at bat. You must learn to be supportive and then, trust all over again. That's part of being a no-compromise leader.

No-compromise leaders are:

• Objective and have no prejudice or bias concerning people or projects. They insist on the truth.

• Sensitive and able to understand their team's needs and fears. They make the welfare of the organization a top priority.

• Fair, yet willing to do unpopular or unpleasant things.

- Consistent. They apply the same rules to everyone and communicate a consistent message.
- Humble, preferably with the ability to laugh at oneself.
- Steady and calm under fire.
- Supportive of staff with a belief in their talents and abilities.
- Able to easily forgive missteps and able to look at mistakes as learning opportunities.

They have:

- the vision to spell out clearly what they will do for those who depend on them.
- the drive to share that vision with those who have a stake in the company's success.
- the courage to challenge status quo, stimulate change and make decisions to move the business forward.
- the ability to inspire people to action, individually and in teams, to achieve goals.
- the foresight to empower people to learn new skills and stretch their capabilities.
- the wisdom to listen and learn, and translate that knowledge into tangible results.
- the integrity to serve as a good example through actions that consistently reinforce basic values.
- the willingness to recognize accomplishments, and celebrate both individual and team successes as well as contributions.

Empowering your staff is good leadership

No-compromise leaders know that they can't do everything themselves. More than that, they understand that they aren't the best person to accomplish every task. No-compromise leaders assemble the best teams possible, make sure that everyone understands the goals, and then have the trust to let go.

Letting go is a key element of effective leadership, and can be one of the hardest things to do. If you want your business to grow, you must loosen your hold on tasks and trust your players.

When you are able to do so, the sum will truly be greater than any of the individual parts. Everyone contributes to the design and improvement of business systems. Help your staff to have a whole-systems view of the business. All team members need to understand their roles in the growth process, in order to best serve the company's goals.

Leadership's role is to nurture and strengthen the salon, spa or medspa culture by keeping it focused and responsive to change. It's a concept that most leaders agree on – in theory. Two common traps often defeat the practice of that concept in the day-to-day world.

Trap #1: Good intentions, no follow-through.
Leaders will often say that they want the team to step up and develop systems and strategies to help the company grow. The reality is cloudier. If a leader is used to making all decisions, he or she may have difficulty not micro-managing. If staff members are used to not having their opinions and suggestions

considered, they may be leery of putting themselves out there for fear of rejection.

It takes a highly evolved leader (yes, a no-compromise leader) to contemplate and put into practice ideas that they personally didn't come up with. It takes a great deal of trust on both sides, and that confidence isn't developed overnight. Don't default back to your "take control" methods. Give team members a chance to come up with solutions. Give them another chance. Repeat your commitment to not wanting to micro-manage. It's a process.

Trap #2: Sudden control.

Trap #2 is the opposite of the first trap. If you've relied on chance to run your business and are now trying to go "no compromise," you may have pushback from employees. When staff has just been doing their own things, putting systems in place is going to be a challenge. Be patient and consistent. When your staff see that you are serious about this new reality and how it benefits them and the company, they will come around. Don't change everything at once. At every stage, communicate the reasoning and expectations fully.

Don't back down when the going gets tough; otherwise you're reinforcing the opinion that it's just another half-baked idea and they were right not to bother getting onboard.

Culture shifts take time

Changing your leadership style in hopes of having a no-compromise business is a game changer. In his book *No-Compromise*

Leadership: A Higher Standard of Leadership Thinking and Behavior, Neil Ducoff advises that a leader allows a full 18 months to achieve a culture shift. That may sound like a long time; however, to fully integrate every aspect involved, it does take a year and a half. This doesn't mean that you shouldn't take incremental steps to achieve the culture that you (and your employees) want and need. Far from it!

1. Develop an operations manual. You'll find it an invaluable playbook.
2. Surveying your employees will help pinpoint holes in your culture.
3. Know thyself. Be aware of your leadership style, strengths and weaknesses. Use your leadership team to fill in the gaps.

In fact, it's important to the culture shift to have defined goals along the way. Map out specific objectives and make it easy to achieve wins. Include plenty of positive feedback for staff. While the first 90 days are critical to your culture change, in some ways, launching the shift is the easy part.

Sticking with it after the initial excitement calms down is the mark of the true no-compromise leader. Don't quit when your staff tries to slip back into old habits. Don't quit when you start backsliding.

Make adjustments, as needed, but make it clear that the standards have changed. Keep communicating and what was once considered a major overhaul will simply become the standard of doing business.

The temptation to charge ahead in reengineering is hard to resist, but doing so without a well-conceived plan can stir up resistance, fear and even sabotage of new programs. Change needs a plan to give it direction. Change needs to come by "baby steps." Change is a long-term process.

Use these three rules as your guide – refer to them often during your reengineering process:

Reengineering Rule #1

You cannot reengineer halfway. No one person, group or system can be excluded. You must be prepared to go all the way – or don't reengineer at all.

Reengineering Rule #2

Don't expect new behaviors and team performance if your pay program still rewards the old behaviors and performance you're trying to change. (Check out the chapter on compensation for an in-depth look.)

Reengineering Rule #3

Relentlessly communicate the new vision of the business and its new culture, values, systems and pay program. The starting point for business success is a well-designed processes.

To successfully lead your company through a reengineering process, you must understand the "why," the new terminology and thought processes that inform your shift. And you must be able to share that "why" with your staff.

There are many factors in play, but it all comes down to one basic concept: What worked yesterday, won't work today.

Here's why:

Yesterday you built stars.
Today you build teams.

Yesterday you encouraged staff to build followings.
Today you build business clients.

Yesterday you tracked request rates.
Today you track client-retention rates.

Yesterday you based pay solely on sales.
Today you base pay on overall performance.

Yesterday staff were responsible for their own "book."
Today everyone is responsible for every hour the business has available for sale.

Yesterday commissions inspired individual growth.
Today team-based incentives inspire team growth.

Yesterday followings limited client access.
Today clients are serviced by the skills of the entire team.

Yesterday waiting lists were a status symbol.
Today waiting lists symbolize gridlock and inefficiency.

Yesterday staff income stalled when their "book" was full.
Today team-based pay offers continued income growth.

Yesterday staff saw their income security in their followings.
Today they see their income security in the business.

Yesterday staff walk-outs were commonplace.
Today, with new business thinking, they are not.

Forming a leadership team

In almost every sport, assistant coaches (and often niche coaches, such as the batting coach), support the head coach. Beyond that, there's usually a team captain as well. It's no different in business. Even the most accomplished owner cannot – and should not – bear the pressures of leadership alone.

The size of your leadership team should reflect the size of your business. A general manager can take some of the day-to-day operational tasks off your plate. A front-desk coordinator can zero in on the guest-services area. Department heads can help with training.

You'll know when you need to start or expand a leadership team if you exhibit signs of the following:

1. **Feeling overworked or overwhelmed.** At many salons, spas and medspas, the owner is responsible for every operational aspect of the business. Others may assist with tasks, but the owner is the point person for marketing, human resources, financial functions, etc. When you are overburdened with responsibilities, it is time to develop a management team and truly let go of some tasks. Make sure your managers are aware of the goals and broad parameters (such as money or time), then step away and trust the person to get the job done. Delegation is the key to making any organization work properly.

2. **Inefficiency and poor performance.** Poor performance is usually the result of poor leadership design. If

you are frustrated, the staff is unmotivated and the business is stalled, it's time to restructure your management and leadership strategy. Is anyone responsible for overseeing growth? Productivity? Morale? Take a look at this new-style organization chart that Neil Ducoff developed. While you may not be ready to completely ditch the traditional organizational chart, think about who is responsible for each of the business outcomes and drivers. If the answer is you, you need to reassess.

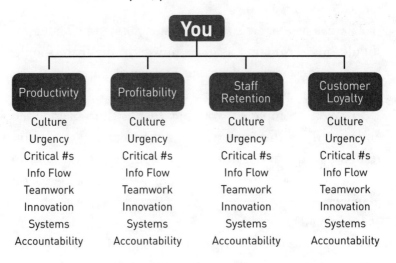

You			
Productivity	Profitability	Staff Retention	Customer Loyalty
Culture	Culture	Culture	Culture
Urgency	Urgency	Urgency	Urgency
Critical #s	Critical #s	Critical #s	Critical #s
Info Flow	Info Flow	Info Flow	Info Flow
Teamwork	Teamwork	Teamwork	Teamwork
Innovation	Innovation	Innovation	Innovation
Systems	Systems	Systems	Systems
Accountability	Accountability	Accountability	Accountability

3. **Lack of clarity, purpose and direction.** If no one on the team knows what anyone else is doing, you must make adjustments. Some projects probably have multiple leaders; others have fallen by the wayside. Clearly articulate who is responsible for what. Otherwise, staff will continue

to bypass any managers to get your approval, while other projects will just be uncompleted.

Choose your team carefully. After all, they are your voice and will help guide the staff to achieve the goals you've set. It's not enough to say, "Sally's been here a long time. I think I'll make her a manager." It takes a different skill set to be a leader, as you well know. Your managers must be able and willing to make decisions (even if they are unpopular), as well as lead the team in your stead.

There is no correct size for a leadership team. Though it should not be so large as to be unwieldy, the team should include representatives from each service department. Each department must have a voice.

In smaller companies, you may even wish to include the entire staff on the leadership team, making each person responsible for various tasks. Larger companies may need to hire dedicated staff for the leadership team, such as a general manager.

Creating a leadership team is simply a form of delegation. The purpose is to persuade everyone on staff to take ownership in the salon, spa or medspa. When everyone feels the same sense of urgency as the owner, the business will take on a life of its own. Though growth is never effortless, it can be made relatively painless through shared responsibility and accountability. Providing an outlet for voicing opinions will provoke ideas and growth strategies from the people you might least expect to hear from.

Structure is a critical component. Each member of the team must know who is accountable for what and where the boundaries are drawn. Those with leadership roles must be provided with the tools and freedom to accomplish the tasks they are charged with.

A cohesive leadership team is integral to the company's stability. Members of the leadership team should be able to relate well to other staff members and command their respect.

They should:

- understand and embody your company's vision and mission, and strive to attain its stated goals.

- be talented in their arena – be it technical, managerial, financial, etc. They should be able and willing to instruct others.

- be authoritative, but not dictatorial. Coercion and strong-arm tactics are a sure way to spread dissension.

- be able to represent the business and promote its interests during staff meetings and events.

- be flexible. Rules and systems are critical for maintaining stability, but so is the willingness to bend them occasionally.

Your salon, spa or medspa needs an effective management structure with specific duties delineated for every layer of responsibility. Team members need to know who to go to when they have questions, who will be evaluating their performances, who decides scheduling, and so on.

No matter what style you choose for your org. chart, the clearer the lines of responsibility, the smoother it will be for

MUST DO!

1. Communicate constantly, including daily huddles.
2. Post the score. Use scoreboards to keep your team updated on goals.
3. Use the Four Business Outcomes and the Big Eight Drivers, as described in this chapter, as the focal point for every action.

the business to operate. When it's not clear who's in charge of what, it's all too simple for things to fall through the cracks.

Owners often give leadership positions to the most senior staff members. While it seems as though it makes sense, that could be a mistake. Just because someone is skilled at providing specific services doesn't mean that they'll be good at – or like – being a manager or department head.

Start by making a list of the tasks that you might want a new manager or department head to assume. Think about interactions between staff members and personalities. Get this on paper before you even begin to match up people with positions.

You may have to think about hiring people to get the best mix of skills and personality. Obviously, smaller companies will have fewer positions. Make sure that the positions are neither too broad nor too narrow. Think about what makes sense for your salon, spa or medspa, not what has worked in other companies. This is your best chance to "get it right" for your business.

If you are creating new positions, make sure that your cash flow will support additional staff or promotions for current staff. Create job descriptions for any new roles so there won't be any question about whether or not a task is a manager's responsibility.

Build your leadership team with care. This is not a decision to rush into, even if a current manager or department head gives notice. Better to be without a manager for a while than to appoint someone to the position without sufficient thought and then have to deal with replacing that person. Have team members wear multiple hats when necessary until the best candidates are secured. You may even discover that someone who is already in your organization is ready to step up and take a larger role.

Mentoring is part of leadership

A mentor is a trusted counselor or guide, an experienced individual who knows the ropes and is charged with the responsibility of transferring that knowledge to another. Mentoring in a business setting is an integral part of the human-resource development process. It's a great way to develop potential in different areas of your company so that there are always staff members who are up to speed and ready to take on more responsibility.

You should regularly be identifying employees in each department who you think have greater potential beyond their current roles. Start mentoring these employees for possible leadership opportunities down the road. Mentees can be helpful during vacations and busy times. By offering this kind of relationship, you are adding to their skills and growth potential while gaining their insight and knowledge.

You may also consider assigning a mentor to each new hire. This will help the new employee get up to speed, as well as helping the mentor to develop new skills and test his or her leadership potential. It is often useful for a new hire to have a "point person" for questions and clarifications.

You may wish to offer a "mentor the mentor" program where key employees are trained in how to best mentor new hires. This provides growth for current staff, as well as ensuring that new employees receive proper training throughout the company. You may also want to link up current employees with mentors. It's a great way for staff to learn new skills and the cross training will be useful during busy times.

Deciding who's ready

Naturally, team members must meet specific performance standards to qualify to be a mentor. It shouldn't be based on just one criteria. Temperament plays as big a part in a rewarding mentor experience as does skill.

Qualifications may include:

- years of service.
- advanced education.
- experience as a trainer.
- skill level in specific technical disciplines.
- personal performance accomplishments.
- professionalism.
- patience and positive demeanor.
- leadership skill, ability and experience.

- communication skills.
- client-retention rates.
- productivity rates.
- average tickets.
- retail sales.
- consultation skills.
- ability to follow through on tasks and projects.
- time-management skills.
- organization skills.
- respect of peers.
- willingness and desire to help others.

Moving into full-time leadership

Most owners get into the beauty industry because they love the technical side. They fall into the leadership and managerial parts seemingly by accident, even considering them a "necessary evil" to keep doing the work they love.

The decision to stop being a service provider is not one to make easily. Your business may need a full-time administrator, but it doesn't necessarily need to be you. However, it is often the logical "next step" on your leadership path.

It's not a decision to just let happen. It's not something you can implement on a whim. The first step is to take measure of where you are and where you want to go.

Think about the following:

• Why are you still on the service floor or in the treatment rooms?

• Will the company's culture allow you to be a full-time leader?

• Are you comfortable in delegating operational responsibilities?

• Is there a system in place to communicate the company's performance and financial goals to the leadership team and the entire staff?

• Do you have the temperament to be a full-time leader?

• Is there an established leadership team in place with strongly delineated responsibilities?

• What are the financial ramifications to the company if you are no longer a service provider? How will this affect your company's profitability? Can you still get paid what you earned as a service provider?

• How efficiently can you manage your time?

• How developed are your financial skills?

It's a lot to think about! For working owners, full-time leadership is an entirely new career. It's a position that will call upon a host of what may be unproven leadership, management and administrative skills.

Too often, this all-important career shift is more spontaneous than planned. Even when time as a service provider is trimmed over a period of time, the lack of a well-conceived plan will doom the effort and lead to enormous deficiencies in terms of time and money. Many owners, with the best of intentions, turn into inefficient office phantoms who are bogged down in paperwork and other mundane projects that should be delegated. They end up drowning in "busy work."

Get focused

Why do you really want to stop being a service provider? What do you want to accomplish? What is your strategic objective? What is your plan? Are you really ready for full-time leadership? Will you miss the creative side?

You must be able to satisfactorily answer these questions before taking the leap to full-time leadership. If you are already a full-time leader, you may want to revisit these questions from time to time to make sure that you and your business are on track. There are no universally right answers.

For the owner who provides services, nothing is usually more frustrating than keeping pace with the bombardment of activities that go on around you. Is Kathy late again? Will UPS arrive in time with what your colorist needs for Mrs. Smith? It's payday tomorrow and the checking account balance is looking rather skimpy. Your front-desk staff is stressed out because your old software program can no longer keep pace with client check-ins, cash-outs and the volume of phone appointments. You forgot that a new technician starts tomorrow, and so you're booked with appointments all day.

Does this sound like your typical workday? If so, take heart; you're not alone. A salon/spa/medspa is an extremely complex and dynamic business. Managing your employees can feel like a full-time job. Add in planning for growth, marketing and financial responsibilities, and your stress level is probably rising. Throw in a full schedule as a service provider and something has to give.

There's too much on your plate. The balls are beginning to drop. Perhaps it's time to reassess your role. Keep answering questions.

• What gives you satisfaction?

• What aspects of ownership do you avoid?

• What price does this conscious avoidance cost the business in terms of stability, profitability, productivity and growth?

Getting your leadership team in place prior to becoming a full-time leader will help you make a reasoned choice. Knowing that you have a mentoring program up and running will give you a measure of peace of mind.

Many owners balance both being a service provider and an administrator. No-compromise leaders know when it is time to transition into a full-time leadership position. Don't rush the decision, but don't avoid it either. When you decide it's time, develop an implementation plan and keep the lines of communication fully open.

What's the procedure?

It may not seem that way at first, but your operations manual is a leadership tool. A complete manual will aid both your leadership team and front-line employees. (It's a must if you're thinking about becoming a full-time leader.)

An operations manual can be a different tool than the policies and procedures manual. Think of the policies and procedures manual as an overall guide for staff. It should have basic information, such as what the procedure is when someone needs to call in sick, how the company handles jury duty and which holidays the business is closed. It is a nuts-and-bolts guide to company policies that affect the staff as a whole.

The operations manual, on the other hand, is the how-to for the entire business. You should be able to hand the book over to your leadership team or BFF and know that the business will run as it should, from turning off the alarm system first thing in the morning to locking the door at night. Every policy, procedure, philosophy and how-to should be included in the operations manual. This will ensure that the business runs as you want it to, regardless of whether or not you're on the premises.

A manual takes all the guesswork out. There can't be any argument about the proper way to do things when it's all spelled out clearly.

If you don't have an operations manual, it may seem daunting to start one. Like skill certification, you won't develop that manual in one sitting. Don't even try!

Begin by breaking down what goes into running the business, starting with turning your key in the lock in the morning. Call upon employees in every department (managers and front-line staff) to write down how they do things. This process may reveal holes in your procedures. Correct them, document them in your new manual, and train to the new standard of excellence.

A manual informs employees of what they may expect to experience and learn while working in your company and explains how they may advance in the business. An operations manual delineates the chain of command. It solidifies your company's fundamentals by defining departments, hours of operation, benefits, etc.

You may wish to begin your operations manual with your company's mission statement. Everything then follows to fulfill that statement, both for employees and customers. The manual should be a complete reference guide that any new employee or manager can consult for step-by-step instructions on what to do and when.

While the document should be as complete as possible, it cannot address every variation of situation. There will still be questions and disagreements. The more in-depth your manual is, however, the fewer these instances will arise. Make sure the manual fits in with your values and ethics.

Still stumped as to what to put in the manual? Consider the following:

• How to schedule appointments.

• How long each service should take and the steps to fulfill each.

• Scripts for every area of the business.

• The organization of the company, including who reports to who.

- Rules of communication, such as huddles and staff meeting schedules.
- Employee relations information, such as holidays, how schedules are determined, benefits, hiring and firing.
- Maintenance for equipment, including who's responsible for maintaining the equipment and phone numbers for who to call when something breaks (such as plumbing issues, computer malfunctions, and so on).
- Cleaning expectations, including keeping workstations in order and laundry.
- Retail displays, including who's in charge of ordering retail and how much product should be in stock/how much should be on the shelf.
- Pre-booking procedures.
- Guest check-ins and check-outs.

Every system delineated in the operations manual must have:

- Who is responsible.
- What is required.
- When does it need to happen.
- How should it be done.
- Where is it conducted.
- Why it needs to be done and the expected outcome.

A comprehensive operations manual is an invaluable tool for running your business. No one – not even you – can keep all that information in one's brain, instantly at the ready in case it's needed. This also means that your managers and department heads won't need to constantly consult you for answers; everything about policies and systems will be in one reference manual. This frees up your time so you can focus on the big picture, as the day-to-day duties will be fully explained in one place.

Conflict resolution

An operations manual can also be a tool for conflict resolution. We've all experienced "he said, she said" dilemmas. When the manual clearly defines expectations, you will be able to stay out of many of these situations. Your team will know where to go to check policy. With the rules spelled out, there will be far fewer cries of favoritism. Consistency will be the rule of the day.

Equanimity in business is largely a measure of co-workers' abilities to speak to, consult with, advise and assist one another. The importance of communication is amplified when disagreements arise. The manual should provide several specific courses of action to resolve conflicts. Management (including you) must stick to the procedures outlined, so that staff members know that there are clear guidelines for resolving conflicts.

Here are some sample ways to resolve conflict that you might want to include in your manual:

- **First course of action, consult the operations manual.** Many conflicts can be nipped in the bud simply by the parties involved referring to the policies already developed. When in doubt, consult the book!

- **One-on-one discussion between the concerned parties.** This is one of the easiest ways to resolve disagreements, yet it's often overlooked. Frequently the "problem" is nothing more than miscommunication. Once each team member understands the other's position, a mutually acceptable resolution is frequently achieved, sometimes just using different words to describe the same situation. A manager should help facilitate these conversations to minimize finger pointing, stereotyping and other negative behavior.

- **Third-party mediation.** If resolution is not achieved with one-on-one discussions, it may be necessary to involve the general manager or owner. As much as possible, disputes should be resolved within specific departments rather than bringing in management. When the conflict is between managers or owners, it may be time to bring in a non-partial third party to help resolve the conflict.

- **Special team meetings.** Gathering the entire staff to make decisions should be used rarely. It can amplify an issue beyond its original scope, which can be positive or negative. It's positive when one question shines light on a broader issue that needs discussion or explanation. Or, for example, if rumors are flying about a business issue, it may be wise to have a full team meeting to nip speculation in the bud and get all concerns on the table.

A final thought on operations manuals: This is an ever-evolving document. Don't let it just gather dust on a shelf. It should be referred to regularly.

Make sure that it is reviewed periodically. As you refine systems, you will need to edit the book. Policies may change. Situations (such as new technology or services) may arise. Once the operating manual is completed, you don't want to change it willy-nilly either. Think of it as a legal document, such as a will. You need to change it periodically but not every day.

It's easy for people to come to you, especially if the operations manual is a new tool. Get in the habit of saying, "It's in the book." The purpose of the manual is to give everyone equal access to the same information. You undermine that purpose when you freely dole out answers.

Get the word out

Communication is a key leadership responsibility. For every leader who has ever cried, "Why don't they get it?", there's usually a leader who gave up on communicating or didn't communicate well. Communicating is a never-ending effort, every day at every level.

Shared knowledge within an organization keeps it competitive, creative and flexible. To function efficiently and remain focused on company goals, every member of the team needs to be well informed.

It starts with the leadership team being on the same page. From there, information flows to the entire staff. Communication isn't one-sided though. It should be flowing up, down, sideways – you name it!

Many companies rely on a monthly meeting or occasional posting on the bulletin board. This is dangerous. Staff must know the who, what, when, where, why and how of projects and goals. Otherwise, they will all be headed in different directions. And leaders wonder why things aren't getting done!

The question of how often you should meet varies from organization to organization. Monthly staff meetings are important for outlining big goals and company initiatives. They're also a great time to bring staff together to rally the troops and improve morale. (You'll find lots of great ideas in Mara Dresner's *Super-Charge Your Staff Meetings: 52 ways to create fun, meaningful, memorable meetings that your employees will love,* available at www.strategies.com or on Amazon.)

You may need daily or weekly meetings with your leadership team as well. Regular meetings with your leadership team can help head off problems and identify patterns of behavior. A daily e-mail summary to the leadership team may be helpful, including daily sales and the next day's goals.

Remember, people process information differently. A quick conversation in passing may work for some staff members. Other employees need things written down. The more effort you make with communication, the more likely your team will fully understand and implement what you want to see in the business.

Huddle up!

One of the most important ways to communicate with your team is through daily (yes, daily!) huddles. Unlike meetings, huddles are quick hits. It's a chance to review goals for the day and week, talk about special promotions, introduce new hires, etc. Huddles are all about the information that is needed that day. They're not the time to introduce a new strategic plan!

Huddles should be just five or ten minutes long. You may wish to have a separate huddle for each department. If you do that, it's still important for the whole team to gather regularly to hear about the accomplishments and challenges of the other areas of the company. Otherwise, departments become isolated.

Huddles should be both a communication and a motivational tool. If they denigrate into "You didn't do this," and "You didn't do that," staff will quickly lose interest and enthusiasm. It's important to keep the huddle balanced, while sharing pertinent data. If the team hasn't reached goals, you need to state that, but work to identify something that someone is doing right, so that the huddles are energizing, not demoralizing. Ending huddle on an upbeat note will help inspire your staff to serve your customers better.

Once you've instituted huddles in your business, you may wish to share "huddle captain" duties with key staff members, or even rotate responsibility throughout your entire team. You'll be surprised by the creativity your staff brings to huddles! Remember to update the scoreboard at the huddle, so everyone knows where they are and how close they are to achieving goal.

Keeping score

How do you expect your team to play full on if they don't know the score? Scoreboards offer a visual way to see where the company stands on goals, every day. Before you can put the numbers out there, you need to understand them well enough to explain them to your team.

The scoreboard can help staff understand exactly what the company needs to do to succeed and why. Most staff want the company to flourish and want to feel as though they are making positive contributions. Understanding how individual performance influences company-wide success often spurs employees to exceptional performance. There is a shared sense of responsibility and pride at the company's accomplishments.

If you want your employees to think and act as if they were owners, it's crucial for them to know the score and how everything influences the bottom line. Open-book management companies – companies that share their financial numbers with employees – see tangible results.

Staff members:

- stop thinking of themselves as "hired hands" and start thinking of themselves as "business people."
- stop doing as little as they think they can get away with and start doing whatever needs to be done.

- try to do their best work all the time because they know it influences the bottom line of the business.

- care about the success of the business because they know that's what puts money in their pockets.

You can devise a scoreboard to track nearly any performance indicator in a business. Here are some suggestions of what you can scoreboard:

- New client acquisition

- Client retention

- Pre-booking

- Retail sales

You can scoreboard anything that has a number attached to it. Goals should require staff to reach, but it is counterproductive to constantly set unrealistic goals. You may want to ask staff about what they feel are reasonable goals. Help them break down big goals into small steps. Celebrate wins along the way. Include everyone. Scoreboards should motivate employees to do better. If your scoreboards aren't functioning in that way, look at how you're presenting them.

Make sure that scoreboards are prominently displayed, perhaps in the break room, where all staff members will see them. You don't have to open your books all the way to use scoreboards; but you do have to be willing to share some numbers.

- Be original with scoreboards.

- Involve the staff in developing goals.

- Use your team's creativity in designing scoreboards.

There is no wrong way to design a scoreboard. It just needs to be clear what the goals are. Update the scoreboard daily for best results.

Here are a few examples of scoreboards:

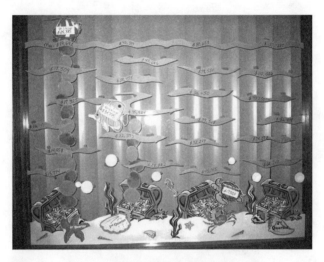

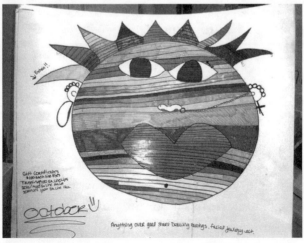

Leadership and culture survey

You know how you think you are as a leader. You know the type of culture you want to have. The question is whether your staff would agree. If you are truly ready to be a no-compromise leader, you must have the willingness to accept criticism and realize that every leader can get better. To help you identify and measure your leadership strengths and challenges, and how your culture is perceived, you may wish to send a survey to your staff. Only do this if you are truly willing to listen with an open heart and change! You will do more harm than good if you ask staff to complete the survey and then aren't willing to improve your skills. (If you need assistance with upgrading your culture, talk to Strategies about a No-Compromise Excellence assessment and game plan.)

A staff survey will:

• offer a sense of the company's culture.

• enable you to pinpoint some aspects of your culture that may need improvement.

• help you measure progress within a changing culture.

• get a view of how staff interprets leadership initiatives.

Begin with a staff letter. You may wish to adapt this sample:

Dear staff member of XYZ Company:

To better ensure the best operations of our company and set the course for success, I need your input. To achieve the most honest input possible, I've decided to use this survey, which is being sent to every member of the XYZ Company staff.

Please answer these questions freely. There are no correct answers to this survey. Answers should represent your candid opinion, not what you feel the answer "should" be.

Unless all staff members elect to openly share their responses, individual responses will remain confidential. You need not put your name on the survey. The leadership team will compile responses and communicate a summary to the team. The survey is meant to provide data which can be used to identify and clarify critical assumptions, beliefs, values, perceptions and behaviors in our company. We want to get your views on what we're doing well – and what we need to do better. Your opinion is vital to this effort.

Thank you for being part of the team at XYZ Company. Please let me know if you have any questions about this, and know that I always welcome your feedback.

Sincerely,
Owner's name

Survey instructions

Write in the number 1 to 5 that most clearly represents your opinion at this time. Select from the following list:

5 Totally agree
4 Partly agree
3 Neither agree nor disagree
2 Partly disagree
1 Totally disagree

The survey

__ 1. Communications are too informal throughout the business.

__ 2. There is a clear picture of where leadership is leading the company.

__ 3. The company's vision and mission have been shared with all team members.

__ 4. Team members are rewarded fairly for their performance.

___ 5. All staff members participate in creating action plans to specify what needs to be done, how it will be done, who will do it and by when it must be done.

___ 6. Team members receive all the information they need to complete quality work.

___ 7. Team members are excited about their work.

___ 8. Staff are recognized and praised when they do a good job.

___ 9. Performance standards are clearly defined and communicated to everyone.

___ 10. Staff members have the opportunity and support to develop and grow within the salon.

___ 11. Mediocrity is unacceptable.

___ 12. The company's decor creates a visually pleasing environment.

___ 13. Staff members have sufficient time to perform quality work.

___ 14. The team receives frequent, useful training.

___ 15. A skill certification process is in place and working.

___ 16. This is a fun place to work.

___ 17. Clients are booked in a way that is equitable.

___ 18. Staff meetings are held regularly.

___ 19. The leadership team cares about the physical health and safety of the staff.

___ 20. Leadership supports decisions made by staff, provided members are acting in the best interests of the company.

___ 21. The chain of command and organizational structure are clear.

___ 22. Staff have the authority to make decisions to get their jobs done.

___ 23. Employee training is viewed as a long-term investment, not just an expense.

___ 24. Staff know and understand how their performance is measured.

___ 25. Every team member receives honest answers from the leadership team on issues of concern to them.

___ 26. Clients are assigned to staff in a way that makes the best use of team members' skills.

___ 27. Compensation is fair, and administered consistently throughout the company.

___ 28. Staff members have a strong desire to complete quality work.

___ 29. The team receives a variety of informal rewards for work done well (e.g., praise, memos, time off).

___ 30. The company's furnishings and equipment are up-to-date.

___ 31. Client satisfaction and loyalty is the company's primary goal.

___ 32. New hires are carefully selected.

___ 33. Policies and procedures are clearly communicated to all team members.

___ 34. Team members enjoy working here.

__ 35. Staff members are able to assess various pressures and demands, and identify which ones are really important.

__ 36. The company is ideally located for both attracting and retaining clients and staff.

__ 37. Team members feel their jobs are secure (i.e., no worries about being laid off or the company going out of business).

__ 38. When staff members are faced with personal situations that interfere with their ability to work effectively, the leadership team is supportive while also ensuring that work is performed according to established standards.

__ 39. A dress code and grooming policy enables the company to present a unified and professional image to clients.

__ 40. Leadership treats all team members consistently.

__ 41. Each owner or manager is a strong leader, seeks the counsel of staff, coaches and supports staff, delegates responsibility and authority, and praises the staff to clients.

__ 42. Client retention is high (greater than 50%).

__ 43. People in the company help one another.

__ 44. Mistakes are seen as an opportunity to learn and improve and, unless repeated or clearly in violation of known rules, are not usually subject to disciplinary action.

__ 45. Products sell well and appeal to clients.

__ 46. Staff members are not stressed by excessive job pressures.

__ 47. The leadership team is receptive to new information, suggestions for improvement and constructive criticism.

___ 48. In-house skill training is done well and immediately useful on the job.

___ 49. To get the job done, staff members have the freedom to act as they need to.

___ 50. The owner or manager coaches me to help me do my job better.

___ 51. Performance standards are challenging, yet achievable.

___ 52. When there is a business crisis, the team pulls together to help relieve the situation.

___ 53. Personal conversation between staff is discouraged while serving clients.

___ 54. The company has the best possible range of staff talent for the clients served and the services offered.

___ 55. Co-workers put the good of the client, other staff and the company ahead of their own interests.

___ 56. Practices subject to disciplinary action are made clear to all staff in advance.

___ 57. Distributors are courteous, knowledgeable and helpful.

___ 58. The leadership team is ethical and moral in business dealings.

___ 59. The leadership team discusses the financial aspects of the business with staff members in a way that everyone understands.

___ 60. Staff are highly skilled and quality-conscious.

___ 61. Any behavior which is potentially distasteful to either clients or staff is frowned upon.

__ 62. Staff have the tools and supplies needed to deliver quality work.

__ 63. New hires always receive training on performance standards and practices.

__ 64. The current hours are best for the clients.

__ 65. The leadership team and staff trust one another.

__ 66. Staff are encouraged to take risks in getting their job done if they think the risk makes good business or ethical sense.

__ 67. The safety of clients and staff always concerns management.

__ 68. The team knows and understands the company's long-term growth strategy.

__ 69. The leadership team takes appropriate steps to help any staff member not meeting expectations.

__ 70. Adequate time and preparation is allowed when a major change, such as introducing new systems, is planned.

__ 71. Decisions relating to staff's work are made without unnecessary delay.

__ 72. Work schedules and hours are fair.

__ 73. Any questions or complaints with policies and practices can be openly discussed.

__ 74. Staff members are proud to be a part of this company.

How to score the survey

1. Tally each team member's score. The highest possible individual total is 370 (74 x 5). If you notice clusters of high and low totals, there are significant differences in the way your team perceives the company's culture. Don't try to

figure out who said what. Instead, look for trends and discuss the findings with the entire staff to get more input.

2. Some statements may have received low-number responses on a significant number of surveys. Total the responses for these statements on all the surveys and divide by the number of respondents to determine the average. This will pinpoint areas for improvement.

3. Repeat step two for statements that received high-number responses. Discuss these positive areas during team and individual meetings. Accentuating the positive aspects of the company is a great way to reinforce behaviors and provide praise.

Don't conduct the survey and not act on it. Enlist staff in improving weaker areas. Make this an ongoing topic of discussion. Add your own questions in, and repeat the survey from time to time.

Leading through conflict

Do you get anxious working in or around conflict? If so, is the thought of resolving that conflict unsettling enough that you put it off as long as possible?

Most people don't like conflict. That's natural. But if you avoid resolving the conflict, your business will suffer and it's likely the conflict will continue, even morphing into something bigger than the original dispute.

As we discussed earlier in this chapter, having an operations and a policies and procedures manual will reduce the number of disagreements in your salon, spa or medspa.

Still, when you add in the human factor, conflict is going to occur. There's simply no way to totally eliminate it. The issue then becomes how to deal with it.

In the most basic of terms, leaders lead through conflict. You cannot lead without being accountable to the tough stuff.

• You will cut costs and take away jobs.

• You meet with your best customer to apologize for a mistake.

• You will discipline a subordinate whom you consider a friend. You will fire that person if that is what makes sense for your business.

• You enter the fray of conflict between clashing personalities and differing opinions. You will remain a neutral party,

The key is to handle conflict from an unbiased position of what's best for the company. Your staff will respect you when you do so, even when they don't like the outcome. It's when you avoid all conflict that resentments simmer and grow, leading to a lot of backroom chatter, negativity and lackluster performance. It is your job as leader to do the right thing for your company, without blaming and finger-pointing. Dialogue usually leads to a resolution. It's the leader's role to be the catalyst for that dialogue, before the situation escalates. Leaders cannot ignore interpersonal conflict. Poor communication and follow-through will add to the conflict. These issues rarely (if ever) go away on their own. Be an involved, caring leader.

Crisis resolution

Like conflict, crisis is inevitable, no matter what the type of business. There are two classifications of crisis: those that are created externally and those that are created internally. External crises include such things as natural disasters (hurricanes, blizzards, floods, etc.), new competition and other situations that are out of your control. Leaders who rise to the challenge of an external crisis and shift those they lead into a "we can overcome this" mode can use the impact of an external crisis to move through it quickly and efficiently, even morphing into a stronger company on the other side.

Internal crises, on the other hand, can cause real damage to a business. Unlike external crises that usually occur and do damage quickly, internal crises often have deeply rooted issues that fester over time before surfacing. Leadership directly influences the nature, severity and duration of an internal crisis through its behavior and the decisions it makes – or avoids making.

Consider the following to see if you're creating crises in your company:

- **Leadership entitlement:** Every great leader nurtures a special connection with his or her followers. They don't put themselves above their employees. They know the importance of rolling up their sleeves and working side by side with their staff. Leadership entitlement widens the gap between leaders and employees by feeding the "us against them" thinking. Leadership entitlement is fuel for every conceivable internal crisis.

- **Emotional blockages:** Failure to make difficult and necessary decisions, deal with challenging employees or address sensitive issues is the essence of poor leadership. This type of crisis never goes away. It only festers and grows in complexity. In this context, leadership is all about engaging and executing the plan. Trace any crisis back to its point of origin and you will find a leader who failed to engage – over and over again.

- **Contaminated culture:** The leader is the keeper and protector of the business culture. This non-negotiable responsibility cannot be ignored or delegated. Contaminated cultures are a breeding ground for drama and, just like hurricane season, they can churn out one crisis after another. Stop the crisis while it's just a drizzle before it reaches monsoon capacity.

On an ordinary day, being a leader tests your abilities, work ethic, judgment and tenacity. A crisis pushes these skills into overdrive. The key is making sure that the crisis is bringing out your best, not your worst; that after peeling back all the layers, the crisis was not of your doing. If your salon/spa/medspa cruises from one crisis to another, it's time to be honest with yourself and acknowledge the source of the problem.

Simple steps to no compromise

"No compromise" is a leadership mindset. It is a non-negotiable commitment to growth. When leaders allow compromise to enter into their thinking and behavior, they also invite its faithful companion, drag. The more compromise that occurs in business, the more drag there is on growth. (You could write an entire book on the topic of No-Compromise Leadership – and Neil Ducoff has. To truly understand the topic, check out his *No Compromise Leadership: A Higher Standard of Leadership Thinking and Behavior.* Here, we would be remiss in not bringing up the topic at all, so this is a brief overview of the subject.)

No compromise means playing the business game at its highest level. It means doing what needs to be done. It means the ability to overcome emotional blockages that cause leaders to hesitate or avoid seemingly difficult tasks. It means making tough decisions. It means managing what's on your plate.

There are five key elements to no-compromise leadership, and they are all non-negotiable.

1. **Build and maintain the right business culture:** What would your business look like if it had a no-compromise culture? Culture is everything. It defines every behavior and performance in the company. A no-compromise culture's point of origin, and therefore its energy, begins with the leader.

2. **Empowerment:** It's the shared responsibility of growth throughout the company. You get there by incorporating levels of authority: Operating decisions are made at the

operations level; management decisions at the management level; and executive decisions are made at the executive level.

3. **Team:** The collective power of team can accomplish the extraordinary. Nurture and encourage teamwork.

4. **Innovation:** Everything changes. Innovation is what drives change and leaves your competition in the dust. It's the leader's job to drive and encourage innovation. Push the envelope.

5. **Systems:** You lead people; you manage systems. Systems create the structure to create predictability in business. If you don't like the results you're getting, change or create a new system.

No-compromise leaders relentlessly drive the Four Business Outcomes:

1. **Productivity:** Create a high-productivity culture with systems that lock it into company goals and performance standards.

2. **Profitability:** Build a culture that is profitable and value-driven.

3. **Staff retention:** Employee loyalty cannot be mandated. It is earned.

4. **Client loyalty:** That's the litmus test. Do your clients come back? Do they sing your praises to others? More than anything else, client loyalty demands the right culture.

A culture that's focused on driving the Four Business Outcomes is a culture that can execute and create sustained growth for the company. Should one of the outcomes slip, all will tumble. No-compromise leadership is the mandate.

Think about where your company is for all of the Four Business Outcomes. Here's a helpful tool to see where you're out of balance.

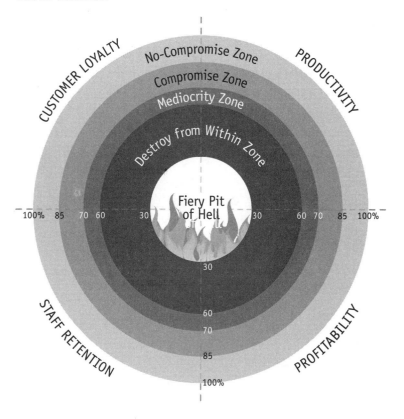

Each of the Four Business Outcomes can be divided into eight sub-categories, known as the Big Eight Drivers. These are simply a collection of rules that, when combined, create a natural, powerful focus on achieving results. It doesn't matter who you are as an individual or what your leadership style is, your company will succeed as long as you are disciplined to adhere to the Big Eight Drivers.

Take a moment to study this chart. Be honest where you are in each driver.

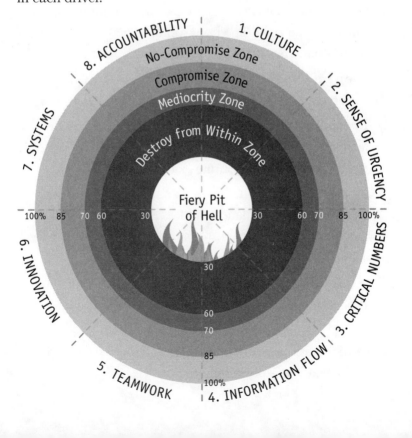

Here's how to use the Big Eight Drivers for maximum effect:

1. **Create the right business culture.** Great leaders create business cultures that define and support the thinking and behavior needed for success.

2. **Maintain a sense of urgency.** Urgency drives performance and growth. It can fizzle in a heartbeat if you don't pay attention.

3. **Drive your critical numbers.** Critical numbers, when moved in the right direction, can have a profound impact on company performance. Define yours.

4. **Keep information flowing freely.** Top down, bottom up – everyone needs to know the score and what's going on.

5. **Promote true teamwork.** You can't be an effective leader if you don't create and appreciate teamwork. Walk the talk every day. Celebrate examples of teamwork.

6. **Inspire innovation.** Get out of the box and stay out! Do what you do better than any other competitor. Keep finding new ways to wow your customers. Leaders either inspire or stifle innovation among their staffs.

7. **Systematize everything.** Systems create predictability. Procedures and structure produce results. If you don't like the results, change or tweak the system.

8. **Enforce accountability.** Always deliver what was promised when it was promised.

Leadership cheat sheet

Being a leader is a never-ending, exhausting, exhilarating role. There are so many tasks to accomplish, so many balls to keep in the air. When it all seems overwhelming, take a few moments to review these key components of building your no-compromise culture. They'll help put you back in touch with the no-compromise leader that resides within.

- **True leadership:** Stay laser-focused and hardwired into the realities of the business. Relentlessly maintain a sense of urgency because urgency is the energy of business. Drive the Four Business Outcomes to create value.

- **Team:** Everyone is responsible for growth. Your team can do great things. Give them encouragement and let them soar.

- **Know your numbers:** Your financials are your business scorecards. Know what every number means, where it came from and what can drive it in the right direction.

- **Information flow:** It must be fast, furious and constant. You must communicate what, why, how, when, who, and the score.

- **Invest in your people:** The game of business is a team sport. Develop the competencies and abilities of the people who play the game for the company.

- **Reward the right behaviors:** Don't expect new behavior and team performance if your pay program continues to reward the behaviors and performances that must change. What gets rewarded gets repeated.

My personal goals for
Leadership:

_____

_____

_____

_____

_____

_____

_____

_____

_____

_____

_____

_____

_____

_____

_____

_____

CHAPTER TWO

Human Resources

*Hiring, training, firing,
morale and more.*

*Hiring, training, firing,
morale and more.*

Human Resources

When it comes to dealing with employees, many owners prefer a hands-off strategy. They don't know what to do, so they do nothing. They take "management by walking around" to a whole new level, basically reducing it to "walking around."

However, human resources and employee relations issues are nothing to be feared. So much is just following the Golden Rule: Do unto others as you would have others do unto you.

You shouldn't fear employee encounters any more than your employees should be afraid of talking with you. While you'll need to consult your state's Department of Labor for specifics (and an employment attorney for any sticky situations), much of good employee relations is about maintaining open communication and promoting an atmosphere of understanding and tolerance where staff members are encouraged to grow and learn. Not so scary, right?

To help with all those forms – from job applications to blank W-2s – you may wish to utilize an online service, such as Google Docs (www.docs.google.com) or one of the services from www.37signals.com. You'll also find it may be more convenient to keep notes from interviews, job descriptions, etc. in one easily accessible online location. (You decide who has access to what. As a side note, these services can be great when collaborating on projects, especially if you have a large business or multiple locations.)

Let's start by examining the hiring process. After all, you can't have employee relations if you don't have any employees! You should have written job descriptions for each position in your company. That way when you need to hire, you'll know exactly what you're searching for.

A good job description includes:

- An overview of the position. This may also be called the job summary or purpose statement. It should be a paragraph of three to four sentences that concisely states the nature, level and objective of the position.

- A list of essential functions. These are the non-negotiables. You may call them tasks performed or job duties. Fully describe each essential duty.

  › A list of secondary requirements. These are the ones that are nice, but not necessary. Someone else on the staff could pick up these tasks, if necessary.

- Job specifications or qualifications.

› Any physical requirements, such as "must be able to lift 25 pounds."

› Skill requirements, such as knowing a computer program, being trained in a certain technique or being able to speak Portuguese.

› Educational requirements.

• License requirements, if applicable.

• Intangibles, such as team player or leadership qualities.

• Hours to be worked.

• Salary range.

• To whom the position reports and any employees that the position supervises.

Remember to pull out those job descriptions at least once or twice a year to make sure they're still accurate. Then, you won't be scrambling when you need to begin the hiring process.

Here's a sample of how a job description might look. Notice how key functions are tied to accountability areas:

Job Description Outline

Customer Loyalty
• Retain clients
• Smile and be friendly
• Follow service systems

Service to Team
• Be on time
• Be agreeable and helpful
• Do the work that you can do

Service to Facility
• Maintain facility per guidelines
• Use products sparingly
• Report needed repairs

Sales
• Sell all that we offer
• Meet sales goals

Professionlism
- Have a winning attitude
- Meet appearance expectations
- Communicate respectfully and clearly

Technical
- Meet performance expectations
- Pursue continuing education
- Strive to be better

Recruitment

Never fear; sooner or later you will need to hire. In a perfect world, that will be because you're growing and need additional staff. In a less perfect world (i.e., reality), it might be because a stylist joined a competitor or a massage therapist decided to strike out on her own.

Before you embark on a recruitment campaign, step back and assess your real needs. Say a stylist has just given notice. Is it necessary to immediately replace the individual? Just because someone leaves doesn't mean that you have to hire right away.

In our example of the stylist leaving, analyze the total productive hours of the remaining stylists. Do you really need to hire a full-time stylist? Perhaps a part-time stylist can satisfy your production needs, and thus save on both payroll and benefits. When performing a staff assessment, analyze the technical skills needed by your salon/spa/medspa. Will a color technician boost color sales? Will a manicurist or massage therapist attract more business? Will a color expert raise the skill level of all stylists? Think, "What does my business need?", rather than: "We have to replace the person who just left."

Job Description Template – Sample

Job Description

Position Title: **Service Provider**

Reports To: **Salon Manager**

Objective: *To provide high-quality services as outlined below by consistently satisfying guest expectations and demands, as well as meeting performance expectations as outlined by leadership. Retain Clients!*

Areas of Accountability

Accountability Area	Key Functions
Customer Loyalty	❖ Never lose a client! ❖ Smile a lot and be friendly. ❖ Build strong, professional relationships with guests. ❖ Be welcoming, warm and genuine. Greet guests by name. ❖ Provide facility tours for all first-time guests. ❖ Follow all service protocols, systems and processes consistently with each guest. ❖ Take initiative and appropriate action to resolve guest complaints – work with leadership to resolve guest challenges. ❖ Support team members servicing guests. ❖ Promote positive first and last impressions for each guest experience. ❖ Meet guests "where they show up" and adapt to their demands in order to best service guest needs.

Job Description Template – Sample *(continued)*

Accountability Area	Key Functions
Service to Team	❖ Never say *no* to a team member – always help out, even when you're busy. ❖ Arrive to work in an agreeable, calm temperament. ❖ Perform your job duties as outlined. If you're caught up, help someone that isn't. ❖ Make yourself available at all times. ❖ Work with the team to hit goals. ❖ Maintain positive words and actions at all times towards co-workers. ❖ Attend work as scheduled. ❖ Work to your full potential.
Service to Facility	❖ At all times make sure the environment is pleasing and safe for the guest and meets our service brand promise. ❖ Care for the environment, equipment, and furnishings with the utmost respect. ❖ Products & Supplies - Use only what is needed. ❖ Perform all daily opening and closing duties as required. ❖ Report "wear & tear" to management as you encounter it in order for it to be repaired.
Professionalism	❖ Adhere to all company policies and procedures. ❖ Arrive to work ready for work: hair and makeup (if applicable) done, adhering to dress code. ❖ Communicate clearly with respect and care to all guests and team members. ❖ Conduct yourself all times in a manner that supports our brand. ❖ Arrive to work on time and as scheduled. ❖ Support our company, our vision and values. ❖ Accountability – no assigning blame.

Job Description Template – Sample *(continued)*

Accountability Area	Key Functions
Technical	❖ Seek to constantly improve your performance, skill and ability - challenge yourself daily to be better than you were the day before. ❖ Meet all requirements for job as outlined by the state department of licensing and regulations. ❖ Meet all requirements for ongoing training as outlined by management. ❖ Attend all company trainings. ❖ Meet all individual performance goals as outlined by management. ❖ Pre-book guests.
Sales	❖ Sell all that we offer. ❖ Meet performance goals for service, retail and gift certificates. ❖ Cross-sell services and products. ❖ Close sales. ❖ Assist walk-in guests with product choices. ❖ Product expert. ❖ Consistently follow all retail systems and recommendation protocols. ❖ Charge appropriately for all services.

Job Description Template – Sample *(continued)*

QUALIFICATIONS: To perform this job successfully, an individual must be able to perform each Key Function satisfactorily. The requirements listed below are representative of the knowledge, skill, and/or ability required. Reasonable accommodations may be made to enable individuals with disabilities to perform the essential functions.

LICENSES:

COMPUTER SKILLS:

PHYSICAL DEMANDS The physical demands described here are representative of those that must be met by an employee to successfully perform the key functions of this job. Reasonable accommodations may be made to enable individuals with disabilities to perform the essential functions.

While performing the duties of this job, the employee is regularly required to stand; walk; use hands to handle or feel; reach with hands and arms; talk or hear; and smell. The employee is occasionally required to sit; climb or balance; and stoop, kneel, crouch, or crawl. The employee must regularly lift and/or move up to 10 pounds and frequently lift and/or move up to 25 pounds. Specific vision abilities required by this job include close vision, distance vision, color vision, peripheral vision, depth perception, and ability to adjust focus.

DISCLAIMER: The above statements are intended to describe the general nature and level of work being performed by people assigned to this Job Role. They are not intended as an exhaustive list of all responsibilities, duties and skills required.

EMPLOYEE ACKNOWLEDGEMENT

I have read the duties and expectations of me in this job role and agree to perform these duties as outlined.

_____

Employee Signature

_____

Employee Name (Printed)

_____

Date

Before you make any moves to hire, make sure you are optimizing the production capability you already have. Are there staff members who aren't working at peak productivity? Make appropriate adjustments prior to looking for new hires.

After doing this review, you'll know if it's time to hire. You have the job description. Here's how to begin the recruitment process:

- Ask your staff for recommendations. This seems obvious, but many people overlook this great resource. Your current staff knows exactly how things operate (yes, the good, the bad and the ugly). They're likely to know whether someone has both the skill set and the personality to be a good fit.

- Put a notice up on your website and Facebook page. Again, people who know you and your business just might know someone who's looking for a position similar to what you're seeking.

- Advertise. This might be an ad in your local paper. (Stick with local sources, as much as possible, rather than large, regional papers.) Try online sources, such as Craig's List (www.craigslist.org) and Career Builder (www.careerbuilder.com). Other online resources include industry-specific job banks, such as at the Professional Beauty Association (www.probeauty.org) and the International Spa Association (www.experienceispa.com). Some people like to run so-called blind ads, where they don't mention the company name. However, you're more likely to get qualified applicants if they know exactly who you are.

> › The more information you include in the ad, the more of a chance that you'll hear from qualified applicants. Include job responsibilities, hours, etc. Mention any benefits that you think make the position special.

> › Allowing people to respond by e-mail simplifies the process for both you and your applicants.

> › Prior to advertising have a procedure in place as to how the applicants will be screened, including who will review the applications.

> › Respond to every applicant, even if it's a generic "thanks, but no thanks." You want to leave the applicant with a good impression. You never know when you will have a job opening that's right for a specific applicant, and you want them to have good feelings about your business. Job applicants are potential customers, too!

- Contact local schools and training programs. Everybody has to start somewhere.

- Utilize networking groups, both in your industry and outside your industry. For example, a front-desk coordinator may have worked in an insurance company and has transferable skills. People who work in retail or the hospitality worlds frequently have the same types of personalities and skills you want interacting with your clients.

- Look for under-served populations, such as veterans and people with disabilities. Your local labor department can help you find new ways to promote your job openings. You may also be eligible for government grants. Think outside the hiring box!

Interviewing

Once you've culled the best applicants from those who applied, it's time to set up interviews. Interviewing can be an intimidating process – for both the interviewer and interviewee! Remember, the applicant is checking out you and your business, just as you are trying to determine if someone's a good fit.

Decide if you're going to have one round of interviews or two. You may want to start with a phone interview to come up with a list of viable candidates. If you're doing one round, it may be helpful to either have a team interview with each applicant, or to have the applicants meet with a few people back-to-back. If you're doing more than one round of interviews, it's good to have different people interview during each round. Your manager and a staff member who will be working with the new team member might be ideal to interview the first round. Then, they cull the list down to three applicants or so, and you interview the finalists.

Everyone involved in the process should take notes! You may even wish to take photos of each applicant (with permission, of course). After a while, it's easy for everybody's skills to run together.

Here are some ways to maximize the interview experience:

- Make things as comfortable as possible. The applicant will be nervous. (You might be, too!) Be kind to the applicant. If you're drinking coffee, offer a cup to the interviewee. Hold the interview in a quiet part of your business. Give a quick tour of the business prior to the interview.

1. Keep up-to-date job descriptions for every position in your business.

2. Have a skill-certification program to ensure consistency for quality customer experiences.

3. Be a company of excellence, and expect top performance from your staff.

- Review the applicant's resume prior to the interview. Just as you should require the applicant to be prepared, you need to prepare, as well. A well-written resume tells the story of a job candidate's career and education. It should be on a neutral paper and should not contain typos. Be on the lookout for long gaps in employment and frequent job changes. Be sure to ask about these things in the interview.

- Be on time. As much as possible, stick to a schedule. How would you react if a candidate arrived 30 minutes late? That's how the applicant feels when you are a half hour late.

- Interruptions should be kept to a minimum. Ideally, you should tell your staff to hold all calls and not to interrupt you.

- Take note about the non-verbal things. Did the applicant dress appropriately for the interview? Did she shake your hand firmly? Did he appear interested when you talked about the job and your company? Was she engaged? Did he turn off his phone? Was she prepared?

• After the interview, ask everyone who talked with the candidate to offer his or her opinion. If someone was rude to the receptionist, for example, you probably don't want him or her on your team, even if they have great technical skills.

• Ask questions that allow the applicant to showcase his or her personality, as well as skill. Don't use questions that can be answered with a short response. It's hard to evaluate a candidate when all you've heard is "yes" and "no"!

• Remember, it's not about you. During interviews many entrepreneurs get wrapped up in telling their own story. Don't forget the prime objective of the interview: to ask leading questions that will reveal the true qualities and potential behaviors of the applicant. You should do more listening than talking.

• Keep it legal. While you know that you can't discriminate based on say, race or religion, you also cannot screen out candidates based on age or disability. Avoid questions that cross into illegal territory. Don't ask things, such as, "Do you plan to retire in the next few years?" or "I see you're limping. Is that from a sports injury?" or "Several of us go to St. John's Church. Which church do you go to?" If you're not sure if a question is illegal, don't ask it! Your labor board can be of help in separating the legal from the illegal, as can an employment law attorney. You can also check with an online

employee to be enthusiastic. Therefore, you should ask questions in several categories.

- **Motivation.** Ask: Why did you apply for this position? What will you bring to the position that another candidate won't? What are your long-term goals? How do you plan to reach these goals? Where would you like to be in five years? What do you want from your next job that you are not getting now? What's your favorite part of your current job?

- **Stability.** This is where you want to uncover the reasons for gaps in employment and frequent job changes. Ask: Why do you want to leave your current job? What were the reasons for leaving your last job? (Feel free to ask this about any job listed on the resume.) How have your goals changed over the years? What's your greatest disappointment so far in your career? What are you most proud of?

- **Resourcefulness.** You want to be sure that the candidate is a self-starter and can think outside the box. Ask: What was a challenge you faced in your last job, and how did you solve it? Describe a time when an employee of another business treated you rudely. How did the person act? How did you react? Tell me about a time when a client was angry or disappointed. What did you do to help solve the situation? How would you deal with Situation X?

- **Compatibility.** This is where you're trying to match the characteristics of your business with your applicant. Ask: For what characteristics or actions has your last manager complimented you? Describe a time when he or she criticized you.

How did you react? Describe your perfect workplace. What are three adjectives that you would use to describe yourself?

• **Values.** You want to hire someone whose values are in line with your company's. (Work with your team to create a set of values that your team lives by. Use the form at the end of the chapter to get started.) If one of your values is teamwork, for example, you might ask: Tell me about a time when you were working on a team, and all the work seemed to be falling on one person. How did you handle it? Tell me about a time when your team pulled together to accomplish a challenging project. What made that team successful?

Want a few more things to think about? Consider:

• Appearance

• Professional demeanor

• Communication skills

• Openness

• Teamwork

• Reliability

• Ethical standards

• Follow-through

• Technical skills

• Specialty skills

• Poise

• Consultation/selling skills

- Years of experience
- Ability to work under pressure
- Organizational and time-management skills

OK, you've completed a round of successful interviews and you've taken copious notes on the ins and outs of every candidate. Yet, you're still not ready to hire.

After the interview:

- Notify everyone who did not make the final cut. A simple e-mail is fine. Just thank the applicant for coming in and let them know that there were other candidates who were a better fit for the position. If you're going to keep their resume on file, let them know.

- You may want to add one more round of interviewing, a "shadow" or "working" interview. This is where a candidate is allowed to come into your business and follow an employee around. This is where you can really see if someone takes initiative, how they'll be with clients, etc.

- Check the references of your final candidates. You can request these during the interview (or on a job application), or contact the candidate after the interview to request references. Many large companies have a policy of only releasing dates of employment and job titles. If that's not the case, you want to determine:
  › Dates of employment
  › Positions held

> › How would you describe the employee?
> › The reason for separation
> › Salary
> › What are the candidate's strong points?
> › What were the candidate's weak points?
> › Would you hire this person again?

• It's time to choose which candidate will fit best in your culture. Look at skills and experience. Be honest about the "feeling" you got from each candidate. (These gut feelings often prove right. Don't ignore them and hire a candidate who has more experience, even though there was something that didn't "feel" like a good fit.) Remember that someone may have left a job because of a poisonous culture. Many businesses have been combining staff and expecting more, due to the difficult economic times. Review the full picture for each finalist, and consult with your staff. Make your decision. Call the person you want to hire, then confirm the offer in writing.

• Once the candidate accepts, notify all the finalists to let them know someone else was hired. Try to find the time to add personal touches to your note, such as things you were impressed with. If you intend to keep a resume on file, let them know. In fact, it's great to keep an active file of possible hires, so that you're already well on the way to hiring, should a staff member leave.

The high cost of turnover

Now that we've talked about what goes into hiring, let's look at what turnover really means to your business. Of course, a certain percentage of employees will leave for a wide variety of reasons. You must take personal responsibility for ensuring that you have a steady workforce.

Staff turnover disrupts business, disappoints and confuses clients, and causes stress for all involved. Moreover, it's expensive. It drives up operating, recruitment and training costs.

Turnover means:

- Lost management time invested in training the former employee.
- Recruiting costs.
- Compensation paid to the former employee while he or she was in training.
- Lost sales while the position was vacant.
- Management time spent interviewing candidates to fill the position.
- Training a new employee.
- Compensation paid to a new employee before he or she becomes productive.
- The extra time management and key staff must invest in the new employee.
- The mistakes a new employee makes when first on the job.

- Disruption at the front desk, and paperwork expense caused by the departing employee.

- The impact of the person's loss of expertise on business and client satisfaction.

- Productive time lost due to the internal gossip and speculation that often follows an employee's departure.

That's why it's so important to hire the right people. Sometimes, you can feel pressured to hire someone right away, and you end up choosing the wrong person. Take your time hiring, and make sure the person is right for your team.

Training new staff

Each new staff member carries remnants of their previous jobs into your workplace. Some of these may be admirable, such as a passion for cutting-edge techniques and being a team player. Others, not so good, such as talking on their cell phones in client areas or a disregard for the specifics of the dress code.

Poor behavior and work habits can develop quickly during the first days and months of employment, and they take a long time to correct. When it comes to servicing clients, maintaining quality standards and supporting your vision, nothing can be left to chance. You must train staff continuously.

Ongoing education is crucial for the following reasons:

- It provides an opportunity to communicate and emphasize your company's vision.

- It provides the concrete skills staff need to succeed at your business.
- It allows employees to work with management to create new ways of serving clients better.

Good training enables people to develop the "right" skills and behaviors quickly. In a service-oriented industry, new employees must immediately live up to established customer expectations. There's no room for, "Sorry about that. I'm new here," when clients expect the best on every visit.

Define what behaviors you want to see and what standards must be lived up to. Put it in writing in your policies and procedures handbook. From dress code to breaks, policies should be in one book that each employee reads and signs off on.

Take the time to ensure that new employees are truly trained in the culture and ways of your business. This is not a one-day process. Online retailer Zappos hires for fit. Then, all new hires go through four weeks of training. During that time, they're offered up to $4,000 to leave if they feel Zappos isn't for them.

Extraordinary skill and talent can do damage to a company if it comes with the wrong thinking and behavior. If teamwork is the hallmark of your company, hire team players. It's not enough that someone has great technical skills. To get the right fit, you must not only screen applicants, you must immerse new hires in your culture and help them understand what's expected of them.

Zappos does it for four weeks. What does the first month at your company look like? Read more about life at Zappos.com in CEO Tony Hsieh's *Delivering Happiness: A Path to Profits, Passion and Purpose,* available in the Strategies bookstore at www. strategies.com.

Know that if a new employee sees long-term employees flaunting the rules, that will become the norm. Ensure that all staff knows what's expected for consistency's sake. Refer to the policies and procedures manual. Make sure that the manual is reviewed during orientation. Remember to update that manual as policies change.

During the first days on the job, newly hired employees are highly impressionable. No matter how much experience a new employee has, everyone must still complete the same training program. It's not just about the technique; it's about vision, attitude, performance expectations, client handling procedures, client-retention programs, quality standards and other specifics that will directly impact their ability to succeed.

Training for all new employees should last at least five days. The goal of this is to quickly get buy-in and understanding from new staff that supports the behavior patterns that support your vision. Many behavior problems could be avoided if all companies instituted a formal, rigorous training process.

One way to approach new-hire training is to focus each day on a specific aspect of behavior, such as customer service.

- Begin by describing the procedure's objectives, and why they are integral to your business' service quality program.

- Show the new employee where to find information about how to do the process.

- Demonstrate the behaviors you expect in a variety of customer-contact situations: telephone calls, front desk greetings, client check-in and checkout, as well as technical standards.

- Role-play until the process becomes natural for the new employee.

- Allow the new employee to shadow an exemplary long-term employee. Let that employee mentor the newbie.

- When the material and procedures have been covered thoroughly, allow the new employee to answer the phone, do a client service, etc., all under the supervision of a manager or mentor.

Think this is a lot of work and not necessary? The Disney Corporation teaches this process at Disney University. New employees go through several days of training to learn the company's vision, procedures and other key aspects vital to maintaining superior service standards. Then, for example, if a visitor asks a groundskeeper the location of a particular ride, he'll have the right answer. You may be smaller than Disney Corporation, but you can have the same commitment to customer service. If you want to read more, check out Dennis Snow's *Lessons From the Mouse: A Guide for Applying Disney World's Secrets of Success to Your Organization, Your Career, and Your Life*, available in the Strategies bookstore.

Here are a few more ways to get the most from your training program for new employees:

- **Teach part of the program yourself.** Prove your commitment to the principles and behaviors your business expects of employees. It shows how serious you are about this and makes a new staff member feel extra welcome when the "big boss" takes time to review key points.

- **Drive home your company's vision, and give new team members an immediate opportunity to use it with various tasks, such as answering the phone or greeting clients.** Remember, this goes for everyone – no exceptions, including the "star" you just hired with15 years of experience. Make sure your training program is "soup to nuts." Help new employees understand the why and how of the tasks they'll be doing.

- **Involve key staff in every department.** Ask new staff members to work with the receptionist or coordinator on one day, and a senior technician the next. A new staff member should know who the lead person is in every department, who they should go to if they have questions. A new hire should have a basic understanding of how the company works and who is responsible for what.

- **Make it all encompassing.** Each day of training should be packed with information, demonstrations, role-playing and hands-on work. This isn't fill-out-some-paperwork-and-get-on-the-floor. Every new employee should feel immersed in your culture and experience a feeling of accomplishment, teamwork and camaraderie at the program's conclusion. Be careful not to overwhelm, though. Schedule breaks and lunch, and be prepared to answer lots of questions.

- **Include every department, and don't forget the "basics."** Every employee needs to know how to answer the phone, transfer a call, greet a client and book an appointment. This is just as important as knowing how to do a color or signature pedicure. Spend as much time as is needed on this process.

- **Write it down.** If you don't have your program committed to paper, key components may be forgotten. Prepare a three-ring binder, with extra paper for notes. The program should be as structured as possible. Have a checklist for each step, so that nothing is missed. Or develop a chart that shows the progress of the training, such as the one on page 87.

- **Follow up.** Check in with the new employee throughout the first couple of weeks to clear up any confusion. Once it's learned wrong, it's tough to unlearn.

Knowing what to expect is key for the success of every employee, new or long-term. When a new staff member starts, you have a unique opportunity to set up their expectations.

Tell new employees:

- **What they should expect in their daily routine.** The simple act of telling people what to expect can save a great deal of pain. Don't push the "ups" and hold back the "downs." If new employees must sweep floors, shampoo clients and rinse color for the first six months, tell them. This is what it is. But don't assume you know which tasks they'll love or hate. Present everything in a neutral, matter-of-fact tone. They may find folding towels to be a soothing way to end the day. Don't prejudice them by saying they'll hate a task.

- **How you will measure their performance.** Nothing is more important to new employees than knowing how their performance will be evaluated. Offer a detailed explanation of your performance and evaluation program, including what, how often and why.

- **How you will recognize and reward them.** Raises, bonuses, prizes, promotions and other types of recognition show employees that you value them and their work. Understanding how these things work is a great motivator, right from the start.

- **How exemplary customer service is a non-negotiable.** Make the standards clear and explain how this will be measured. It will encourage them to pursue maximum levels of excellence and customer satisfaction.

Reviews

After the initial training period, it's important to give each employee lots of feedback. There's a saying in Human Resources that nothing said at a performance review should ever be a surprise for the employee. Problems should be dealt with as they arise, and not saved for a formal review. And be generous with your praise. What gets rewarded, gets repeated!

Training Modules:

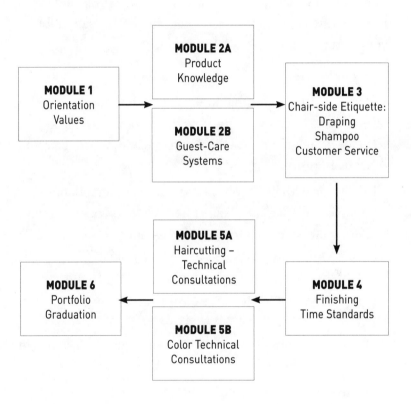

The first year, an employee should receive reviews at the one-month, three-month, six-month and one-year marks. Notice this doesn't say raises. These are simply performance evaluations. Determining an employee's pay grade and raises is a separate issue. (See the chapter on Compensation for all you need to know.)

In a performance evaluation, you should:

• Have a written form that addresses each job responsibility. Use it as a guide to discuss how the employee is doing. Use a scale of 1 to 5, or terms such as Excellent, Good, Fair and Needs Improvement.

• Be specific with both your praise and recommendations for improvement. Never say someone needs to do better without offering tangible ways to do so. For example, don't say, "You need to improve your customer-service skills." Say, "Our policy is to greet every client who comes into our view. I notice that you often turn your head as you walk past clients. Please start greeting clients every time."

• Go over any corrective action forms and discuss progress in previous trouble areas.

• Discuss achievements and acknowledgements, such as positive customer feedback.

• Talk about training that's been accomplished, or that needs to be done. This includes both skill-certification and other training, such as business education.

- Beyond job responsibilities, have a list of other items, such as being in dress code, following cell-phone use rules, etc.

- Rate the employee on teamwork, enthusiasm, communication, and other culture-related things.

- Allow the employee to give his or her side of things. She may believe that she is fulfilling a certain job requirement. You also may not see everything that's going on, so be open to changing your mind.

- Ask your managers and key employees for their input prior to the performance review. Have the employee's immediate supervisor sit in on the reviews and offer direct input.

- Continually jot down notes to help you remember details of an employee's performance. Praise it in the moment; then praise it at the review. Correct it in the moment; don't mention it in the review, unless it's a chronic problem. It's not productive to have a laundry list of negative behaviors that have already been corrected.

- Always find something to compliment. Look for it; it's there.

- Don't make up your mind about an employee after the first review. It sometimes takes a while for a new staff member to find his or her groove. There's so much to learn in a new working environment. Help the employee to know which job responsibilities are most important. Their success is your success.

- Make sure the employee understands what needs to be improved and the steps that need to be taken to improve, as well as the consequences if improvement is not achieved within a stated time period. Both you and the employee should sign off on such actions.

• Document, document, document. If you ever need to fire an employee, you must have records of conversations you had that detailed what needed to be improved.

• Be sensitive. People's identities are frequently wrapped up in their jobs; that's not just for entrepreneurs. Criticism is difficult to hear. Offer a dose of kindness and compassion, but be honest. An employee can't learn and grow if he or she doesn't know there's a problem.

After the first year, many companies offer quarterly reviews. While that might seem excessive, developing an evaluation process will help ensure that employees know exactly how they're doing and can make needed adjustments before too long a period of time has lapsed. It gives management a structure through which to objectively judge performance and ensure that behavior is held to a consistent standard. The guide for this is the broadband, which offers clear standards for each step on the growth path.

With an effective evaluation process, you can:

• emphasize client satisfaction and retention.

• create a unique image based on appearance, ambiance, ability, etc.

• foster business growth and build profits.

- build strong, cross-trained teams.

- enhance the skills of every staff member.

- provide a way to compare actual performance to established standards.

- increase staff's productivity and quality of service.

Without an evaluation system in place, you may have little basis for comparing actual performance (based on individual objectives, work standards, skill certification and job descriptions) to the company's stated goals. In the absence of black-and-white criteria, an evaluation becomes little more than an opinion. Using broadbands and job descriptions will hold staff to similar standards. There's no room for favoritism in an effective review program.

If behavior doesn't change after a review, it's time to reconsider your process.

- Does your evaluation system rely on subjective ratings? (It shouldn't.)

- Is appraisal based on personality traits, which bear little relation to work behavior? (It shouldn't.)

- Will the rating process stand up to a consistency test? (It should.)

- Does your appraisal system recognize star qualities over team qualities? (It shouldn't.)

- Is there a clearly defined and communicated standard, objective or expectation? (There should be.)

- Is the method of collecting and measuring data clear? (It should be.)

- Is evaluation data above suspicion in accuracy, consistency, completeness, and in how and by whom it is collected and reported? (It should be.)

- Is the evaluation approach and the data used sensitive to areas and situations over which individuals may have no control? (It should be.)

- Are the employees aware of the criteria by which they will be evaluated? (They should be.)

Evaluation guidelines

An effective employee evaluation should include:

- performance criteria relating directly to client satisfaction goals.

- clear standards and measurements.

- procedures and descriptions that promote a positive, forward-thinking view rather than a negative focus on past deficiencies.

- a formal process to inform staff of what they must do to improve performance before the next evaluation.

- employee opportunities to receive (or provide their own) feedback to help them keep track of their progress.

- an understanding of the support you will provide to help the employee improve performance and enhance skills.

• a clear-cut understanding of the link between performance, pay and career growth.

Encourage staff to offer their own feedback about their performance. An evaluation should be a give-and-take between the leader and the employee. Always remain calm. Focus on offering constructive criticism rather than negative. Evaluations should not be demoralizing for you or the employee. They are an excellent way to ensure that communication is clear and that employees are on the right path to achieve personal success and success for the company.

What if it's just not working out?

Problem employees can make life miserable for everyone in the business, clients and staff alike. Their behavior must be addressed before it disrupts the rest of the business or impacts client service.

Be assured that these problems won't simply go away. Ignoring the troubling behavior will just make it worse and will send a signal to other employees that subpar performance is an acceptable way to do business.

A lack of training or a poor understanding of the company's vision brings on most employee-behavior problems. Address the behavior as soon as it comes up; don't let it become a chronic habit. It might be as simple as reminding an employee of a policy from your company's policy and procedures manual, or you may have to review the procedure for doing a specific service.

GOOD TO KNOW!

1. Little things mean a lot to staff. Find ways to surprise and delight them on a regular basis.
2. Document everything about your employee behavior, both positive and negative.
3. Update your benefits package to meet changing employee needs.

When you speak to an employee about an area that needs improvement, keep your emotions out of the conversation. Simply review the facts. If it's a one-time incident that is not of major importance, you may not need to have an in-depth conversation. A reminder of the policy might be enough to solve the issue.

However, when there's a major policy violation or recurrent problem, you should strive to get to the root of the problem, discuss corrective measures and develop a verbal and/or written contract through which the behavior will be corrected. Early communication will usually resolve the issue. Document every conversation and have the employee sign any written reviews/contracts. If it becomes necessary to fire an employee, you'll need this back-up material. When in doubt, contact an attorney who's a specialist in employment law, or contact your state's Department of Labor.

You may wish to have a Corrective Action Form. (See a sample on page 96.) This will help you be consistent when speaking with different employees about various employment issues.

Employee files

You should have a file for every employee. These files must be kept under lock and key; employees have a right to expect privacy. You need to have hard copies of documents required by the government, as well as a record of reviews. Some things you need to have in an employee file:

• Application and resume; any written references

• Copies of applicable licenses and permits

• I-9 form

• W-4 form

• Salary information

• Performance reviews

• Documentation of corrective conversations, including signed contracts of performance requirements

Why build a skill-certification program?

Help every employee flourish with a skill-certification program. A skill-certification program is a formal, organized approach to evaluating staff ability in a variety of technical and customer service areas. The program's objective is to ensure the quality and integrity of your salon/spa/medspa by allowing staff members to perform only those services for which they have been certified.

But a skill-certification program must go well beyond technical skills. It must also include customer-service standards, communication and other non-technical skills. Designing a certification program requires great attention to detail and being attuned to the specifics of how services and behaviors feed into your vision.

Here is a sample of the Corrective Action Form:

Corrective Action Form

Verbal   Written

Employee: _____

Date: _____

☐ Customer Service
☐ Team Service
☐ Facility Service
☐ Technical Skill
☐ Performance Requirments
☐ Employment Relationship
☐ *Attitude*
☐ *Appearance*
☐ *Attendance*
☐ *Punctuality*
☐ *Time Management*

Performance Area

Incident Description   Excused   Unexcused

_____
_____
_____
_____
_____
_____

Action Plan   Followup Date:

_____
_____
_____
_____
_____

_____   _____
Supervisor Signature   Date

_____   _____
Employee Signature   Date

Since skill certification is specific to each business, begin with clearly defined objectives that reflect your vision. When fully designed and implemented, your skill-certification program becomes your image: quality technical service, superior customer service, and all the intangibles that separate your company from the competition – and there's plenty of that!

The program's objective is to ensure the integrity of your business, by allowing staff members to perform only those services for which they have been certified. The client's experience should be of the same quality, no matter which technician does the service. Beauty-industry businesses, including salons, spas and medspas, need a formal skills program to train new staff, monitor and update the skills of veteran staff members, and help them grow.

Let's examine some of the main facets of a skill-certification program:

You can't have consistent quality without it.

Service is your product. To deliver any service consistently, you must have established processes, objectives for quality and specified standards of performance. No one – including you and your managers – should provide a service of any form (technical or interpersonal) unless he or she can perform to established standards.

Size doesn't matter. If you're already thinking your business is too small to justify a formal skill-certification program, you're wrong. Size is not the issue; customer satisfaction is. How good do you want your business to be? Are you willing to accept mediocre technical and customer service? Are you willing to accept the costs of redoing services because they weren't up to par? Are you willing to accept low client-retention rates? Are you willing to fund the costs of inefficiency and poor productivity? Of course you're not. Even the most basic certification program will pay major dividends and give your business a competitive advantage.

Clients notice its absence. Often, clients are assigned to staff based on availability. This practice, combined with a lack of quality assurance mechanisms, produces dismal first-time client retention rates. What's your first-time client-retention rate? The only surefire way to improve your company's client-retention rate is to implement a skill-certification program.

It helps offer growth paths for your staff. What does it take to succeed in your company? What's expected of new staff? How can they move into the higher pay levels? A skill-certification program helps provide the answers. Skill-based pay systems encourage employees to develop and perfect new skills. These programs benefit the company, employees and clients. Yet many beauty-industry businesses are stuck in, and limited by, "percentage of sales" pay methods. The promise is: Sell more, earn more. Sales are clearly important, but where do quality assurance and customer service fit in? When pay is based solely on individual sales, everything else takes a back seat. (Check out the chapter on compensation to learn more.)

It's a powerful marketing tool. Don't keep your skill-certification program a secret. Promote it through advertising and in all potential and existing client contacts. Help clients and potential customers understand the benefits of your skill-certification program: consistent quality on every visit.

Designing your skill-certification program

Too many business owners rush to complete a skill-certification program only to get frustrated because it's not an instant fix. Plan on three or four months to complete entry-level technical and non-technical portions. Intermediate and advanced certification programs could take up to six or eight months to complete.

Where do you start? Commit to developing a customer-driven, high-quality, consistent business. Add solid leadership and a clear vision. Then delve into the following program blueprint. It contains everything you'll need to build a basic skill certification program.

The elements of the plan

Nearly all salon/spa/medspa skills which require certification fall into one of three major training areas: technical, professional/organizational, or personal/cultural.

- Technical training encompasses the skills which generate revenue for the business. They include retailing; performing hair, nail, spa and medspa services; and telephone and consultation skills.

- Professional/organizational behavior supports an understanding of the company's vision and goals. Examples of these skills include the ability to understand retail goals, etiquette, decision-making, profiling, profit and loss, client treatment and retention rates, and how to handle complaints.

• Personal/cultural skills relate to working relationships: staff to staff, staff to client, and staff to leadership team. They include upholding cultural requirements which contribute to the over-all environment: participation in meetings, relating to co-workers, maintaining and enforcing the company's culture, working on and leading projects, contributing ideas, and supporting the business's mission and vision.

These are only partial skill listings. You may add or subtract skills, depending on the specifics of your business. Your list may not be all-inclusive on the first go; keep searching.

Here is a diagram of what your program should look like. Simply identify the skill to be certified in the box at the top – and get started.

You may find a few items that seem to fit into more than one category; it's your choice as to which category each skill best fits into.

The heart of your program

The written, practical and benchmark sections of the program includes the bulk of training information, and can be used for any skill in any of the above categories, from a technical training program for hair color to the personal/cultural skill of handling complaints. The plan can be used for any skill needing certification.

To gain a better understanding of the system, let's use a technical skill from the salon industry, "perming."

The written portion

Writing down all aspects of a skill solidifies teaching methods and makes it black-and-white for you and your staff. Preparing each part of the written section will help you methodically list the skills to be learned. Once it's written, continually refer to it. Skill training should not become a guessing game. If a step needs to modified or additional information is required, make sure to change the written portion of the skill-certification program. All skill-certification materials should reflect your company's current processes and standards.

To create a comprehensive written analysis for a particular skill, gather as much support material as possible: magazine articles, notes from other training sessions, anything to enhance the learning process. Don't forget to include key members of your staff in this process. The people who do the skill most frequently will have crucial information to add.

After gathering the materials, create a topic description explaining how to master the skill. Make bullet point notes. For our perming example, topic descriptions would include hair analysis and consultation, perm selection, wrap and processing.

A procedural breakdown consists of all of the bullet points from the topic description. Precisely outline the steps for performing that particular skill. This will give the staff an agenda to follow, and ensure the skill is performed correctly every time and without confusion. Remind your staff that shortcuts will not be tolerated.

A perming example:

Step One: Perform detailed consultation with client to determine the goal for the procedure and to explain to the client what to expect.

Step Two: Shampoo hair with a deep-cleansing shampoo.

Step Three: Begin perm wrap using technique outlined by perm consultation.

Use your procedural breakdown to develop worksheets. Key points can be used to form review questions. Utilize these worksheets as quizzes to reinforce the learning process.

Here is a diagram of what your program should look like. Simply identify the skill to be certified in the box at the top – and get started.

The practical portion

The major thrust of the practical portion of a skill certification program is visual learning or learning by showing.

Hands-on demonstrations reinforce the written material already covered by allowing staff to see a particular skill applied in a real-life situation. When showing the steps for perming, for example, actually wrap a model. Show all aspects, including section size, rod placement and wrap technique. Demonstrate the entire process so that there is no room for misunderstanding or confusion.

You may wish to demonstrate the skill yourself, or you can select a key employee to teach the skill. Then, allow staff members to duplicate the process. Role-playing encourages staff to repeat new skills, and lets them try new techniques and methods in a controlled environment. Staff can work on mannequins, each other, or even friends and family, repeating the techniques they have seen. Videotaping may be effective in critiquing some skills.

Situational testing, much like written testing, allows staff to be evaluated on their newly acquired practical skills. Testing can range from role-playing to observations about the hands-on demonstrations and the end results.

The benchmarks

When written and practical training are completed, it's time to establish benchmarks: parameters which measure how well staff members retain new skills. Certain benchmarks must be achieved before certification is granted; others must be achieved afterward, to ensure consistency.

Pre-Certification Benchmarks include:

• Written test scores, which should range from 85%-100%.

• Practical test scores, which are rated pass/fail, as scored by a person that you designate.

• Establishment of goals means setting attainable, realistic objectives to help your staff master new skills and become certified. An example: Perm wraps must consistently be completed within 25 minutes.

Post-Certification Benchmarks include:

• Goal maintenance ensures that skill levels remain consistent and comply with certification requirements. It also encourages staff to master new skills. For perming, staff may be required to perform a minimum of 10 perms per month to remain certified.

• Efficiency problems isolate aspects of new skills that trouble staff. For example: Excessive re-perms may indicate the need to review the process, and retrain staff if necessary.

A skill-certification program must grow and change with the business. It needs adequate time to incubate. Staff, especially new members, must be certified before performing services. This will keep quality high and decrease mistakes. Technicians who are already performing services should continue to do so, but also be trained and formally certified within a specified time period. (Strategies offers a *Skill-Certification Manual*, which includes templates that will be valuable in establishing your company's skill-certification program. Visit the Strategies Bookstore at www.strategies.com to learn more.)

Get help developing your training program if necessary. Consider your staff when looking for qualified trainers. The benefits of a certification program will far outweigh the time spent building and maintaining it. A skill-certification program is a cost-effective way to improve quality, consistency and efficiency. Your staff and customers will appreciate the changes.

Getting your staff to do their best

While money is obviously a reason that people work, you have to look beyond salary to motivate staff members. People need a reason to work in your business, not just in the industry. And those reasons go far beyond compensation. When your employees talk about their company, do they shrug and say, "Well, it pays the rent"? Or are they excited to come to work every day and be a part of a bigger vision?

Often the companies where people are happiest offer a variety of seemingly small incentives and rewards. If you need inspiration, check out www.greatplacetowork.com. Keeping morale high and employees happy is an ongoing process. And if you're thinking, "Well, they should be happy they have jobs," then you're definitely not on track to be a world-class company. Inspired employees go the extra step, every time, without being asked. Customers know when an employee is turning in a lackluster performance, and they know when staff members love their jobs. It shows in everything they do. That's more work on your part (and the part of your management team), but you will see the difference on the bottom line.

Top employees and job candidates will be attracted to a company that has:

- No-compromise leadership. Inconsistency and compromise starts at the top. Employees want to know that leaders are willing to take the accountability to steer the ship – especially in challenging times.

- A captivating vision. A business needs a higher purpose to guide it.

- An engaging culture. A company's culture embodies its emotional, behavioral and moral values.

- Complete transparency. There cannot be double standards or hidden agendas. Open information builds trust.

- Amazing teamwork. Teamwork happens when everyone is working toward the same vision.

- Compassion and social consciousness. Show kindness and understanding toward your employees and appreciate your role in the greater good of the community.

- A commitment to consistency. Have an eye for attention for detail. Hold your staff to the same discipline.

Now, start a list of all the benefits of working in your company, as well as listing little ways that you can keep your staff happy.

- Begin with your benefits package. Is it competitive? Ask your staff what benefits are most important to them, then work to find ways to include them in the package.

- Offer flexibility, such as job sharing or flexible hours.

- Look at your vacation and days off policies. What can you tweak to help out your employees?

- Engage your staff in conversation and really listen. Don't be one of those bosses who only speak to employees when they're mad about something. Make an effort to connect with every employee, and help each to feel like an important member of the team.

- Treat staff members fairly. No playing favorites.

- Ask for employee input when looking to institute new policies.

- Spruce up the break room.

- Talk to local businesses to see if they'd like to offer a discount to your employees.

- Look to catch employees doing something right, whether it's on the phone with a potential client or an employee taking extra care with an elderly customer.

- Praise your employees frequently. Offer recognition one-on-one, to your management team, in staff meetings and publicly. In the day-to-day rush, that often falls by the wayside. Don't let it. Otherwise, employees can feel as though their efforts don't make a difference.

- Put on a happy face. That doesn't mean that you don't acknowledge problems. When you storm through the business looking baited for bear, you send a message to your staff. Your bad mood will send ripples through your organization.

- Once a week or monthly, take an employee or small group of staff members to lunch or out to coffee. In a relaxed setting, you'll learn new things about your employees. What's more, you might just hear some new ideas that an employee has been too shy to bring up in a more formal way.

- Model the behavior you want to see. If it matters enough to expect it of your staff, it matters enough for you to do it yourself.

- Bring a sense of fun to your organization with unexpected surprises:
  › Bake cookies.
  › Treat your staff to pizza.
  › Have a picnic or cookout in the parking lot.
  › Bring in flowers for staff members.
  › Bring in a variety of specialty coffees and teas.
  › Have a drawing for small-denomination gift cards, movie tickets, etc.
  › Be the one to organize a holiday lunch.
  › Celebrate everything! Bring joy to your organization.

› Leave notes for your staff, complimenting them on specifics of their job performance, or just to say how glad you are they are with your company. Make a bigger impact by sending the note to their homes.

What are your values? – a team exercise

The point of this exercise is to come up with a list of values that your team lives by. Once your team has agreed to a list of values, this is the code that guides every action and decision in your company. Plan for a good deal of discussion about what's most important. Don't rush the process. After you and your staff have come up with your list of company values, post them where the entire staff can see them. Be sure that discussing the list and how they apply in the company is reviewed extensively with each new hire.

Here's a plan for developing a list of salon/spa/medspa values:

• Compile a comprehensive list of values you see or would like to see in the salon/spa/medspa, or use the list provided on page 111.

• Put the list aside. When you can be objective, choose the three values most important to you.

• Make a copy of the complete list for each employee. Ask each to select three values from the list or to write in their own.

- Create a new list using everyone's choices. Values chosen by more than one person do not receive "favored" status. All are equal on the new list.

- Repeat the selection process until you've narrowed the list down to fewer than 10.

- Discuss these values as a group, ultimately deciding on the three most important to the company.

- Post these three values throughout the business. They should guide all management and staff decisions.

Choose from the list of values on the following page. Use these lines to write in any values that aren't listed.

_____

_____

_____

_____

_____

Our company values:

1. _____

2. _____

3. _____

Here is a suggested list of values:

truth	persistence	sincerity
fun	relationships	wisdom
flexibility	perspective	commitment
recognition	learning	honesty
originality	candor	prosperity
respect	fairness	order
spirituality	adventure	cooperation
humor	collaboration	efficiency
initiative	environmentalism	power
control	courage	competition
excitement	creativity	happiness
honor	innovation	obedience
financial growth	community support	integrity
peace	loyalty	clarity
security	love	resources
dependability	trust	excellence
teamwork	service	profitability
freedom	friendship	influence
justice	quality	hard work
responsiveness	fulfillment	purposefulness
strength	self-control	cleverness
success	artistry	support

My personal goals for
Human Resources:

_____

_____

_____

_____

_____

_____

_____

_____

_____

_____

_____

_____

_____

_____

_____

_____

_____

CHAPTER THREE

Compensation

*Is your pay system working
for your company?*

*Is your pay system working
for your company?*

Compensation

B e honest. Did you just cringe even reading the word "compensation"? It's certainly a topic that many owners and managers don't like to think about. It can be sticky – and give host to a variety of employee issues, from bad feelings to gossip to walkouts.

The truth is that pay doesn't have to be an uncomfortable topic. The key is that you must be willing to open your mind to a system that goes far beyond traditional commissions. It's called team-based pay and it's been revolutionizing compensation throughout the beauty industry. Strategies developed the team-based pay concepts, and believes it is the best way to compensate employees.

Compensation is a complicated issue. Your compensation is part of the package you use to reward and motivate your employees. There's no one golden number to reach that will work for every business. There's no right percentage for increases and bonuses that works in every situation. You must find the right formula that works for your salon, spa and medspa. Then, you must explain it in a way that inspires employees.

GOOD TO KNOW!

1. It takes time to change to a team-based system. Don't expect overnight success. Get the help you need to implement it in your company.

2. Communicate company goals, individual performance markers, etc. over and over again.

3. Celebrate the wins along the way – every time.

Before we discuss team-based pay, let's review other types of compensation. Let's start with commission, the traditional way to pay in the beauty industry.

Commission pay is easy for everybody to understand. No matter how you look at it, commission rewards employees for individual sales performance. For example, if a technician is paid a 50% commission and her chair, station or treatment room produces $1,000 in one week, she will earn $500. Simple. It's a safe choice for those with weak cash-flow management skills because, unlike the fixed expense of salary and/or hourly wages, a commission payroll rises and falls with the level of sales. To get a "raise," the employee must either take on more clients or negotiate for a higher rate of commission.

Many salons/spas/medspas are paying commission rates, which, even after product-cost deductions and service charges, guarantee such a high percentage of sales revenues to technicians that profit, if ever achieved, is impossible to maintain. Standard commission rates hover between 45-55% – a number that has gone unchanged for decades. However, other costs of business have increased dramatically. Consequently, the commission rates of the past no longer fit the costs of doing business. They are the primary force behind chronic cash-flow crises and can cause the eventual collapse of many salons/spas/medspas.

Compensation must reward the right behaviors.

What exactly does commission pay reward, and does it advance your company's vision and culture? If your business rules state that "the higher your sales, the more you make," and "the higher your request rate, the higher your value," what message are you sending to staff and which behaviors are you rewarding?

The messages employees hear are, "sell more to clients" and "build my following."

Question: What happens when a staff member, pushed on by commission, attempts a service he or she doesn't have the skill to perform?

Answer: Quality is compromised and client-retention rates suffer.

Question: What if, due to a lack of technical or selling skill, a staff member chooses not to recommend a service that would benefit a client?

Answer: The client, business and staff all lose, simply because there was no formal system to efficiently "move" that client to another chair or treatment room.

Followings and full books

The strongest message that commission pay delivers is: Build a following. Yet, that is at odds with having a culture that is customer oriented. Clients deserve access to salon, spa and medspa services when they want them. Unfortunately, they often encounter stylist and technician gridlock because compensation and other traditional operational systems discourage team service. After all, why would a technician who is paid commission and rated by his or her individual request rate encourage clients to visit other technicians?

No other element of the beauty industry is more worshiped than followings and full books. For most technicians, they are prestigious indicators of success. But owners and managers universally fear them because they are used as leverage to hold management "hostage."

As individual followings build, loyalty and income security gradually shift from the company to the employee's column in the appointment book. The employee's mode of thought then becomes: "I'm paying the company 50% of what I bring in." This attitude is a sure sign that your culture has been compromised.

Employees will do what your pay program rewards them for doing. Your compensation system needs to encourage the behaviors and culture your business needs to grow.

What vision- and culture-specific behaviors does your current compensation system reward and/or discourage? Because commission rewards individual sales, performance behaviors such as client retention, productivity, skill development and referrals go unacknowledged. If these and other performance factors are not tied into your compensation plan, employees often will regard them as nothing more than interruptions to their work. Remember, they will receive their sales commission whether or not they adopt the company's vision and culture.

How then can you address behavior problems such as lateness and absenteeism, poor attitude, lack of communication, being out of dress code, or not being a team player? An effective compensation system rewards overall performance.

Take a hard look at your current pay program by filling out the chart at right.

Everyone needs to be responsible for growth.

Just like the rest of the business world, salons/spas/medspas are finding that delivering a good product or service guarantees neither success nor customer loyalty. To stand out from the crowd, you must focus on fundamental competencies that reach far beyond technical skill. The company's vision and culture, and its operating and compensation systems, must be engineered to meet the demanding expectations of today's client.

Commission-based pay: A piece for me, a piece for you

Because commission is the predominant compensation structure for the industry, it has become part of the culture of the many salons/spas/medspas. There are many reasons why commission is the most common pay method, but they can

How good is my current pay program?

The process: Rate your present pay program on a scale of <u>one</u> (very little) to <u>five</u> (very much).

The objective is two-fold: First, we want you to focus on the inherent characteristics of your present pay program. Where does it fall short; where does it excel? Second, we want to get your creative juices flowing by opening up the traditional confines of salon/spa compensation. Once you understand that compensation can influence virtually every performance behavior necessary for business success – not just sales – you're over the biggest hurdle.

The total possible score for this analysis is fifty. The lowest score is ten. Any single statement that scores a four or less represents an element of the pay program that needs reengineering. If your total is forty or less, consider reengineering your entire pay program.

Complete this statement:

"My present compensation system encourages ..."

	Very Little			**Very Much**		
Client retention	1	2	3	4	5	Score _____
Productivity	1	2	3	4	5	Score _____
Client sharing	1	2	3	4	5	Score _____
Quality	1	2	3	4	5	Score _____
Teamwork	1	2	3	4	5	Score _____
Years of service	1	2	3	4	5	Score _____
Continuing education	1	2	3	4	5	Score _____
Above-average wages	1	2	3	4	5	Score _____
Business growth	1	2	3	4	5	Score _____
Profits	1	2	3	4	5	Score _____
						Total Score _____

be summed up in one thought: The beauty industry loves to celebrate the individual.

Everything else is predicated on that idea. Clients are loyal to technical staff rather than the salon, spa or medspa that employs them. And management in many salons/spas/medspas is best described as laissez-faire, resulting in a culture which allows employees to "do their own thing" with work schedules, customer service, technical competency and overall performance.

Why does the industry celebrate the individual through the legacy of commission? The three primary causes are:

• **The client ownership factor.** In the old days of weekly wash-and-sets, for example, there was a much closer bond between stylists and clients. (Seeing someone every week can do that.) Clients wanted to be "owned," especially when encouraged to be so by a stylist with whom they had developed a close, personal relationship.

• **The motivation factor.** The commission incentive is meant to motivate technicians to produce more. But in reality, commission is not a sales and productivity driver.

• **The management factor.** Many owners and managers never gain practical human-resources experience in the salon/spa/medspa environment. Many work as technicians themselves, leaving them little time to handle day-to-day operations.

Commission pros

In the interest of presenting a balanced picture, we can think of a few reasons why owners like the commission structure. (But we still don't think it's the best way to pay.)

- **Commission may motivate technical staff.** By paying staff on commission, the salon/spa/medspa owner effectively says, "Your value to this company and the client base is directly proportional to how hard you work." This is particularly effective with staff who have a strong work ethic and career drive. They're the ones who stay to service the last customer who walks through the door.

- **Commission makes it easy for service providers to open their own businesses.** Without a commitment to a fixed payroll, new owners can hire all the people they need. (Incidentally, this approach also spawned the practice of looking for technicians with large followings. "Stealing" clients has long been a by-product of commission.)

- **Commission offers an equitable means to distribute income.** Most technical staff understand the concept of working harder to earn a higher wage, and few find inequality in the administration of commission.

- **It's simple.** A given percentage is all you need to determine payroll for any period. Many companies pay 50% commission, which makes splitting sales right down the middle the basic calculation. Commission variations include sliding scales, service charges, product-cost deductions and multi-level pricing. Deductions and service charges lower commission payouts by giving the illusion that commission rates have not been reduced. Multi-level pricing, though it may be used to reward years of experience, is just a tool to increase pay without increasing commission rates.

Commission cons

Let's get right to them:

- **Commission tends to trap owners and top producers in production roles.** These people are so busy making a living that they cannot find the time to teach new service providers and help them become productive. Thus, the company's greatest asset – the skill of senior staff – is lost to each new generation.

- **It can restrict profits.** Often, up to 60% or more of all service income is consumed in payroll and related taxes. It's difficult to make money when only forty cents of each dollar is left for overhead, taxes and reinvestment in the business. The difference between successful and unsuccessful salons/spas/medspas can often be traced directly to their commission percentages.

- **Commission limits productivity.** It can actually demotivate a significant segment of technical staff because it tells them that they can make as much or as little as they choose. Many settle for less money and avoid the "pressure" of being busy or working more.

- **Commission is purely sales-driven.** When technical staff is paid for the amount of work they do – with no regard for how well they do it – quality and related behaviors can suffer. The underlying assumption is that if a technician does good work, he or she will become more popular and "do better." However, many believe it doesn't really matter if a client comes back, as long as their station or treatment room is busy, or their column is full.

- **Staff aren't rewarded for retaining clients.** Client retention is the single most important growth indicator of any salon/spa/medspa, and should be the focus of any compensation system.

- **Commission burns out many new technicians before they get the chance to become successful.** Many leave the profession after only one or two years because it's difficult to build a following and thereby earn a living.

Other considerations

Perhaps the greatest flaw in commission compensation is its inherent tendency to promote individualism. Commission encourages service providers to build personal clienteles which are often used as leverage against management. And yet, many owners and managers continue to judge technical staff's value by the size of their followings. Even the most experienced and competent stylists, nail technicians, massage therapists and estheticians find that when they relocate to a new town, they command little or no income security and must start all over simply because they don't have a following.

Ten sobering pay questions

The following questions will indicate the ability of your present compensation system to contribute to the culture you want to create. Use the comments that follow each question to help you to assess your responses.

1. **Where did your current pay program come from?** Most pay programs are mirror images of the ones owners previously worked under at other salon, spas and medspas. They typically are commission-based designs. Commission pay seldom allows for the other operational costs of the business.

2. **Which vision- and culture-specific behaviors was your pay program designed to reward?** If client retention, productivity, skill development, communication, attendance and other performance elements are not addressed through compensation, the company's culture can be compromised. Most commission-based programs do not encourage these behaviors.

3. **Which negative behaviors was it designed to discourage?** If your current pay program does not address negative behaviors such as tardiness, absenteeism, attitude and failure to recommend retail products, they will continue.

4. **If you pay a commission percentage on sales, how did you arrive at the percentage rate(s)?** Most commission rates reflect "the going rate" (i.e., what the other guy is doing), or the rate paid in the business where the current owner was previously employed. But if the original template was poorly designed, its inefficiencies will exist in all cloned versions.

5. **How did you integrate the compensation system into the company's overall financial plans?** Few commission programs are designed around the financial realities and operational costs of a business.

6. **Are controls designed into the program that will allow the business to adjust to increased operating costs?** When the largest operating expense is the fixed percentage of sales allocated to payroll (usually 50% or higher), any other cost increases will compromise profits.

7. **How does your pay program offer continued income growth to senior staff, who are typically booked solid?** When commission-paid employees are booked solid and their individual service prices cannot be increased, their income is gridlocked.

8. **How is the compensation system meant to encourage staff to develop their skills?** "If you want to earn – you've got to learn." What could be more important to one's earning potential in a service business than skill development?

9. **What strategies did you include to encourage teamwork?** In a team-based business, everyone is responsible for every hour available for sale, and focuses on achieving the company's sales and service goals. Commission pay focuses on individual sales.

10. **How does the compensation program benefit clients?** Clients serviced by the collective skills of the entire team can truly experience world-class service. A team-based pay program makes it possible.

Are you ready? Let's talk team-based pay.

The mechanics of team-based pay

There are many indicators that it's time to reassess a company's pay structure. In salons/spas/medspas, the most common are shrinking profits, less-than-motivated staff, lack of a clear direction for growth, marginal client retention and low productivity.

Commission and team-based pay directly conflict in three ways:

1. Commission is driven entirely by individual sales – Team-based pay is driven by overall performance. Consider a salon paying 60% commission and falling steadily deeper into debt because payroll is out of control. A decision is made to implement a new compensation system that is based on overall performance, both as individuals and as a team.

The first step of the conversion process is to calculate each technician's starting salary by examining their previous year's earnings, gross pay for the last four to six months, and overall performance. For our model, assume a salon scored only 37% on first-time client retention. In the time frame assessed, only fifty-eight of 158 first-time clients returned. During the pay-calculation process, red flags may go up for technicians with low client-retention rates. Particularly if they have been with the business for a number of years, they can still be paid quite a bit of money via commission, yet lose 70%-80% of the new clients assigned to them. The importance of a technician's "busy factor" pales beside his or her retention numbers. It's impossible to calculate the long-term costs of lost and dissatisfied clients.

A popular conversion strategy – and one that works well for a low-retention salon, such as our model – is to compensate technicians at their income level of the previous year, with a ninety-day window from the date of conversion in which to improve their retention and other performance factors. The owner's role is not to dictate improvement, but to coach and encourage specific and measurable results. Discrepancies between compensation earned and paid are erased in a performance-based framework.

2. Commission puts production control in employees' hands; team-based pay awards control to owners. Most salons, spas and medspas cannot continue to fund their present commission rates if they hope to keep pace with rising

operating costs. Product-cost deductions and service charges are not the answer; they simply cannot keep pace with increasing overhead expenses, and often cause significant staff upheaval.

Companies that succeed (yes, even during economic downturns) have realized they could not expect new behaviors and levels of performance if they didn't also reengineer compensation.

- **Reengineering Rule #1:** You cannot reengineer halfway.

- **Reengineering Rule #2:** Don't expect new behaviors and team performance if your pay program still rewards the old behaviors you are trying to change. You'll only confuse staff and stall the reengineering effort.

3. Commission does not inspire team performance – team-based pay is defined by it. Commission rewards individual sales and creates natural roadblocks to team service and performance. Team-based incentives are perhaps the most powerful performance-driven tools to arrive on the management scene in the last half century. They focus employee energy on growing the business. Few (if any) commission programs can make that claim. Since many salons/spas/medspas already pay out more in commission than they can afford, there's no room left for team incentives. Thus, reengineering the entire pay program is the only logical alternative.

The basics

Team-based pay is an hourly and/or salary program, which ties a team bonus to the achievement of critical numbers (e.g., revenue, gross margin, client retention, productivity, net profit). Individual growth is tied to overall performance − not just the employee's ability to generate revenue. A team-based pay system is designed to reward the right behaviors and performance − those that support the company's goals and culture.

If you change your pay system, especially to a team-based system, your business will go through a culture shift. The wider the gap between the five non-negotiable criteria (listed on page 133 and 134) and your current program, the greater the shift will be. The most significant shift will occur if you're moving from commission to team-based pay. Remember, commission encourages an "I/me" culture. Team-based pay encourages a "we/us/the team/the customer/the company" culture. The shift will be dynamic. Best of all, your customers will notice the change, and identify it as positive.

Shifting into "new pay" thinking

There is no "gold medal" for reengineering your pay program. It will not solve all your business woes, or instantly inspire staff to raise the performance bar. A compensation system is a reward system and nothing more. How efficiently you manage the program will determine its success or failure.

The most common mistakes business owners make while rolling out the pay program are:

- Introducing it without a vision (i.e., goal, objective and purpose). Employees must understand the vision in order to understand the changes that must take place to achieve it.

- Focusing on the program itself rather than the behaviors and results it is meant to inspire and reward. The new pay program will drive your business forward only if you steer it toward your vision. The team must know the weekly and/or monthly targets for sales, retention, productivity, average ticket, etc.

- Thinking the program will manage itself. Commission is a simple program because the burden of building sales rests with the employee. Commission says, "If they're hungry, they'll produce." The new pay says, "You and the team must meet these standards of performance." If one team member drops the ball, the entire team may pay the price.

Team-based pay is a better way to do business:

- Consistent bottom-line profits.
- A pay program that makes sense.
- Getting paid as an owner, not just an employee.
- Clients loyal to the business – not to an individual.
- A team culture that is fueled by growth.
- Bulletproof systems.

   The collective behavior of a business defines its operating culture. The method of compensation is at the core of a company's culture.

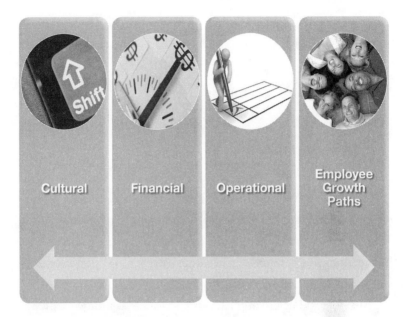

Cultural Financial Operational Employee Growth Paths

Five non-negotiables

Our ever-changing business climate demands a compensation system that meets the following five non-negotiable criteria:

1. Combined with fiscal responsibility, it must fit the financial reality of the business – today and into the foreseeable future.

2. It must be controllable, not a large "fixed percentage" of revenue.

3. It must encourage and reward the right individual behaviors and performance consistent with the vision and culture of the business.

4. It must give clear guidelines and pathways for individual growth.

5. It must inspire and reward teamwork, team culture, and attainment of the company's overall performance and revenue goals.

The leadership factor

Pay systems are foundations that great companies are built upon, but a pay system alone does not change behavior, performance or culture. Leadership must step up to the plate. Communication, goals, standards, skill development, financial accountability, openness and integrity are non-negotiable elements of a successful pay conversion.

Businesses that fail at pay conversions are managed by leaders who pick and choose which elements they want. They compromise the system from the beginning. They fall asleep, and then wonder why it didn't work. They sink into the blame game. Leaders need to be tenacious. No compromise.

Team-based pay is an exciting way to grow a company. Change gets the business juices flowing. The reward at all levels is extraordinary.

You may believe that you have effectively communicated the focal point of the business. You may feel that a job well done is rewarded handsomely. The bigger question is: If you altered the way you rewarded your employees, would you get different results? Aha! You shook your head yes, didn't you?

Then you do recognize that the way you compensate people influences their behavior.

The most important challenge is: How do you create a true team environment from a commission mindset and system? After all, you get what you reward. Have you ever heard an employee say, "I'm not paid enough to do that!" Or, "That's not what I was hired to do?" Typically, the task at hand is necessary to grow the business. However, the compensation plan and the agenda of the employee are focused on growing their bank accounts. It is impossible to have a team atmosphere with individual agendas.

Pay must reward the right behaviors.

Consider the behaviors your current pay model rewards. Is this in alignment with your business and company culture? Commission is entirely sales-driven and rewards only individual performance. It also encourages customers to build relationships with whoever is responsible for their account.

Today's business world is slowly waking up to the fact that, together, a team can accomplish more than any individual alone. Delivering a service does not guarantee success or the level of customer satisfaction that drives loyalty and retention to new heights. To shine brightly, you must focus on fundamental competencies and capabilities that go far beyond the basics of servicing a customer.

Today's employees are more demanding and less loyal. They want to see career growth paths. They want to know their income can continue to grow, even when their schedules are completely booked.

If your goal is to move toward a total team mindset, then you must evaluate the method in which behavior is rewarded. Look at your business with a magnifying glass. Peel back the layers and look at the behavioral outcomes. Are you rewarding what the company needs most from the employees?

If people are showing up late, does your current system ignore this behavior – or worse, reward it? When someone is struggling to reach a sales goal, do other employees volunteer to coach that person? After peeling back the layers and getting to the heart of your business, do you think the people who make up your company culture understand and get rewarded for the overall well-being of the business – or just their slice?

What's in it for you. What's in it for staff. What's in it for the business.

- Imagine how your business might perform if everyone was forging ahead in the same direction.

- The way an employee is compensated is typically the launching pad for all the operational systems within a company

- What would your company look like if you built the vision and mission first – then designed a compensation plan to support the desired behavior? With team culture as the objective, how would you design systems to support this?

- If you reward employees for individual accomplishments, they will forge ahead with running their "own clientele" businesses within yours.

- If you reward employees based on overall performance and for growing the company, they'll grow it faster and bigger than you can imagine.

Communicating your new pay program

As you move forward with your new pay program, it is vital to remain focused on the objectives of the transition. A conversion to team-based pay is not a ploy to force pay cuts or take anything away from staff. It is not another smoke-and-mirrors, variable commission, product cost/service charge, multi-level pricing, request-driven, inefficient, hostage-management pay program. (So there!)

Remember, what gets rewarded gets repeated. If one rewards only sales (i.e., pay service provider via commission), sales will occur with varying degrees of success. With team-based pay, increases will not occur unless overall individual and team performance meet the standards you establish. At the heart of the program is the team-based incentive which unites the efforts of the entire staff – not just service providers – to move the numbers in the right direction: revenues up and costs down.

Understand that team-based pay is not a quick fix or panacea. It will not solve all your operational, financial or growth problems. It requires planning and constant attention to detail.

It requires leadership, honesty, teamwork and open communication. It is simply a compensation system, but one which rewards the behaviors that enable a business to grow.

Broadbands: the fuel behind team-based pay

When it comes to assessing employee performance and compensation, broadbands are an invaluable tool. They visually link compensation levels to skill requirements, and help employees and management plot growth paths. They define skill sets, pay ranges and income potential. They are an effective way to share critical information and eliminate claims of ignorance of standards at performance reviews. They are integral to fair hiring practices, graduated skill acquisition and consistency in performance reviews. They outline the responsibilities associated with each position within a business and define the reward potential for goal accomplishment.

In short, broadbands provide a complete picture of an employee's position within the business. They not only draw the outlines of job responsibility; they paint in all the colors. While every purpose they serve is important, perhaps the most significant is establishing a correlation between skill and compensation.

A broadband derives its name from its function: It separates, into "broad bands," the specific skills, competencies and contributions that are required at each level of compensation within a business. The bands are broad so that employers and evaluators have a little wiggle room, and are able to incentivize accomplishments without guaranteeing what could be a significant pay increase to someone who may be only marginally deserving.

Broadbands are not a replacement or substitute for detailed job descriptions or position contracts. (See the chapter about human resources for more on those.) They are not designed or intended to provide the same level of detail concerning a position's duties, responsibilities and desired outcomes. You don't want the broadbands to be overly complicated. Over-building will just confuse or even demoralize staff.

When designing broadbands for the various positions in your business, you're building a guide for career growth and income advancement. Broadbands should not be so rigid that an employee's performance is strictly measured against it. Remember, team-based pay is about overall performance, creating the right behaviors, and business culture. That's why we stress that broadbands are a guide – not an absolute.

Broadbanding establishes concise performance guidelines. Although there is no fixed or "proper" number of bands, try to have as few as possible, perhaps one for each staff group.

The purpose of broadbanding

With broadbands, jobs are grouped based on the tasks involved and the skills required. This means that employees can move up the compensation ladder without traditional promotions and job delineations, because their growth is based on skill attainment and performance rather than their tenure with a business or in a certain position.

1. Evaluate your pay system to ensure that it makes sense.
2. Reward behaviors that go beyond providing a service.
3. Change your culture by changing your pay system.

An effective broadband will be fairly rigorous to move through, especially in the upper levels, where skill levels and competencies are already high. It will demand not only skill attainment, but also the ability to put those skills to use during client services, team meetings, brainstorming sessions, and leadership and mentoring scenarios. It will demand a depth and breadth of growth from employees that reaches far beyond technical capability. And, finally, it will show employees the personal and professional rewards they will attain as a result of their efforts.

You may be thinking that broadbands will only work in businesses that have strong teams. In reality, they will only work in businesses that have a culture strong enough to support a team. Everything needn't be "just so" in order to build and use broadbands – but they do work better in some businesses than in others. Broadbanding works best in companies ready to let go of traditional employee roles and job classifications that support outdated management systems. If you want to create a high-performance, team-oriented workplace that offers greater flexibility, cross-training and employee involvement in decision-making processes, you'll likely need to change a few things in the way the business is managed.

The manner of employees' work, and the way they are compensated for it, is the heart of the matter.

Broadbands can also reduce the number of pay levels, or at least help you get a handle on them, by tying pay advancement directly to factors other than seniority and client lists. This results in greater control over allocation and total payroll costs. Of course, broadbanding can be used with any compensation system – whether salary, commission or seniority-based. But it work bests when some sort of skill-based element is incorporated. While nothing about broadbanding or certifying employees' skills is meant to diminish the current importance or integrity of the individual, it is meant to increase their value to the business by ramping their skills upward and involving them more deeply in the decision-making processes.

Performance-based broadbanding:

- should focus on ongoing and effective communication and employee trust.
- works best in businesses where the existing culture encourages improved performance.
- works best in businesses that have strong performance management systems.
- needs adequate funding. Increases in pay should be meaningful to employees and appropriate to their contributions.
- requires adequate controls in order to keep total costs in line with the company's true capabilities.
- requires high levels of training for employees.

• requires innovative reward systems.

• should result in growth for employees and the business.

The following example of a broadband shows five levels of skill sets (pages 146-147). You may label the bands, but do not use names that imply superiority. Focus on performance, not titles or status. You may construct broadbands for any staff group (e.g., junior stylists or spa specialists), as long as their overall performance criteria are clearly defined and understood.

Planning the pay program launch

Traditionally, people don't talk much about pay, except to complain about it. Compensation systems and formulas are a great mystery in many companies. If compensation guidelines are not articulated in a way everyone understands, trouble can erupt. In the case of a new pay program filled with incentives, bonuses and reward systems, employees must know the details. Otherwise, they will have no idea what their goals are, or what the rewards will be for meeting them. With a team-based pay system, goals and objectives are the foundation of the entire program. Staff must be clued in to what's happening or goals will never be met.

Your team depends on you for information. They have faith that you will make decisions in their best interest – and in the best interest of the salon, spa or medspa. Only when they suspect foul play do they begin to lose faith. Owners must maintain the integrity of their actions and alleviate the staff's (natural) fear of change through detailed communication.

Strong communication can eliminate the rumor mill. Leadership announcements and personal communication with staff must start well before the program is implemented and last long after. Once the staff hears about it from the source – team leaders and management – rumors won't have the chance to form.

During times of dramatic change, people become overly sensitive. The communication process must ensure a clear and concise message, which is understood by everyone.

• The means of communication should agree with your current salon, spa or medspa culture. Thoroughness, detail and a willingness to listen are key. If the culture is self-directed (i.e., hostage management), your communications must define a new vision and commitment from the top. No matter how well-managed your business is, changing the way people are paid will always create unrest.

• Communication must encompass everyone at every level. It's the only way a new compensation system will succeed. Every team member wants to have a voice in change. Give it to them. You'll be surprised at the ways different ideas and opinions can improve the outcome.

• Any significant change in operations must complement your company's vision. Compensation must be discussed in terms of changes already made, as well as those to come.

Why? Compensation is the true force behind most successful change initiatives.

• The message must be consistent and clear. Teach the team to play a new game with new rules. Focus on the growth opportunities the new program offers. Explain new terminology, performance criteria, skill certification and team-based incentives. Employees' fears stem from what they don't comprehend. Help them understand. Without proper communication, a pay program may never reach its true potential.

Compensation Checklist

Before introducing and launching a new pay program, complete the following:

• Research current compensation trends in business. Explore all your pay options.

• Compile a detailed list of every performance requirement and behavior that is important to growing your company. Involve your staff in this process.

• Determine your breakeven point and prepare a twelve-month revenue and expense projection to guide your efforts and control expenses.

• Calculate the average paycheck for each employee.

• Define the standards of overall performance you want the program to reward. These might include client-retention and productivity rates, continued skill development, service and retail sales, and teamwork.

• Get help. A new compensation program is a huge change. Strategies is the expert on team-based pay and can assist you in rolling it out right and getting your team on board – from the start.

Team bonus: designing your team's brass ring

The mandate of team-based pay is simple: Everyone is responsible for growing the business. These words are powerful, but words alone aren't enough to inspire dynamic team performance. A pay program alone cannot instill a business-wide sense of urgency to drive revenues up, manage costs and build net profit. Given this, team-based pay uses team bonus as a means of driving the Four Business Outcomes: productivity, profitability, staff retention and customer loyalty.

Before going any further, let's be clear. A team bonus is not an entitlement that employees receive simply because the business hit a goal or generated profits. Entitlement-based bonuses cannot shape or encourage dynamic team behavior.

For example, an annual Christmas bonus that is not attached to any performance goal is an entitlement. Employees will expect it every year and, should it stop, there will surely be a fuss.

Every business has critical numbers that, when achieved, have a profound impact on one or more of the Four Business Outcomes. More specifically, driving a critical number shapes team performance and behavior in a lasting way.

Clearly the most obvious critical number is net profit – but it can also be productivity rates, client retention, gross-margin

	Level 1		Level 2	
	Minimum	Maximum	Minimum	Maximum
Yearly	$18,600.00	$26,040.00	$24,738.00	$34,633.20
Hourly	$8.94	$12.52	$11.89	$16.65

Team-Based Broadband Pay Scale

This model of a Team-Based Broadband pay scale details five skill levels and their corresponding pay ranges, performance criteria. Individual and team performance bonus structures are clearly identified. The model also shows how growth potential is tied to all key areas of performance.

Level 1

Performance & Critical Numbers
- New client retention = 40%
- Existing client retention = 75%
- Productivity rate = 75 - 80%
- Pre-book ratio = 40 - 50%
- Retail to service ratio = 10 - 15%
- Units per client = 1.0
- Avg service/retail ticket = $45 - $52
- Average service ticket = $35 - $42
- 100% product recommendation

Skill Requirements
- Greeting/consultation/front desk basics
- Draping/shampooing
- Manicures and pedicures levels 1,2,3
- Service time protocols
- Round brush styling
- Curling and straight ironing, texturized
- Color formulations
- Cutting
- Service recommendation/prebook
- Product recommendation
- Guest awareness and relations

Culture & Teamwork
- Lives no-compromise culture
- Strives and supports company values
- Interpersonal relationship skills
- Cooperation: up, down and around
- Positive and supportive attitude
- Delivers results
- Supports company and team initiatives
- Seeks to mentor others
- Strives to set the right behavior
- Embrace and support change
- Communicate problems quickly
- Actively participate in huddles
- Team problem solving

Strengths
- Knowledge of the work
- Quantity of work
- Quality of work
- Initiative
- Dependability & accountability
- Quality of interpersonal relationships
- Attendance
- Punctuality
- Supervisory abilities
- Communication abilities
- Trust
- Strives to get better
- Listening skills
- Maintains a sense of urgency
- Keeps commitments

Level 2

Performance & Critical Numbers
- New client retention = 40% - 48%
- Existing client retention = 80%
- Productivity rate = 80 - 85%
- Prebook ratio = 50 - 60%
- Retail to service ratio = 15 - 20%
- Units per client = 1.0 to 1.3
- Avg service/retail ticket = $52 - $64
- Average service ticket = $42 - $54
- 100% product recommendation

Skill Requirements
- Greeting/consultation
- Draping/shampooing
- Service time protocols
- Round brush styling
- Curling and straight ironing, texturized
- Highlights/lowlights
- Cutting
- Service recommendation/prebook
- Product recommendation
- Guest awareness and relations

Culture & Teamwork
- Lives no-compromise culture
- Strives and supports company values
- Interpersonal relationship skills
- Cooperation: up, down and around
- Positive and supportive attitude
- Delivers results
- Supports company and team initiatives
- Seeks to mentor others
- Strives to set the right behavior
- Embrace and support change
- Communicate problems quickly
- Actively participate in huddles
- Team problem solving

Strengths
- Knowledge of the work
- Quantity of work
- Quality of work
- Initiative
- Dependability & accountability
- Quality of interpersonal relationships
- Attendance
- Punctuality
- Supervisory abilities
- Communication abilities
- Trust
- Strives to get better
- Listening skills
- Maintains a sense of urgency
- Keeps commitments

Level 3		Level 4		Level 5	
Minimum	Maximum	Minimum	Maximum	Minimum	Maximum
$32,901.54	$46,062.16	$43,759.05	$61,262.67	$58,199.53	$81,479.35
$15.82	$22.15	$21.04	$29.45	$27.98	$39.17

Performance & Critical Numbers
- New client retention = 46% - 58%
- Existing client retention = 80%
- Productivity rate = 85 - 92%
- Prebook ratio = 50 - 60%
- Retail to service ratio = 20 - 25%
- Units per client = 1.3 to 1.5
- Avg service/retail ticket = $60 - $72
- Average service ticket = $50 - $62
- 100% product recommendation

Skill Requirements
- Greeting/consultation
- Draping/shampooing
- Service time protocols
- Round brush styling
- Curling and straight ironing, texturized
- Specialty services
- Color formulations
- Highlights/lowlights
- Cutting
- Service recommendation/prebook
- Product recommendation
- Guest awareness and relations

Culture & Teamwork
- Lives no-compromise culture
- Strives and supports company values
- Interpersonal relationship skills
- Cooperation: up, down and around
- Positive and supportive attitude
- Delivers results
- Supports company and team initiatives
- Seeks to mentor others
- Strives to set the right behavior
- Embrace and support change
- Communicate problems quickly
- Actively participate in huddles
- Team problem solving

Strengths
- Knowledge of the work
- Quantity of work
- Quality of work
- Initiative
- Dependability & Accountability
- Quality of interpersonal relationships
- Attendance
- Punctuality
- Supervisory abilities
- Communication abilities
- Trust
- Strives to get better
- Listening skills
- Maintains a sense of urgency
- Keeps commitments

Performance & Critical Numbers
- New client retention = 56% - 70%
- Existing client retention = 85%
- Productivity rate = 85 - 92%
- Prebook ratio = 60 - 75%
- Retail to service ratio = 20 - 30%
- Units per client = 1.5 to 1.7
- Avg service/retail ticket = $68 - $82
- Average service ticket = $58 - $72
- 100% product recommendation

Skill Requirements
- Greeting/consultation
- Draping/shampooing
- Round brush styling
- Curling and straight ironing, texturized
- Cutting
- Color formulations
- Base color
- Highlights/lowlights
- Service time protocols
- Specialty services
- Service recommendation/prebook
- Guest awareness and relations

Culture & Teamwork
- Lives no-compromise culture
- Strives and supports company values
- Interpersonal relationship skills
- Cooperation: up, down and around
- Positive and supportive attitude
- Delivers results
- Supports company and team initiatives
- Seeks to mentor others
- Strives to set the right behavior
- Embrace and support change
- Communicate problems quickly
- Actively participate in huddles
- Team problem solving

Strengths
- Knowledge of the work
- Quantity of work
- Quality of work
- Initiative
- Dependability & Accountability
- Quality of interpersonal relationships
- Attendance
- Punctuality
- Supervisory abilities
- Communication abilities
- Trust
- Strives to get better
- Listening skills
- Maintains a sense of urgency
- Keeps commitments

Performance & Critical Numbers
- New client retention = 70%+++
- Existing client retention = 95+%
- Productivity rate = 92 - 100%
- Prebook ratio = 75 - 100%
- Retail to service ratio = 30%+++
- Units per client = 1.5 to 1.7
- Avg service/retail ticket = $78 - $92
- Average service ticket = $68 - $82
- 100% product recommendation

Skill Requirements
- Greeting/consultation
- Draping/shampooing
- Round brush styling
- Curling and straight ironing, texturized
- Cutting
- Color formulations
- Base color
- Highlights/lowlights
- Open air processing
- Service time protocols
- Specialty services
- Service recommendation/prebook
- Guest awareness and relations

Culture & Teamwork
- Lives no-compromise culture
- Strives and supports company values
- Interpersonal relationship skills
- Cooperation: up, down and around
- Positive and supportive attitude
- Delivers results
- Supports company and team initiatives
- Seeks to mentor others
- Strives to set the right behavior
- Embrace and support change
- Communicate problems quickly
- Actively participate in huddles
- Team problem solving

Strengths
- Knowledge of the work
- Quantity of work
- Quality of work
- Initiative
- Dependability & Accountability
- Quality of interpersonal relationships
- Attendance
- Punctuality
- Supervisory abilities
- Communication abilities
- Trust
- Strives to get better
- Listening skills
- Maintains a sense of urgency
- Keeps commitments

goals, product and material costs, etc. Tying a team bonus to the achievement of a critical number makes the business game interesting. It also adds flexibility and variety to your program, which will help maintain the all-important sense of urgency that drives team performance. Give careful consideration to defining your critical numbers. Begin with a number that, when achieved, will have the most profound impact and give cause for major celebration.

A team bonus is not about maintaining status quo performance. The thinking is simple: If you want growth, team performance has to stretch. When we say "stretch," we mean incremental growth steps, not giant leaps. A team has to win regular-season games before going to the Super Bowl.

But at most companies, nobody understands the program. Employees don't know what bonuses are tied to. They don't know how the company is doing, so they have no idea whether they'll hit a bonus. Nor do they understand how their own jobs contribute to company performance.

Sometimes, the very best a bonus program can do is make you feel good about the company you work for. When somebody hands you a bonus check, you're inclined to think: Gee, this is a pretty good place to work after all. On the other hand, those warm fuzzies can quickly evaporate. If there is no bonus, or if the check is smaller than before, it's hard to avoid feeling: "Gee, I've been burnt once again by the company I work for."

If people don't know why they get a bonus and what they have to do to get one again, they can't be expected to move any numbers forward. How can people work to increase profits if they don't know what the goals are or how their job helps achieve them?

Companies that use team-based pay take a different approach to bonuses. The bonus plan is expected not only to motivate employees but also to help them learn. It's also expected to leave the company stronger at the end of the year than it was at the start. An open-book bonus plan isn't an afterthought. The bonus is everyone's reward for boosting the company's performance. It makes it possible for employees to think of themselves as businesspeople.

Here are some bonus basics:

• **It has to be self-funding.** Nothing will demoralize a team more than to achieve their goal, but be told, "Oops, there's no money for a bonus." Whether your team bonus is based on hitting net profit goals or some other critical number, your system must be self-funding. Achieving the goal must create net profit – cash – at the bottom line. Caution: Do not play the team bonus game if you and your leadership team are not committed to being fiscally responsible. One way to create a self-funding bonus program is to set minimum net profit targets that must be achieved before the bonus is awarded.

  › Here's an example. If net profit currently averages a lackluster 5%, you may set a new baseline of 7% - 8%, which needs to be achieved before any money drops into the team bonus pool. This approach ensures that current profit levels are not only maintained, but are increased before the team bonus is calculated. (Securing the company's future must be part of the team-based bonus program.)

Once net profit exceeds the baseline set for funding and activating the team bonus pool, you can schedule monthly, quarterly or annual payouts. To keep the game interesting, consider ramping up the payout in progressive stages, leading up to the big-game payout at the end of the year. How much of the gain goes into the team bonus pool requires careful consideration and a thorough understanding of the current and near-future financial realities of the business.

• **It has to be super simple.** There's nothing worse than a team bonus program no one understands! Resist the temptation for elaborate formulas and payout schemes. Focus instead on creating a program that every employee can understand. Try quizzing employees on the final plan, to see if they can explain it. If they can't, it's too complicated.

• **You have to keep score.** Since team bonus is tied directly to performance and hitting your critical numbers, your program must include a rapid-fire communication system. To accomplish this, incorporate daily huddles and scoreboards, which keep everyone informed, engaged and focused on achieving goals. Strategies' clients that do report faster growth, significant cost reductions and stronger profits. Daily huddles and scoreboards maintain that essential sense of urgency. Don't overlook this key piece of the team bonus. (More on this in the Leadership chapter.)

- **Everyone wins.** Team achievement means everyone on the team gets a share of the bonus payout. Some businesses take the "everyone gets a fair share" approach – from top management to custodial. Others use a system of differentiated levels to distribute the bonus based on decision making and accountability – not excessively so, just enough to reward and recognize their leaders. A balanced team bonus program should also include qualifiers for participation. Nothing will dash teamwork more quickly than players who don't contribute or play the game.

- **It has to be generous enough to matter.** If the company is doing well, the bonus must reflect that. (Nobody wants to come to work every day to make the boss rich.)

- **It has to be fair.** A bonus plan that leaves out any group of regular employees runs counter to the basic idea of open-book management.

- **It cannot be a substitute for base pay.** A bonus is an addition to competitive base pay.

- **The bonus is an educational tool.** Employees need to understand some business basics, such as how the company makes money and the critical numbers that they can affect. If you tell staff the payout is based on client retention, they will make themselves client-retention experts. They'll do everything possible to get clients back in the salon/spa/medspa. If a bonus is to be an educational tool, it must be coupled with instruction, reminders and communication. (It's another reason for using scoreboards and other open-book management tools.)

• **The bonus makes the company stronger.** Every business has specific challenges in any given year (e.g., decreased service sales, low retail). These are the problems that keep owners up at night – and they rarely share them with employees. But what would happen if you identified a challenge, set a goal for improvement, and then tied part of the bonus payout to hitting that goal? Bingo! Now everybody is worrying about that problem and working to rectify it.

Designing your bonus program

What you want a bonus system to do is simple: Focus everyone's attention on the critical elements of business performance in order to build a stronger, more profitable company. Stronger companies provide more job security and opportunity, and generate more wealth to share.

Everyone has a powerful interest in establishing a bonus program that works. By helping people understand critical goals, they learn how they can move the numbers in the right direction. That leads to better performance. Hint: It's one thing to change the way a company is supposed to work, but another to change the way people actually think and act. It takes time, careful attention to detail and lots of communication and follow-up.

The easiest way for salons, spas and medspas to set goals is to base them on sales and tie the bonus directly to net profit.

This works because the relationship of people's jobs to how the company makes money is easily understood. For most salons, spas and medspas, it's simple: The business makes money when productivity is up and costs are down. More services generate higher revenues and, if costs are kept down, profit goes up.

- Set the sales goal high enough for the business to cover all costs and have something left over as net profit.

- What must the business do in one month in order to cover all expenses?

- How much more is necessary to have a nice amount drop to the bottom line?

These numbers are the basis for your goals. And, if the goal is hit, you will have enough to cover all expenses before paying out a bonus.

- Determine the critical numbers that will drive the sales goal. They may be productivity, retention, retail sales, etc. These numbers will move the business toward its goal.

- Pick your target numbers carefully.

- How high is reasonable?

- Targets too easily reached won't do much to improve the company's performance.

- Those that are too high, that seem impossible, will make the whole bonus plan seem like a sham. The targets that trigger a bonus payout should be a stretch, but also reachable.

- **Create the bonus pool.** Your salon/spa/medspa hits its targets. How much money will be distributed as bonus? Tie the bonus to net profit by allocating a percentage of net margin to team bonus.

- **Include everyone.** This is a team bonus and a team effort. Everyone is part of the team, so everyone should be included in the bonus – except owners. Owners get what's left over: the rest of the profit.

- **Set up disqualifiers.** Many salons, spas and medspas like a "three strikes and you're out" program. As a team, the entire staff should decide what constitutes a "strike," such as showing up late for work, missing a huddle, violation of dress code, not participating in product-recommendation systems, etc. If an employee earns three strikes in one month, he or she is disqualified from team bonus. That means everyone else's share gets a little bigger. The slate is wiped clean each month.

- **Decide how much each person gets.** There are several methods used to divide team bonus. The method we like best is equal shares. Under this method, all employees receive an equal share based on time worked. For example: A full-time person receives a full share, and a part-time person, a half share. (Shares may even need to be divided into quarters, depending on the range of hours employees work. If you split the shares in quarters, someone working forty hours would receive four, someone working thirty hours would receive three, etc.)

- **Some companies offer a percentage based on actual hours worked.** Some offer the same percentage across the board, while some give percentages based on job responsibilities. Still others give employees the same percentage of bonus that their gross W–2 earnings represent of overall payroll.

- **Celebrate! When you pay a bonus, put on a party.** This is a time for celebration. Whether it's coffee and doughnuts or a picnic, show its importance by passing out bonus checks at a special time.

Don't forget about the pay.

It's not just about the bonus. Pay is obviously a key part of the compensation package. Pay evaluations are frequently a touchy subject. How do performance numbers tell an owner when it's time to reward a team member?

Before we go further, remember that there is a tremendous difference between performance evaluations and pay reviews. Performance evaluations are one-on-one meetings with team members for the purpose of discussing performance only. Pay is not discussed during performance evaluations.

A pay review is only scheduled after one or more performance evaluations indicate that a pay raise has been earned. (This is where cash-flow projections are essential. You cannot grant a raise before plugging the increase into your monthly payroll expenses and projecting its impact on overall cash flow.)

Key criteria used in performance evaluations may be first-time and existing client retention, productivity rate and average ticket. When an employee's performance is consistently at or above performance goals in all categories, it's clear that he or she is contributing to overall salon/spa/medspa growth and should be rewarded in some fashion. This could mean a raise, a bonus, time off, free education or special privileges. Of course, a service provider can only operate to a certain productivity level before having to pass sales to other people, but that is the whole point of the team system.

When you have retention and productivity numbers right under your nose, you will discover patterns of activity. Employee strengths and weaknesses become clear within a few months.

Understanding Pay Raises

One of the most perplexing aspects of working with a new pay program that encompasses all aspects of performance is how to determine raises. Commission is easy because sales performance takes care of raises automatically (often in spite of tardiness, poor client retention, attitude, etc.).

Here are some guidelines to take the mystery out of pay raises on the new pay system:

• Pay raises are granted when it makes sense for both the business and employee. Raises are not entitlements. They are earned through individual and team performance.

• Just because an employee meets the skill-certification requirements for a skill set doesn't mean an automatic raise or promotion is in order.

- A series of "good" or "excellent" performance evaluations will indicate if and when you should schedule a pay review.

- Always consider overall performance when determining employee pay increases. If an employee is habitually late, has an attitude problem or displays behavior contrary to the salon/spa/medspa's culture, the employee must know that his or her behavior is preventing a pay raise.

- Pay increases are long-term commitments. No matter how small or large, pay raises must be worked into the cash-flow plan.

- Pay raises do not have to start with the next paycheck. Set a start date for raises that fits the cash-flow plan – for example, thirty to ninety days from the pay review. Don't delay a raise needlessly. Be fair and honest.

- When an employee asks for a raise, it is an opportunity to refocus his or her attention on performance or behaviors that may need improvement. Together, set realistic, time-based goals, and the reward for achieving them.

- Salary reviews should be held, on average, once per year. A salary review does not mean a raise will be awarded. Overall performance and cash flow are the deciding factors.

- Employees (new and existing) with superior overall performance, skill development and individual achievement may qualify for special salary reviews.

- A raise is usually awarded as a percentage increase in the hourly rate or annual salary (e.g., 3%–5% annually).

• All planned payroll increases (including taxes) must be added to service and/or general and administrative payroll.

Finally, it's important for your pay program to complement the vision, mission and culture of your business. Make sure that every employee understands how this relates to his or her job. These are the standards that everyone in the company must adhere to in order to achieve the highest levels of customer service. Here's a sample on the facing page.

Aligning pay & performance with vision, mission and culture

VISION - What is your objective?

Total Quality Commitment ... Strive to meet and exceed standards of performance and excellence, follow pre-established processes, do what's best for the customer

Service Driven ... Listen and respond to the needs of the business, the team and the clients we service

Technical Excellence ... Education and technical skill orientation

No Re-Dos ... Quality and consistency come first

On-Time Service ... Sensitivity to customer's time value, meticulous booking procedures, organized and controlled front desk

Customer Responsive ... React quickly to customer needs, takes action

Team Service ... Skills of the entire staff are available to each and every client.

MISSION - How will you achieve your vision objectives?

Maximum Client Retention ... Client retention is the most important factor to the business's success. Given this, the business's – and every individual's – overall retention rate will be tracked and monitored. It is the key quality and growth indicator

Maximum Productivity ... Every revenue producing hour must be efficiently used and accounted for. This means that every staff member is responsible for every hour the business has available for sale. It doesn't make sense to have clients on the waiting list while other qualified staff are waiting for something to do

Skill Certification ... Every staff member must be skill certified before delivering any service to a client

Everyone Is Responsible ... Every staff member, from the front desk to the dispensary, is responsible for growing the business

Access ... We will not deny any clients access to our salon/spa and its services due to grid-locked technicians or waiting lists

Team-Based Incentives ... We use team-based incentives to reward all staff members for their efforts to grow the business and control costs

CULTURE - What are your values?

Ethical Behavior and Practices ... We never compromise our business, professional or personal ethics in our behaviors or our actions

Integrity at All Times ... We display and practice the utmost in professional integrity with all clients and all team members at all times

Uncompromised Teamwork ... We cooperate with each other in order to maintain the best possible work environment and to achieve business goals and objectives

Professionalism ... We practice and adhere to the highest standards of professional excellence

Open and Honest Communication ... We listen and respond to all team members and customers with understanding, patience and self-control

My personal goals for
Compensation:

_____

_____

_____

_____

_____

_____

_____

_____

_____

_____

_____

_____

_____

_____

_____

_____

_____

CHAPTER FOUR

Stress Relief

Finding a balance between work and everything else.

*Finding a balance between
work and everything else.*

CHAPTER 4 # Stress Relief

Picture this: You've been working 12 hour days because you're down a service provider and there's no one to take up the slack. You're trying to make up next week's schedule when your manager comes in and asks a question, her 10th this morning. Three people want Tuesday off. You haven't eaten since the two doughnuts you grabbed hours ago in the breakroom, unless you count the artificial creamer in your six cups of coffee. Lately, you've been snapping at your staff, your family, even your dog. If you were a cartoon character, your face would be bright red and there would be smoke coming out of your ears.

We all have days like that. But constantly feeling as though you're at the breaking point means that there's something wrong – and you have the power to do something about it. Beyond just not being a good way to live, constant stress can lead to bad habits, such as not getting enough sleep, eating poorly and not exercising. Ultimately, your health can suffer, perhaps leading to diabetes, high blood pressure or heart disease.

Possible health ramifications aside, no one wants to feel stressed all the time. The antidote to long-term stress is finding the balance between work and "life" that works for you. Unlike profit-and-loss statements, there's no easy formula for cultivating mind-body balance. There's no set amount of time that you need to spend away from your business each week. There's no recipe for the number of "oms" it takes to be in balance.

Just as elevators and trucks have weight limits, you too have a limit of how much you can handle. While it's different for every person, when you're at or past your limit, you simply cannot function well in any area. No exceptions. It will show up in your business and personal lives.

Make a list

Start with writing down what work/life balance means to you. You might want to think of daily, weekly and long-term goals. Work/life balance and manageable stress levels are different for everyone. There is space at the end of this chapter for you to do this. You should have a variety of goals that you want to achieve.

Here are a few suggestions:

• A zen state of mind.

• To be home in time for dinner three nights each week.

- To be able to take two consecutive weeks of vacation – and not to have to call in every day.

- To have a weekend off.

- To be able to attend your child's soccer game or piano recital.

- To sleep well at night.

- To work out four days a week or to get home in time to take an evening run before it gets dark.

No matter what your goals, you need to take a similar path. You must make a plan for work/life balance just as you do a cash-flow plan. Having balance in your life is an ongoing process; it takes work. Whatever your path, don't imagine it's going to happen on its own; it won't.

Like other habits, once you start leaving in time for dinner or taking a yearly vacation, it will become second nature. The opposite is true, as well. Stay late a few nights in a row, and you'll probably start falling into your former habits. Cancel one weekend away, and you're less likely to schedule another.

Step by step

You can do it! Now that you know what some of your goals are, start with the following steps to integrating them into your life:

- Review your goals as often as necessary to remind yourself of what you're trying to achieve. Once a week, every day or every 20 minutes, whatever it takes to ingrain them in your mind.

- Share your goals, as appropriate, with your staff, family and friends.

- Develop an action plan to achieve your first goals. If you want to go to the gym before work, the plan may be as simple as:
    › Lay out gym clothes the night before.
    › Set alarm earlier.
- If it's a longer-term project, such as wanting to take a vacation in six months, you need more steps:
    › Pick your dates for vacation.
    › Let your staff know that you will be taking a vacation.
    › Write down all of the tasks that will need to be covered in your absence.
    › Decide which staff members will be assigned which tasks.
    › Start training so that you are comfortable that things will get done in your absence.
- Develop a timeline, so you know what you must do every day/week to achieve each goal.
- Make a pledge – both to yourself and a trusted friend or colleague. Ask that person to check in with you to see how you're progressing on each stage of your goal(s). Don't get angry when you haven't achieved what you hoped. Merely recommit yourself to your goal and look at your steps/timeline to see why you fell down. Come up with strategies to ensure that you succeed going forward.

Look inside

Now, start to think about your role in your company. If you feel stressed too frequently, it's time to examine how you run your business:

- **Let go.** Figure out which tasks you absolutely have to do yourself and delegate the rest. Take a few minutes now to make a list of tasks you've been doing yourself that you could assign to other employees. Remember, this is not an abdication of power; it doesn't mean that you are less of a leader. Quite the opposite, in fact. What you're doing is freeing yourself up for the more crucial tasks of running your business and your life.

- **Decide which tasks you truly enjoy and what you'd like to delegate.** Stop hanging on to tasks you don't enjoy. It's draining. It doesn't even make you a better person. You probably have someone on staff who loves the things you hate, whether it's event planning, updating your website or designing retail displays. Talk to employees and help them grow.

- **Can't completely give up a to-do?** Give parts of a task to an employee. Have confidence in your staff. Give them opportunities to grow – and lessen your load. More will get done with less stress.

- **Review the talents of your employees.** Don't pigeonhole any staff member. Even if an employee doesn't have the exact experience, don't be afraid to assign new tasks. Most people will rise to the occasion, given the opportunity to shine.

- **Be clear and specific in what your expectations are.** Remember to share the what, the why and the when. Leave the how up to your employees. They'll often find newer, easier, more time effective and/or less expensive ways of doing things.

- **Be flexible.** No one can do things just the way you do. And that's perfectly fine for many tasks. It doesn't mean that you should skimp on quality or results. It does mean that your way is not the only way. If the job gets done well, open your mind to the possibilities.

1. You need to have a plan for work/life balance; it's not just going to fall into place.
2. You are responsible for finding balance in your life. No one can do it for you. Basics – eating well, exercising, getting sufficient sleep – must be the foundation of your day.
3. Systems, systems, systems. Getting your systems down will take the crisis out of your day.

- **Give thanks.** Always acknowledge genuine effort. Offer kind, constructive criticism. Celebrate successes. And don't forget to say, "thank you." Your positive feedback nurtures your employees. Your appreciation will make them glow.

Finding your work/life balance is not easy. Even beyond getting to the gym or "happy hour" with friends, you want to reduce the stress in your life. It's hard to face, but a lot of business stress is self-created. Yes, there are numerous challenges to being an entrepreneur. Often, the "rush" that occurs in owning a business means that you live in the fast lane. The stress you used to thrive on starts to take a negative toll. The trick is to make some long-term changes so that your relationship with your business – and it is a relationship – stays positive.

Just like any other relationship, it can be difficult to find the right balance of emotions and time. The challenge is figuring out how your business fits in with the rest of your life. (You do have a life outside of your business, right?) That's a challenge that exists whether you've been in business a day or decade.

Sometimes, you need to pour yourself into your company 100 percent. That means nights, weekends, holidays. That can only work for so long. When you stay at that pace, there's one sure path you'll find: burnout, exhaustion, unrelenting stress.

Finding a balance in your work and personal lives is especially difficult for entrepreneurs. So much of their identity is caught up in the business. Entrepreneurs spend a lot of time and energy just to get the business open – and then, to grow it to each new level. That's all right; it's what gives you the drive to want to open and operate your company.

Develop your game plan

Being an entrepreneur, however, is not all who you are. And to sustain the energy you need to bring to the business, you must first feed your own soul and ensure that you – body and mind – are being cared for.

• **Know yourself.** Are you a morning person or do you like to burn the midnight oil? When do you like to do hands-on work, have meetings, make phone calls? Part of reducing stress from your business is connecting your tasks to your daily rhythms.

- **Be honest about what you keep putting off.** We waste so much mental energy by not making decisions. Have that awkward conversation, or make that challenging choice. Once you get in the habit of doing these things, you'll find that your stress level drops. And you might just find that these things aren't that difficult after all.

- **Let your staff know what's on your mind.** While you don't have to share every detail of your business, it's important for your employees to know where your head is. If you're worried about sales, tell them. If your new line of retail isn't taking off, let them know. Often, your team will help develop a solution. It's not all on your shoulders. And never announce a problem without talking about how to resolve it in specific terms. It's stressful to hear that sales are bad. It's less stressful when everyone knows what the plan is to improve.

- **Don't leave a trail of destruction.** Your staff takes its mood cues from you. When you're in a bad mood, it trickles throughout your company and makes everybody tense. Then, everybody feeds on everybody else's tension. Ultimately, clients feel it, too. And who wants to frequent a place that doesn't have a relaxing atmopshere? Make an effort to be pleasant, to smile and to treat staff and clients with kindness and patience. Reduce your stress; reduce your staff's stress.

- **Get out of your rut.** If you always do everything the same way in the same order, maybe part of your problem with stress is boredom. Mix up your tasks. Do them in a different order or approach them in a new way. Try taking a different route to work. Order something new for lunch. Drink herbal tea instead of soda. Keep it interesting.

- **Focus on the big picture.** When we're drowning in details, it's easy to feel overwhelmed. On a regular basis, take some time to think about why you opened your business, your dreams, what you want to accomplish. Yes, there is a lot to get done, right now, this very second. But the doing should be feeding into your vision. If it doesn't, it's time to rethink how you spend your time.

- **Find the positive.** Catch your staff doing things right – and tell them you've noticed. Take notes on what you find. It will be helpful both at performance review time and when a certain employee is just driving you up the wall. When you only find fault, you cultivate an atmosphere of negativity. Who could be happy working in that kind of culture? How can you be happy in that sort of business?

- **Count your blessings.** Every day. Be grateful for the opportunity to be an entrepreneur, for the food you eat and the clothes you wear. Be grateful for friends and family, for trees and singing birds. Write these down, so you can refer to the list on days when things threaten to get out of control.

- **Keep a master calendar.** Include all your commitments, work and otherwise. That way, you can see all your commitments in relationship to each other. It's not as easy to over-schedule yourself when you view your day as a total package, rather than separating out work events and home events.

- **Plan out your day.** Don't treat each to-do as a crisis. Know what needs to be done and how you'll do it. Leave time for true emergencies or unexpected circumstances.

- **Use technology wisely.** Part of the reason that we're so stressed and feel as though we have so little "down time" is technology itself. Don't be available 24/7. Use the old standby of "If it's not on fire and nobody's bleeding, don't bother me." It doesn't have to be so extreme, obviously, but let your phone go to voicemail sometimes and don't check your e-mail or texts during certain hours. Chances are that things will run smoothly without your instantaneous response. The flip side is to use technology to your benefit. Download apps that will help you relax. Send yourself reminders to leave work early or meet a friend for lunch. Technology is a double-edged sword. Don't let it contribute to your stress levels.

- **Develop and use your cash-flow plan.** When you know what's coming up financially, you reduce the worry about "what ifs." Use this tool as a stress reducer. Live by an organized plan.

- **Make sure systems are in place for every area of your business.** Small problems stay small when everybody knows how to handle a situation. Systems offer predictability and ease of operation. Don't create stress where there isn't any. Develop your systems, so each employee knows step-by-step what to do.

- **Measure it, and share it.** Every goal has a starting point, which means that everything in between can and must be measured and communicated daily, weekly and monthly to everyone. A business stays in balance by charting its progress. The entrepreneur stays in balance by having a solid plan.

- **Have the proper staff in place.** If there are gaps in your staffing structure, there's going to be extra stress. Hire right for your company's needs and ensure that staff are properly trained. Communicate constantly, so that your employees understand both the "big picture" and the necessary details.

- **Celebrate.** All wins, large and small, must be celebrated in some fashion. Why do the all the work if there's no opportunity to celebrate and be rewarded? Celebrate to reinforce and maintain balance. It will remind you and your staff that business is not a grind. It is a chance to achieve, to accomplish goals that will impact the lives of others in a positive way. Cultivate an atomosphere of joy and fun.

- **Ask for help.** Know when you're in over your head. Ask your managers, employees, friends, family and physician for assistance. Sometimes, just talking about it is enough. Other times, you'll need to ask for something concrete. It's not a sign of weakness.

- **Remind yourself that you are only human.** You can't influence the weather or whether people get sick or if a car hits a pole and knocks out power to your business or if there's a recession. Take control of what you can control. Let go of the rest.

Don't forget the basics

The last big piece of finding work/life balance is taking care of yourself. No one can do this for you. It's important for reducing stress, for staying healthy and for not feeling as though you're a hamster on a wheel. The rules are basic and non-negotiable.

Let's start with the "big three."

- **Eat a healthy diet.** This includes eating regularly – no meal skipping or being too busy to eat. No grabbing a candy bar and calling it lunch. Focus on whole grains, fruits, vegetables, lean protein and low-fat dairy. This will keep you fueled up for the challenges of your day. Learn which foods make you feel awesome – and which sap your energy. Limit your caffeine intake. There are lots of healthy eating plans available. Find one online if you need assistance. Start with the United States Department of Agriculture's website at www.choosemyplate.gov.

- **Get enough sleep.** No one functions at their peak when they are sleep-deprived, and it only takes one night for performance to suffer. You can't counteract it with lots of coffee, either. Yes, there are a small group of folks who only need four hours a night. Be honest about whether you're one of them. Most of us need seven or eight hours to feel our best. It's not a failing to get that much rest. You owe it to yourself – and to your staff and clients.

• **Incorporate movement into your day.** Sure, going to the gym is one option. But so is taking an after-dinner walk, gardening, biking, playing catch with your dog. It doesn't have to be a dedicated, traditional workout. Just be as active as you can, every day.

These should be part of your regular routine, as well:

• **Limit your bad habits.** You know that smoking is bad for your health; don't do it. See your doctor if you need help quitting. As far as drinking, eating fatty or fried foods, or not being active enough, well, take control as much as you can. One espresso in the morning is fine; three Red Bulls before 10 a.m. probably isn't.

• **Meditate.** It's not about twisting your body into the lotus position and saying ancient words. Meditation is about calming your mind and accepting the current state of things – body, mind and spirit. Go online, get a DVD or take a class. It's easier to get started led by a professional. Try guided meditation, walking meditation or yoga nidra, a deep form of physical relaxation. Inner peace isn't going to happen overnight. Ongoing practice will help with day-to-day challenges.

- **Get a life.** You can't have work/life balance when you don't have interests besides your business! Take a class in cooking, knitting, ceramics, flower arranging, growing herbs or auto repair. Cultivate a circle of friends who are not involved with your business.

- **Network.** Join your local business networking group or Chamber of Commerce. It's good to see that some challenges (like finding and retaining staff) are universal. Attend meetings to learn from others and to see that you're not alone.

- **Volunteer.** Whether it's at a soup kitchen, homeless shelter or Humane Society, volunteering takes you out of the day-to-day concerns in your life. Give back to your community. Yes, it's important to donate gift certificates to charity auctions and the like, but nothing beats the feeling you get when you serve a meal to the hungry or give haircuts to homeless women. Be hands on.

- **Don't forget to breathe.** Yes, this is different from "meditate." When we become stressed, we take shorter, more shallow breaths. Our upper bodies tense up, which only feeds the cycle. Stop yourself throughout your day to check if you are breathing deeply. If you're not, it's a simple remedy. Just focus on your breathing for a few moments. Try breathing in for a count of five and exhaling for the same. Whenever stress strikes – whether it's a traffic jam or an unreasonable customer – take a deep breath. It's an instant stress buster and no one will know you're doing it. By forcing yourself

GOOD TO KNOW!

1. There's no one solution for everybody. Experiment until you discover what works for you.

2. Nobody's perfect. Some weeks will flow smoothly; others will feel like one crisis after another. Roll with it. You and your business are works in progress.

3. Working with your natural body rhythms make the day easier. Plan your tasks accordingly.

to slow down, you may also avoid saying or doing something you'll regret.

• **Take mini-breaks.** Society allows smokers breaks to sneak a cigarette, so why aren't you taking health breaks throughout your day? Go outside for a quick walk or just to stand there and feel the sun on your face. Send an e-mail to a friend or make a phone call to a loved one. Read a few pages of a book, or flip through a non-work-related magazine. Talk to a staff member about the latest reality show antics or last night's game. Clearing your mind for a few minutes will help you refocus on what needs to get done. You'll be more productive and feel better doing it.

• **Laugh.** Laughter truly is good medicine. It feels great, increases endorphins and just improves the quality of life. When you realize that it's been several hours (or days!) since you've had a good laugh, find a way to infuse your day with some ha-ha-ha. Look for ways to turn potentially stressful situations into funny anecdotes. Go online and search for silly animal videos. Watch a clip of your favorite comedian. Buy DVDs of sitcoms that produce sure-fire chuckles. Share a laugh with everyone you know: staff, friends, family, people in line at the grocery store. Laughter is contagious. It feels good, is free and provides health benefits. Why aren't you doing it more?

- **Make time for relationships with those you love and who make you feel good.** No man is an island. When we don't spend time with those we love most, we feel isolated, disconnected. Plus, we can feel guilty about not spending the time. Make a phone call. Text. Smile. Give a hug. Get your friends and family involved in your favorite activities. Start now.

My personal goals for
Stress Relief:

_____

_____

_____

_____

_____

_____

_____

_____

_____

_____

_____

_____

_____

_____

_____

_____

_____

_____

_____

_____

CHAPTER FIVE

Financial Success

It's all about the numbers.

It's all about the numbers.

CHAPTER 5 Financial Success

L et's get it out of the way. You hate numbers. We know. Your accountant or bookkeeper handles all that stuff, so you've never felt the need to be that involved. Well, this is where the demystification process begins.

You absolutely can understand the numbers and you need to for the health of your business. No, you don't have to earn an accounting degree or do advanced math. But understanding your numbers will give you a foundation to grow your business.

Your numbers tell a story about the financial health of your business, how it's performing and whether it's growing. Numbers and financial reports keep you on top of your business. They help identify strong and weak performance areas.

They are the key to making money and succeeding in business. The more you know about the numbers of your business, the better your chances are for success. And just like anything else, the more you use your reports, the easier you'll find the process. There, not so scary, right? (FYI: At the end of this chapter, there's a glossary of financial terms.)

Don't wait until you file your taxes to make an appointment with your accountant. Have your accountant go over your reports, line by line, until you feel comfortable using them. Do it again in a few months to see how things are progressing. Keep asking questions until you understand how to use each report – and are able to explain the reports to your team.

Internal vs. external financial statements

Financial statements and other reports are necessary for both internal (management) and external (IRS, bankers, investors, etc.) purposes. It is therefore important to remember why you're preparing financial reports and how the information will be used.

External users have specific requirements for the format, style, frequency and content of financial reports. Financial statements for tax filing and bank loans, for example, should adhere to generally accepted accounting formats.

Internal reports, on the other hand, can and should be customized to fit the unique needs of your business and the people using them. Internal reports should be user-friendly and help you quickly understand your financial performance in order to identify areas in need of adjustment and/or improvement.

What's an accounting method?

An accounting method is a set of rules which determines when and how to report the income and expenses of a business. You may use either the accrual or cash method for internal purposes.

Accrual accounting will render a more accurate picture of the business, while cash accounting is simpler and less time-consuming. You may not have a choice of which method to use for tax purposes. If you do, either method will have tax consequences, some of which may be significant.

The IRS requires that you file tax returns using the same method each year. Changing methods will require IRS approval. Ask for advice from your accountant.

1. Owners and managers need to become well-versed in the financial reports for the business.

2. Develop a cash-flow plan and use it to guide your decision making.

3. Communicate key numbers to your entire staff and help them to understand what roles they play in the financial health of the company.

Cash basis – Under the cash-basis method of accounting, income is recorded when the money is received. Expenses are recorded when the bills are paid. It's simple: Cash in, cash out.

Accrual basis – Under the accrual basis, income is recorded when a sale is made, regardless of when the business receives payment. An expense is recorded when it is incurred, regardless of when the bill is paid.

There are times when both methods yield the same result. Because the majority of salon and spa sales are paid upon delivery, both methods would yield the same results. A medspa that bills an insurance company for payment would record that income differently.

Gift-certificate (or gift-card) sales are an exception across the board because payment is received prior to the actual delivery of the service or product. On an accrual basis, the income is not considered "earned" until the gift certificate is redeemed for a service or product, or when it expires (if your state allows gift cards to have an expiration date). If gift-certificate sales are a significant part of your business, the tax consequences can be dramatic.

It's worth spending some time on the concept of gift-card sales because there's often confusion about how the dollars should be recorded. The dollars your company receives for gifts cards are not service sales or retail sales, and should not be recorded as such when making deposits. Instead, they are best described as "loans" that clients make to your company, loans that have to be repaid. The proper term is "deferred income."

Let's break this down with two examples:

- A client comes in at the beginning of the day. She gives the front-desk coordinator $80 and says, "Keep this for me until later. I want to be sure to have $80 left for my appointment at the end of the day." Obviously, this money would be put aside until the client returned, and then used to pay for services at the time the sale actually occurs. If the client did not return, the money would be repaid rather than deposited because the business did not earn it. It simply held the funds until the client reclaimed them. If the client did not return by the end of that first day, no entry would be made on the company's book for service or retail sales. You cannot record the "sale" until the obligation is fulfilled.

• A gentleman comes in first thing in the morning and says, "I want to surprise my wife with a hair and nail appointment at the end of the day. I can't be here later, so here is $80 to pay for her services." As in the preceding scenario, had the client not arrived for the appointment, the $80 given to the coordinator would not belong to the business. You could not, in good conscience, deposit those funds and record that $80 as a service or retail sale.

This is exactly what happens with a gift-certificate purchase. A client gives the salon/spa/medspa money not for services themselves, but for the right to receive services at a future date. This right is represented by the gift certificate, which the bearer may redeem for services or products.

Consider it an IOU. The business promises to provide services or retail products when the certificate is presented for redemption. There is no sale but, rather, a liability. The income is deferred until you earn it.

A gift-certificate purchase is an advance payment for services or products. The salon/spa/medspa therefore incurs a liability and, under the accrual accounting method, gift-certificate revenues should be recorded as a "liability" under the heading "Deferred Gift Certificate Income" on your Balance Sheet. (More on the Balance Sheet later in this chapter.) When the gift certificate is redeemed, it becomes a "sale" and moves to the "Income" portion of your Profit-and-Loss (P&L)

statement. (More on the P&L Statement later in this chapter.) Under a cash accounting method, it is considered a sale and recorded as income at the time of purchase. On a cash basis, you cannot defer taxes on unredeemed gift certificates. The accrual accounting method is often best if you have an active gift-certificate business.

To avoid tax penalties, unredeemed gift-certificate revenues should be moved from the "Liabilities" section of your Balance Sheet to the "Income" section on your financial statement after one year. Meet with your accountant to discuss gift-certificate sales, deferred income and setting up special accounts.

Set up a special account (similar to accounts payable or taxes payable, which show the company's other liabilities) on the Balance Sheet of your financial statements. All gift certificates sold should be recorded in a special account called "Gift Certificates Outstanding" when they are deposited in the company's bank accounts. This is not a sales account, but a current liability. When the gift certificate is redeemed (i.e., services are rendered or products purchased), a sale occurs. The income is then earned, and its liability to the bearer of the certificate satisfied.

A gift certificate is simply an alternate form of payment. When the transaction is posted, the company's books reflect the sale, and the "gift certificate outstanding" account is reduced.

What about unredeemed gift certificates?

Unredeemed gift certificates must be reported under "sales" one year after the original purchase date. Leaving unredeemed certificates in the "outstanding" account for longer than one year puts the business at risk for taxes due on unreported sales. If an audit determines that the salon/spa/medspa should have recorded unredeemed certificates as sales, the business may incur penalties and be held responsible for back taxes and interest.

Gift-certificate money is not yours to spend. Ideally, it should be held in reserve to defray the costs of providing services at the time of redemption. Remember, no cash will be generated at the time of service. Prudent cash managers put gift certificate proceeds aside in an interest-bearing account until they may be transferred back into the company's operating accounts for general bill paying.

You may want to transfer one-twelfth of the "gift certificate outstanding" account each month, in anticipation of redemptions and the variable costs of payroll and products.

Controlling your money

All you need to know are two simple things. (See, we told you it wasn't so complicated.)

1. To understand the relationship between money and business activities.

2. To create and implement ongoing and straightforward money-management tools and strategies.

Remember, business is about making your life better – not merely paying your bills!

It's easy to "grow broke" by making financial decisions based on incomplete data.

The Profit-and-Loss Statement, for example, tells only one piece of your company's financial story. Executing a revenue and expense plan is what makes financial reports look great. Business is about building a healthy Balance Sheet.

What you need to know about debits and credits

• Debits are recorded on the left side of a T-account.

• Credits are recorded on the right side of a T-account.

• Debits must always balance with credits.

Here's how it works:

	DEBIT	CREDIT
Assets	Increase	Decrease
Liabilities	Decrease	Increase
Equity	Decrease	Increase
Revenues	Decrease	Increase
Expenses	Increase	Decrease

Two quick examples:

• The business has revenues of $100. Cash (an asset) is debited $100, and sales (revenues) are credited $100.

• You borrow $100 from the bank. Cash (an asset) is debited $100, and loans (a liability) are credited $100.

Financial statements

Now, let's review your financial statements. These two charts will give you a quick overview of your main financial statements, and how they relate over time.

	Balance Sheet	Profit-and-Loss Statement	Statement of Cash Flows	Cash Flow Projection
Describes	The financial **HEALTH** of the business	The financial **PERFORMANCE** of the business	The financial **FUEL** of the business	The financial **POTENTIAL** of the business
Time Period	Snapshot	Specific period of time (month, quarter, year)	Previous periods (usually months)	Projected periods (usually months)
Shows	Assets. liabilities, owner's equity	Revenue and related expenses	Receipts and disbursements	Projected sales and expenses

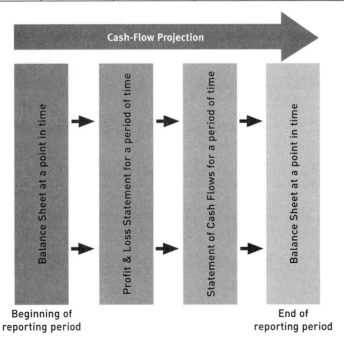

Cash-Flow Projection

Balance Sheet at a point in time

Profit & Loss Statement for a period of time

Statement of Cash Flows for a period of time

Balance Sheet at a point in time

Beginning of reporting period

End of reporting period

Many business owners rely on only one financial statement, often the Profit-and-Loss Statement (income statement). They either do not understand or utilize other key financial statements. However, the information provided by each is powerful. Combined, they are a series of "report cards" for your business.

GOOD TO KNOW!

1. The more you use your financial reports, the easier it will become.

2. You don't need an accounting degree to be financially knowledgeable.

3. Numbers don't lie.

Profit-and-Loss Statement (or P&L): Shows business income and expenses over a period of time.

Balance Sheet: A snapshot of the business for a specific date. The Balance Sheet is divided into three key parts:

1. Assets, such as cash in bank accounts, accounts receivable, inventory, land and buildings, equipment and fixtures.

2. Liabilities, including accounts payable, deferred gift-certificate income, mortgage payable, wages or commissions payable, notes payable, taxes payable.

3. Owner's Equity, such as owner's or stockholders' stake in the value of the business. Ownership consists of the original amount the principal owners or stockholders invested to start or purchase the business, and any subsequent additions (called capital or capital stock); and any profits the company has accumulated and retained in the business since it began operation (called retained earnings). The owner's equity is

the value that remains after all liabilities are met. The resulting "excess" is also known as the company's "book value."

Statement of Cash Flows: Shows cash inflows and outflows over a period of time. This report will explain why an increase in profit does not necessarily equal an increase in cash.

Cash-Flow Projection: A financial worksheet that demonstrates the inflows (revenues) and outflows (expenses) of cash within an organization, and the resulting cash balances. It is usually prepared for future (i.e., projected) time periods.

The Statement of Cash Flows shows what was. The Cash-Flow Projection or Cash-Flow Plan shows what you think will be.

Financial reports:

• Give you an accurate, objective picture of your business.

• Reflect something real.

• Help you understand your business.

• Help you determine the health of the business.

• Allow you to easily measure company performance.

• Are indispensable management tools.

• Help you with external reporting and internal management.

• Allow you to think about your business, the various parts of it and how they work together to achieve a financial result.

• Help you make better decisions.

• Are a model of the vitality of the business.

- Give you objectivity and precision.
- Give you the whole view.

When do you "break even"?

Calculating your breakeven point is easy. And it's vital information to have. Without it, there's no way to tell when your revenues cover your expenses.

Here are some tips:
- Costs and expenses must be recorded differently, depending upon whether they are fixed or variable. These differences can affect your income statement and may have a dramatic effect on the bottom line.

- Fixed costs remain constant from period to period, and are not influenced by changes in sales volume. General and administrative (G&A) expenses are predominantly fixed.

- Variable costs change from period to period, and are influenced by changes in sales volume.

  › "Cost of Sales" expenses are variable costs. These include service payroll, service payroll taxes, retail product costs and professional product costs.

- Few costs are entirely "fixed" or "variable." A number of the costs of doing business have both fixed and variable components.

Breakeven calculations

1. Classify expenses. They are either fixed or variable. If your salon, spa or medspa uses a format similar to the model on page 198, it's easy to identify each. If your financial statements have all expenses grouped under one primary heading, you will need to specify each as either fixed or variable.

2. Determine "variable profit on sales."

Subtract the total variable costs from sales revenues:

$200,000 Total sales
-100,000 Total variable cost (cost of sales)
$100,000 Variable profit on sales

3. Compute "variable profit percentage."

Divide the variable profit on sales (step 2) by sales revenue:

$100,000 ÷ 200,000 = 50%

4. Calculate breakeven.

Divide total fixed costs by variable profit percentage. Let's say that fixed costs are $70,000 for this example:

Total Fixed Costs ... $70,000 ÷ Variable Profit % ... 50% = $140,000

(If the business in this model generates $140,000 in total revenues for the month, it will meet its breakeven requirement; that is, income will equal expenses, and there will be neither profit nor loss. Two significant conclusions may be drawn from this information:

1. There is a dramatic positive effect on profitability once the company's total sales revenue surpasses its breakeven point. In this example, sales exceeded breakeven by $60,000 ($200,000 - $140,000). This means that approximately 50% of every sales dollar beyond breakeven drops to the bottom line as profit. This is determined as follows:

Net profit ($30,000) ÷ Sales beyond breakeven ($60,000) = 50%

2. There is a converse effect on profitability when the breakeven point is not met. Assume that instead of achieving breakeven, the company in this model generates only $135,000 in sales revenue. The following illustrates how this will result in a loss rather than a profit:

$135,000	Total sales
- 67,500	Total variable cost (50%)
$ 67,500	Variable profit on sales
- 70,000	Total fixed expenses
(2,500)	Loss

Proving your breakeven

To limit inaccuracies, it is prudent to "prove" your breakeven calculations by way of a confirming computation:

$140,000	Breakeven sales revenue
- 70,00	Less variable costs (50% of sales)
$ 70,000	Gross profit on sales
- 70,000	Less fixed costss
-0-	Net profit (loss)

BREAKEVEN EXERCISE

MONTHLY PROFIT-AND-LOSS STATEMENT

SALES		
Service Sales	85.00%	$170,000
Retail Sales	15.00	30,000
TOTAL SALES	100.00%	200,000
COST OF SALES ...	(Variable Costs)	
Service Payroll	34.00	68,000
Payroll Taxes	4.25	8,500
Retail Cost of Goods Sold	7.50	15,000
Professional Use Products	4.25	8.500
TOTAL COST OF SALES	**50.00%**	**100.000**
GROSS PROFIT MARGIN	50.00%	100,000
GENERAL & ADMINISTRATIVE EXPENSES ... (Fixed Costs)		
Admin. Payroll & Taxes	8.0	16,000
Advertising	5.0	10,000
Bank Charges	1.5	3,000
Benefits	2.0	4,000
Education	4.5	9,000
Interest	1.5	3,000
Maintenance & Repair	2.5	5,000
Miscellaneous	.5	1,000
Rent	6.5	13,000
Telephone	1.5	3,000
Utilities	1.5	3,000
TOTAL G&A EXPENSES	**35.0**	**70,000**
NET PROFIT	15.0%	$30,000

Are you in balance?

The Balance Sheet lists a company's assets, debts and owner investments as of a specified date.

A Balance Sheet helps you quickly get a handle on the financial strengths and capabilities of the business:

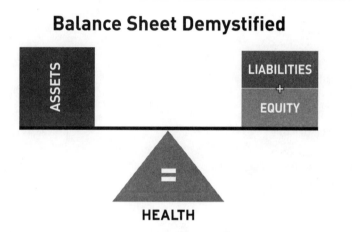

Balance Sheet Demystified

HEALTH

The Balance Sheet (statement of Financial Condition) is so named because it represents the following equation:

ASSETS = LIABILITIES + EQUITY

At any point in time, this basic equation holds true, although the amounts assigned to the individual elements will fluctuate.

Assets: Something of value that the company owns.

Liabilities: Money that is owed by the company. Liabilities can be payable to suppliers, vendors, employees, government agencies or banks.

Equity: Reflects the "net worth" of the company. It consists of the owner's or stockholders' investments, plus any profits retained to date. Also called book value.

Balance Sheet Statement

[Date Report is Run]

Assets

Current assets

Checking	55,929.64
Savings	25,000.00
Inventory	22,615.20

Fixed Assets

Equipment/fixtures	208,110.00
Computers	5,000.00
Total Assets	**$316,654.84**
Liabilities	
Total current liabilities	61,292.20
Total long-term liabilities	164,899.26
Total liabilities	**$226,191.46**
Equity	
Shareholder equity	30,000.00
Retained earnings	54,105.70
Net income	6,357.68
Total Equity	**$90,463.38**
Total Liabilities & Equity	**$316,654.84**

• Is the business in a position to grow and expand? It can help identify and analyze trends.

• Can the business easily handle the normal highs and lows of revenues and expenses? Or should it take immediate steps to boost its cash reserves?

A simplified Balance Sheet includes assets (what a business owns), liabilities (what it owes) and equity. Equity is the money

Balance Sheet
Quick Reference

Everything you need to know about the Balance Sheet, all on one page:

It is a snapshot of the financial health of the business at a specific point in time.

It shows what your business owns, what it owes and its accumulated value.

It tells you if you have enough assets to cover all of your liabilities.

It allows you to monitor if you're accumulating assets or debt.

Comparing starting and ending balance sheets, tells if the business is getting healthier or unhealthier.

The mission of every business is to build a better balance sheet.

a business owes its owners after all creditors have been paid. It is also the "book value" of your business. As with home ownership, you'd like to see the value or the equity of your business increase without taking out a second or third mortgage.

What's on the income statement?

Income statements, otherwise known as Profit-and-Loss Statements (or P&Ls), are a summary of a company's profit or loss during a given period of time, whether one month, three months or a year. The income statement records all revenues for a business during this period, including those that come from sources other than its core business, as well as all operating expenses.

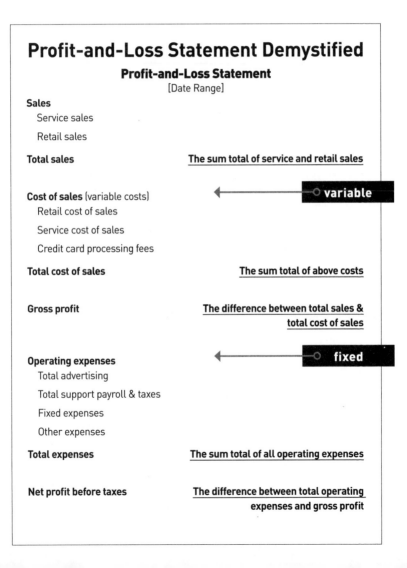

Profit-and-Loss Statement Demystified

Profit-and-Loss Statement
[Date Range]

Sales
 Service sales
 Retail sales

Total sales   The sum total of service and retail sales

Cost of sales (variable costs)   ← ○ **variable**
 Retail cost of sales
 Service cost of sales
 Credit card processing fees

Total cost of sales   The sum total of above costs

Gross profit   The difference between total sales &
                                     total cost of sales

Operating expenses   ← ○ **fixed**
 Total advertising
 Total support payroll & taxes
 Fixed expenses
 Other expenses

Total expenses   The sum total of all operating expenses

Net profit before taxes   The difference between total operating
                                     expenses and gross profit

Profit-and-Loss Statement

[Date Range]

Sales	$	%
Service sales	69,366.00	71.30
Retail sales	27,920.00	28.70
Total sales	**97,286.00**	**100.00**
Cost of sales (variable costs)		
Service payroll	40,303.20	41.43
Credit Card Processing	1,945.72	2.00
Retail Cost of Sales	16,891.60	17.36
Total cost of sales	**59,140.52**	**60.79**
Gross profit	**38,145.48**	**39.21**
Expenses (fixed costs)		
Total fixed expenses	31,787.80	38.00
Total expenses	**31,787.80**	**32.67**
Net profit before taxes	**$6,357.68**	**6.54**

Income statements help determine the performance of your business. Small-business owners and managers use them to find out what areas of their company are over- or under-budget, according to their cash flow. Items that are using more cash than expected (such as phone, rent, shipping and postage, supplies) can be pinpointed.

Income statements can also track dramatic increases in product returns or cost of sales. They can be used to determine income tax liability, as the Cash-Flow Plan cannot. The Statement of Cash Flows can be used to determine income tax liability, as the Cash-Flow Plan cannot.

Income statements contain some of the same information found in Cash-Flow Statements, plus some greater detail:

• Sales revenues – not just the ones generated from "normal" sales, but also any derived from sources other than a company's core business (e.g., any income generated from renting company space for a party).

• Cost of sales.

• Gross profit.

• General and administrative.

• Depreciation. This is an annual expense that takes into account the loss in value of equipment used in your business. Equipment subject to depreciation may include furniture, computers and printers. While depreciation is important to help reduce tax liability, it's not actual cash leaving the business. This is one reason why an income statement cannot replace a Cash-Flow Plan in determining how much cash a business has.

• Taxes. Enough said.

• Net income. This is the amount of money left after the business has paid income taxes.

It is very important to build an income statement that is appropriate to your business, so work with your accountant.

Income statements, along with Balance Sheets, are the most basic elements needed by potential lenders, such as banks, investors and vendors. They will use the information to determine credit extension and financing eligibility.

Profit-and-Loss Statement
Quick Reference

Everything you need to know about the Profit-and-Loss Statement, all on one page:

Shows how much profit was made in a specific period.

Look at them regularly. Compare to benchmarks.

It is a tabulation of revenues and expenses.

It does not measure cash moving in and out of your business. Profit is not cash!

The value of this statement is solely dependent on the accuracy of the reporting of revenues and expenses.

Statement of Cash Flows

Cash is the fuel for your business. Companies can easily "grow broke." Many companies show a profit on paper, while not having the cash they need to survive.

Every year, tens of thousands of businesses fail. Some were showing a profit at their demise. What happened? They didn't have enough cash to stay in business.

The Statement of Cash Flows is a frequently neglected financial report, but it's deserving of your attention. The Statement of Cash Flows tells you everything you need to know in a reporting period about the in-flows and out-flows of cash. This standalone report tells you whether the cash generated is positive or negative for the time period you're looking at

---

Statement of Cash Flows
Quick Reference

Everything you need to know about the Statement of Cash Flows:

Measures in-flows and out-flows of cash in your business.

Illustrates activities from operations, investing and financing.

Cash is the fuel of your business.

Are you turning profits into cash?

You can show a profit and run out of cash.

---

and by how much. Remember, cash is real money; it's what's in the bank.

The Statement of Cash Flows:

- tells you how well you're turning your profits into cash.

- shows how much cash was generated by the operations, how much was invested, and how much was paid out to lenders or brought in from lenders.

The Statement of Cash Flows reports the sources and uses of cash for a period in three major classifications:

1. Operations: Activities include the cash effects of items identified in the Profit-and-Loss Statement, such as sales, costs of sales, operating expenses and extraordinary items.

2. **Investing:** Activities include the purchase of property and equipment and/or the proceeds from the sale of, and also certain investments in securities or other non-operating assets.

3. **Financing:** Activities include the borrowing and repayment of debt, as well as the contribution and redemption of equity capital and the payment of dividends on the capital.

Here's how it works:

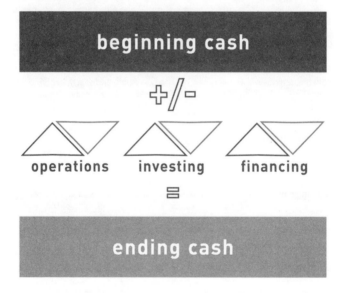

You can operate a long time without profit, but you can't survive without cash. Cash is the fuel that lets your business run. Ignore this report at your peril. End of story.

Statement of Cash Flows Demystified

The Statement of Cash Flows tells you how well you're turning your profits into cash.

Statement of Cash Flows
[Date Range]

Operating activities
Net income (before taxes)
    Adjustments to reconcile net income to net cash provided by operations
Other activities
Net gift card activity

Net cash provided by operations	**The sum total of all operating activities**

Investing activities	Property and equipment or the proceeds from the sale thereof, and also certain investments in securities or other non-operating assets.

Computers

Net cash provided by investing	**The sum total of all investing activities**

Financing activities	The borrowing and repayment of debt, as well as owner's investments and disbursements of the capital

Bank loan

Net cash provided by financing	**The sum total of all financing activities**

Net cash increase/decrease	**The sum total of operating, Investing & financing cash**

Beginning cash	**Cash you started with at beginning of this period**

Cash at end of period	**The sum total of beginning cash plus the net cash increase/decrease for the period**

Cash provided by or applied to operations

Cash provided by or applied to investing activities

Cash provided by or applied to financing activities

Net increase or decrease in cash

Cash-Flow Plan

Your Cash-Flow Plan or Cash-Flow Projector is critical to having a profitable business. (A sample Cash-Flow Projector is on page 213. We've shown three months as an example. Your Cash-Flow Projector should include the entire year.)

Your Cash-Flow Plan:

- Gives you control of all activities that either receive or dispense cash.

- Gives you a reliable, accurate and all-inclusive source of financial information and documentation.

- Helps prevent cash-shortage surprises.

- Identifies strengths and weaknesses in your management systems (e.g., credit policies, payables).

- Helps anticipate cash needs in order to reach financial and business goals.

- Provides tools for communicating with lenders, suppliers and employees.

- Allows you to look at opportunities and make sound financial decisions.

Forecasting and the Cash-Flow Plan

Every expenditure must be planned, and realistic revenue goals set to ensure money is available both when needed and in the amount needed. Cash-Flow Projections alert business owners and managers that revenue and expenditures are either proceeding on course or are deviating from plan.

In this segment, we'll examine Cash-Flow Plans as a tool for monitoring operations and profitability. First, let's dispel a couple of myths.

Myth #1: A Cash-Flow Plan is the same as a business plan.

A business plan anticipates and provides for the future activities of an organization over a specific period of time (usually one, three or five years). It defines what a company will accomplish and how. A business plan, however, does not detail costs, revenue or impact on the bottom line. That's where your Cash-Flow Plan comes in.

A Cash-Flow Plan should be an integral part of a business plan. It should separate the plan into specific sources of revenue and cost, and provide managers with a projection of the financial results of implementing the overall business plan.

Myth #2: A Cash-Flow Plan is just another financial statement.

Not all financial documents are classified as financial statements. Financial statements are after-the-fact records of an organization's financial condition, which may expose situations in need of management attention. The Balance Sheet and income statement are two such "historical" controls.

Cash-flow planning, on the other hand, looks forward in time. A Cash-Flow Plan is an estimate of future revenue and expenses. Owners and managers generally use a Cash-Flow Plan in conjunction with financial statements in order to determine how well the business actually performed (financial statements) in comparison with its objectives (the Cash-Flow Plan).

What do you get from cash flow?

Cash is the fuel that drives a business. The more cash on hand, the greater the company's ability to help get rid of (or at least pay down) debt, provide revenue for company investments, and grant incentives to the team.

Cash-flow planning also tells us:

- when expenses will come due, and how much has to be paid out. Taking a sharp knife to all the company's expenses in order to decrease its cash outlay will obviously increase your cash position. But involving the team in the process can often lead to surprising and dramatic results.

- where the income will come from to pay these expenses. Making realistic goals, or predictions, gives your team a "road map" to success, as well as inspiration for team performance. Periodically reviewing these goals will help keep the fires burning and ensure they are neither too high (which can cause a sense of discouragement) nor too low (thus failing to provide inspiration).

- everyone is fiscally responsible. Accountability is an important ingredient in cash-flow planning. Without the transparency that derives from frequent cash-flow updates, even the best-made plans can go awry. Weekly updates are recommended.

This accountability also instills trust in the company's leadership team.

• where the leaks are. When extra effort is needed to stop the bleeding of certain expenses, or efforts need to be redirected at increased sales, Cash-Flow Plans allow you to put your staff to use where it's most needed. This lets a company turn its financial ship on a dime. If you really want to charge up your company and its growth, there is probably no better way than through excellent cash-flow planning.

A good Cash-Flow Plan is created on a calendar or fiscal year, and broken down by individual months.

Some of the specifics:

• Sales revenues (the top line) are created through sales over a certain period of time, including sales of services, retail goods, and gift cards or packages.

• Cost of sales. This expense usually includes costs directly incurred by the company in providing goods and services: payroll for service personnel and their associated payroll taxes, cost of retail items sold, and cost of supplies needed to provide said services. Each of these expenses is listed separately; the final "cost of sales" line shows the total.

• Gross profit (or gross margin). Subtract cost of sales from the top line to find gross profit.

• G&A, or general and administrative, costs. Here is where all other business expenses are listed, from advertising to utilities. Each is listed separately, and all are normally paid on

CASH-FLOW PROJECTOR

	A	B	C	D	E
1	Developed by STRATEGIES...800.417.4848		www.strategies.com		
2	*Enter Months Here =>*	January	February	March	
3	*Beginning Cash(= ending cash from prior month)*				
5	**Sales & Revenues**				
6	Service Sales				
7	Retail Sales				
8	**TOTAL SALES** (row 6 plus row 7)				
9	**Cost of Sales**				
10	Service Payroll				
11	*Team Bonus*				
12	Professional Use Supplies (6% of Service - row 6)				
13	Retail Products (50% of Retail sold in prior month)				
14	Credit Card Processing Fee (2% of Total Sales)				
15	**TOTAL Cost Of Sales** (Sum of rows 10 thru 14)				
16	**Gross Profit** (Row 8 minus row 15)				
17	**General & Administrative Expenditures (G&A)**				
18	Administration Payroll				
19	Officers' Salaries				
20	Accounting & Legal				
21	Advertising - Web - PR - Printing				
22	Auto Expense				
23	Coaching/Consulting				
24	Debt Payments (Loan / Past Credit Card Debt)				
25	Debt Payments (Business Loan)				
26	Dues & Subscriptions				
27	Education				
28	Equipment Lease				
29	Insurance - Business				
30	Insurance - Health				
31	Maintenance, Repairs & Cleaning				
32	Meals & Entertainment				
33	Office & Facility Supplies				
34	Rent				
35	Security				
36	Taxes - Payroll (9.5% of rows 10, 11, 18 & 19)				
37	Taxes - Other				
38	Telephone				
39	Travel & Lodging				
40	Utilities				
41					
42					
43					
44	Emergency Fund				
45	**Total General & Admin** (Sum of rows 18 thru 44)				
46	**Net Profit** (Row 16 minus row 45)				
47	**Net Profit Percentage** (Row 46 divided by row 8)				

a monthly basis. Again, there is a separate line that shows their total.

• Gross net profit. The amount of cash available after all expenses are paid but before taxes are paid.

Creating a Cash-Flow Plan

To create a Cash-Flow Plan for your business, you will need financial statements for at least the last twelve consecutive months. These statements, combined with your revenue and spending objectives for the next twelve months, will provide the basis for "best guess" assumptions on the Cash-Flow Plan.

The Cash-Flow Plan shows revenue goals and spending budgets for each month. As you progress, revenues may be charted on a scoreboard to help the team remain focused on achieving objectives. Expenses should also be monitored by comparing what has been (or is going to be) spent to what is planned in the Cash-Flow Projector. This simple tool will enhance your bottom-line profits by helping the team reach target revenue goals and control expenses.

Cash-Flow Plan guidelines

• Remember, it's a "best guess." Some business owners labor over projections by overanalyzing or trying to come up with exact numbers. Projections are simply best guesses.

• If your best guess was too high or too low, guess again, and adjust the budget accordingly. Over time, your guesses will become more accurate. Be patient.

› Calculate G&A expense projections first. These are primarily fixed, and are easier to project.

› Calculate service and retail revenue projections next. Consider seasonal fluctuations, staff availability, price changes, marketing efforts and other factors that may influence revenues

› Calculate cost-of-sales projections last. These are variable costs, the biggest of which is service labor. Take your time in this area.

• If you cannot justify the expense, cut it!

Use your Cash-Flow Plan when making any decision involving money. If it's not in the Cash-Flow Plan, don't spend it.

Let your team in on the financials

No, this isn't about sharing information about salaries or perks. It is about getting your whole team on board in working to help the business have a rock-solid bottom line. To do that, you need to communicate the numbers, what they mean and how to improve them.

The best way to generate your staff's interest in the numbers is to show them what's in it for them and how they make a difference. It's to let them know that you understand their self-interest by focusing on their point of view at the start, before you tell them about yours. This will motivate them to tune in.

Teach your staff how to drive sales. Show them how increased productivity and efficiency affects sales. Show them real numbers. Show them where the numbers need to be for bonuses or raises.

People have to know what the goals are and how they can affect those goals, or they won't care. At Strategies, we say, "If you fall asleep, they'll fall asleep." This means that you, as the leader, must always know what's happening in the business and continually communicate with your staff. Keep them informed of what's happening, and inspire them to keep moving forward.

While sharing the numbers may seem scary, it's the key to getting your entire team to move your company forward. You can't expect your team to play to win if they don't know the score.

Tools for communicating the numbers

Scoreboards are the basic vehicles of communicating the numbers to your staff. They're visual reminders of how the company is moving toward specific goals. They are designed to keep staff informed of what the company's goals are, as well as the progress being made toward those goals.

One thing we know about human nature is that "what gets measured, gets done." When staff sees that performance goals are being tracked, and they understand how they can help push them in the right direction, they begin to make those numbers happen.

Scoreboards force a level of accountability and hence, performance, that's missing in many companies. The numbers come in quickly – usually daily, or at least weekly. They then must be passed on to employees, so problems get addressed faster and everyone is working at peak performance.

Communicating the company's progress lets managers and employees see the results of their work. It will definitely have a positive impact on performance, productivity, efficiency and quality.

Huddles are another crucial aspect of the communication process. Huddles are regular, short, structured meetings designed to verbally communicate what's happening in the business. Hold them daily to keep everybody focused.

Huddles and scoreboards go hand in hand. The scoreboards will be more effective if verbally communicated, and this happens in the huddle. Huddles pass vital information through the company. It's when and where employees get to see the big picture: what still needs to get done and how to get it done.

Huddles get and keep people moving in the right direction. They get everyone working together to make the improvements that will determine whether the team will succeed.

Using a system of scoreboards and huddles, and holding everyone accountable for goals, will help drive your business to higher levels of performance, productivity, efficiency and quality.

Key ratios

Here's where it starts to get fun! Data from financial statements can be used to create ratios, which compare various numbers from financial statements in order to reveal key relationships. Many are easy to create, and reveal important information regarding the financial performance and condition of your business.

Here are a few you may wish to calculate:

Profitability ratios

• Return on revenues (also called "return on sales" and "net profit ratio") shows how much net income is derived from every dollar of net revenues:

Return on Revenues = Net Profit ÷ Net Revenue

• Return on equity (also called "net worth" or "return on owner's profit and owner's investment") shows the relationship between net profit and owner's equity:

Return on Equity = Net Profit ÷ Owner's Equity

Efficiency ratios

• Gross-profit margin is a percentage of net revenues. This tells you how well the business is generating funds to cover fixed expenses and to make a profit: The target is 50% or greater.

Gross-profit Margin = Gross Profit ÷ Gross Revenues

• The Breakeven ratio shows the dollar amount of revenues that exactly covers all variable and fixed costs, with nothing left over for profit:

Breakeven Revenues = G & A ÷ Gross-Profit Margin Ratio

• Inventory turnover shows the number of times in the accounting period that inventory is sold, or "turns over":

Inventory Turnover = Cost of Goods Sold ÷ Total Inventory

Solvency and liquidity ratios

- Current ratio measures the company's ability to use current assets to pay off current liabilities. Generally, a current ratio of 2:1 is considered reasonable:

Current Ratio = Current Assets ÷ Current Liabilities

- Quick ratio measures the company's ability to pay its short-term liabilities. Strive for a quick ratio of at least 1 to 1:

Quick Ratio = Cash + Marketable Securities + Accounts Receivable ÷ Current Liabilities

- Working capital signifies the short-term resources available to maintain normal business operations:

Working Capital = Current Assets - Current Liabilities

- Debt-to-equity indicates how much the owners have at stake in the company, compared to how much creditors have at stake:

Debt-To-Equity = Total Liabilities ÷ Owner's Equity

Glossary of Financial Terms

There are numerous financial terms that you should know to keep informed about where your business is and where it is heading. Your bookkeeper and/or accountant will be of great assistance helping you understand these terms and how they relate to your business. Don't be afraid to ask questions!

Here's a cheat sheet of definitions:

Accounts payable. The total dollar amount of money owed by a company, generally due within thirty days.

Accrual method of accounting. This is when sales and expenses are recorded when they occur – e.g., a gift certificate becomes a sale when it is redeemed.

Asset. Something of value that the company owns.

Backbar. An all-inclusive term for professional products and supplies used in the rendering of services. This includes dispensary, station use and other items depleted in rendering services.

Balance Sheet. Reports company assets, liabilities and equities (the owner's ownership portion of the company's holdings) at the end of the accounting period.

Book value. The "worth" of a business, calculated by subtracting total liabilities from total assets. Also called owner's equity.

Bottom-line vs. top-line analysis. This is a comparison of a company's retained earnings vs. the top line of the Balance Sheet or internal cash flow (cash and marketable securities).

Breakeven analysis. This shows at what point a company will make a profit. One way of analyzing breakeven is to look at the point where revenues equal expenses. This is the breakeven point. Another method of determining breakeven is to subtract cost of service/ retail from selling price, and dividing this amount into fixed costs. This will give you the total number of units (service/retail) to reach breakeven.

Budget. A financial plan of all the company's anticipated or planned expenses for a given period of time. Budgets are helpful in properly running a company and planning its day-to-day operations, as well as financing and expansion.

Capital. Money invested or available for use by the company.

Cash-Flow Projection. Also known as Cash-Flow Plan. A financial worksheet that demonstrates the inflows (revenues) and outflows (expenses) of cash within an organization, and the resulting cash balances. It is usually prepared for future (i.e., projected) time periods.

Cash method of accounting. Sales and expenses are reported when cash is received – e.g., a gift certificate is recorded as a sale when it is purchased.

COGS or Cost of Goods Sold. COGS is the cost, at purchase price, of all items resold to the public.

Credit. An entry to the right side of an account ledger sheet. It is usually an amount of money earned by the company.

Debit. An entry to the left side of an account ledger sheet. It is usually an amount of money paid by the company.

Equity. The ownership of a company, usually through shares of common stock.

Fixed costs. Expenses whose amount is not influenced by the company's production level.

Gross profit. Total revenues minus variable costs.

Liability. Money that is owed by the company. Liabilities can be payable to suppliers, vendors, employees, government agencies or banks.

Net profit. Gross profit minus fixed costs. It may also be expressed as revenue minus total costs.

Net worth. Total assets less total liabilities. It is also referred to as stockholder equity.

Overhead. These are your fixed costs, such as rent and insurance.

Owner's equity. The owner's residual interests in assets after liabilities have been deducted. It's the part of the Balance Sheet that reflects the "net worth" of the company. It consists of the owner's and stockholders' investments, plus any profits retained to date. Also called book value.

Profit-and-Loss Statement. Reports revenues and expenses, and the resulting profit or loss, throughout an accounting period.

Ratios. Financial measurements of a company's performance or good standing according to varied criteria.

Retained earnings. Profits accumulated since the formation of the company, which have not been distributed as dividends.

ROI or "return on investment." Or after-tax profit divided into the original investment.

Service payroll. This is the payroll of all service providers or technicians. It excludes any administrative or sales support personnel.

T-accounts. These are used to illustrate the debit and credit entries made to an account's ledger sheet.

Variable costs. Expenses whose amount is influenced by and vary according to the salon, spa or medspa's production level.

My personal goals for
Financial Success:

CHAPTER SIX

Client Retention

What's your number?

What's your number?

CHAPTER
6 Client Retention

Two questions: Who's responsible for client retention in your business? What are your client-retention rates? The answer to the first question should be "everybody."

As for the second question, did you have an answer? A startling number of salon/spa/medspa owners and managers can't answer that second question with accuracy. Not being aware of your client-retention rates – both first-time clients and returning clients – is going to keep you from running a profitable business.

Your client-retention rate is your report card. Numbers don't lie. If your client-retention rates aren't where they should be, you're failing Customer Service 101.

Let's start with some cold, hard facts.

On average, only 3 percent of owners know their retention rates. Half of those confuse request rates with retention rates.

(They are not the same. More on that later in this chapter.) Most have no means to track retention. Even those with point-of-sale systems often find their software doesn't track retention properly, if at all. Without this performance ratio, it's impossible to know how your business is doing. Even those owners and managers who do know their client-retention rates often don't know whether they're on target.

So, where should your retention rates be?

First-time client-retention target range: 45%-60%+
This is the ratio of how many first-time clients return for a second visit within 90 days.

Existing client-retention target range: 75%-90%
This is the percent of multiple-visit clients who return within 90 days.

Here's the sobering truth: Salons, spas and medspas only average 30% new client retention. They should be retaining almost twice that! Scary, right? Client retention is one of the most powerful revenue-producing and productivity-building strategies available.

You cannot argue with the numbers. From a technical standpoint, the beauty industry can offer clients extraordinary levels of skill and expertise. From a customer-service standpoint, salons, spas and medspas often score poorly. No matter how much you want to refute this assessment, it is impossible to argue with industry-wide numbers that show salons, spas and medspas are not retaining seven of ten first-time clients. Yes, that's 70 percent of clients who don't come back. Interestingly, poor retention remains consistent from value-priced salons right up to upscale, service-intensive day spas.

The most important client-retention number to track is the conversion rate from first visit to second visit. For example: How many first-time clients did the business service in April, and what percentage of this group returned for a second visit in approximately 90-120 days?

The overriding objective of every business is to attract and retain customers. That's as basic as it gets. The higher your retention rate for first-time clients, the higher your level of customer satisfaction, the more you can grow profitably. Granted, you want to satisfy clients on every visit, but client-retention tracking begins on the first visit. If your business fails to perform to client expectations on the first visit, there usually is no second chance.

Still not convinced you need to do this? Here's the reality.

It's your company's future. Winning the business game means building a retained customer base that is loyal to the salon/spa/medspa. Your retained customer base is by far your most important asset. There is little resale value for used furniture and fixtures.

The rules for winning the business game have changed. Competition is fierce in most markets, and current customers and potential clients are thinking more and more about where they want to spend their hard-earned money. Unlike food and shelter, visits to the salon and spa fall firmly in the realm of discretionary purchases. If you're not providing the best service, customers will go elsewhere. It's that simple.

If you're not tracking those client-retention rates, there's no way to know how you're doing. Guessing or estimating those rates is no way to run a business! Not paying attention to those numbers will all but guarantee a lack of success. A committed retention effort will produce tremendous growth in your client list. This growth will prove even more lucrative than an increase in average ticket and frequency of visit.

Retention rates tell you if your customer-service programs and procedures are working. The overriding objective of every business is to attract and retain customers. First-time client retention rates are directly in proportion to a company's ability to satisfy customers and offer consistent quality experiences.

You need to know what to track. The traditional process of staff development focuses on hiring a stylist, esthetician, etc., providing training, and then putting him "behind a chair" to assist all the new clients that the veteran, request-saturated technicians cannot accommodate. He is encouraged to build a "request rate" and a loyal personal following. According to the old rules, when the stylist or massage therapist is booked solid with requests – he has won the game.

By design, that method encourages staff members to divert client loyalty from the team to themselves, and is therefore counter-productive to the team-oriented thinking that successful companies live by. It's such old thinking that tracking client retention completely eliminates the need to track request rates. Moreover, request tracking encourages the very followings that owners fear and guard against (as well they should).

Request vs. retention

It's important to differentiate between these two items. "Request" simply tells you who is building a following and who isn't. In the "old days," it made sense to know how many clients were requesting each staff member. The game was to "build your clientele," and request tracking was the best measurement tool.

From all outward appearances, a busy technician producing brisk sales at his or her chair or treatment room is doing a good job – until you examine the technician's ability to retain clients. How would you view an employee's performance – even with a 60% request rate – if his or her first-time client-retention rate was at 26%? Would you still be eager to assign those hard-won and precious first-time clients to this technician? Certainly not until some additional skill and customer service training is completed.

The problem with request tracking today is two-fold:

1. Request tracking fails to accurately show the salon's or spa's ability to retain clients, no matter how sophisticated your tracking procedures. New requests, repeat requests and other tracking codes fail to answer the fundamental reten-

tion question: "How many new clients came in, and how many came back?" The only measurement request tracking provides is the number of clients who ask for a specific individual. It doesn't give the retention rate for all those new requests (i.e., how many actually came back).

- How long does it take to build request rates?
- How many first-time clients are lost in the process?
- How much growth potential is lost?

Without tracking client retention, you'll never know.

2. Retention builds client loyalty to the salon/spa/medspa. It's a rallying point for every area of your business – technical and interpersonal – including customer service. No other score takes precedence.

Retention tracking encourages business growth – request tracking encourages stylist followings.

Retention builds client loyalty to the business and provides a highly reliable score of how your salon, spa or medspa is doing in terms of the overall client experience. It's a rallying point for all salon and spa processes – technical, interpersonal and customer service. No other score takes precedence.

Here's how you start thinking about retention.

Ask the following questions about every client (including clients who haven't been in for a long time):

- Was this the client's first visit?
- If not, when was the client's last visit?

- Has it been more than ninety days?
- Did the client return to the same staff member?
- Did the client willingly visit another staff member?
- What services were performed?
- Did the client visit the salon/spa/medspa a number of times before ceasing to visit the business?

NOTE: If your business is in a resort area, for example, your numbers will be off, as clients often come for a one-time visit while on vacation. The same is true for businesses which have seasonal variations, such as "snowbirds" visiting Florida or Arizona for the winter months. Those businesses must consider these issues when setting client-retention goals.

Get buy-in from your team.

Retention should rally staff around the "team concept," strengthening both individual and group performance. It also helps identify weak skills and services, and pinpoint other areas for improvement. When you know where the weaker spots are, you can train employees and get them on board to improve retention numbers.

Most importantly, everyone has to understand what retention is. Don't assume that everyone on staff understands what it is and why it's important. Make sure that team members know what the numbers are – both their individual numbers and the numbers for the business as a whole. Regularly seek their input on how to improve the client experience and improve the numbers. You might want to request that technical or front-desk staff ask their customers what would improve the experience. It might be an enhanced waiting area, Wi-Fi, different hours or flavored coffee. Take advantage of the relationships your staff has with your clients. Use their knowledge to create the best overall experience for your clients.

When you post retention reports and conduct monthly evaluations, you can focus on an individual's strong and weak points. You can track retention by service and time of day to discover why clients did or did not return. You can discuss the demographics of your clientele or see if there are consistent issues with scheduling.

The most important thing in staff discussions is follow-through. There will always be good things going on with each team member as well as things that need to be worked on. Be sure to keep thorough, accurate records so you can specify these items.

Everyone wants to know if the business is doing well, and have his or her individual contributions acknowledged. But it must also be made clear that mediocrity won't be rewarded – and that everyone is accountable as a team for the company's overall growth.

Improving retention is an ongoing company-wide mission. Distribute reports and discuss performance at meetings. Maintain the urgency. Accurately measuring client retention allows your business to invest in its future by finding its weakest retention areas. Improved retention leads to greater sales in the short-term and unparalleled long-term growth. Make client retention the mandate at your business.

You need to develop a client base not just for today, but for the future. Once you know where you are and have made the commitment with the staff to pursue higher retention goals, you can forecast what your salon is capable of by extrapolating your current numbers.

Here's how:

If you know your average ticket, you can project the revenue gained from an increase in the client base. You can check retail sales to see how close you are to your goal. Retention numbers can even tell you where the bottom line has to be. In fact, every system in your company revolves around retention – especially if you offer salary-based compensation. (Check out the chapter on compensation for all the details about why your pay system matters – and how reaching client-retention goals should be part of what's required to move up the pay scale.)

Without retention information, you can't forecast the number of new clients you can see every month or calculate a team bonus – you can't even figure out where you want your business to go because you have no idea where it is currently!

Let's elaborate on the link between retention and productivity. What does retention tell you about the individual efforts of staff members? To assess productivity, you must have a time standard. In other words, determine how long particular services should take, and hold everyone to that standard. If you have a staff member who habitually takes twenty minutes longer to complete a service than everyone else, there could be any number of repercussions for the business.

When clients get accustomed to a service provider running behind schedule, they take up valuable time of your front-desk staff by calling in to find out if the technician is running on time. That staff person may be with another customer and must now interrupt that transaction to figure out if the technician is running late. There is no way to calculate the lost dollars from appointments that are canceled because clients don't want to wait. Other team members may fall behind because they are trying to help out. Clients may stop coming back because they don't like how rushed they feel. Other clients may feel as though they're "missing out" because their service provider took less time to deliver the service.

But on the opposite end of the spectrum is the technician who is very proficient and always runs ahead of schedule. That service provider will have more time open on the book – reducing gridlock, keeping clients happy through prompt and efficient service. Clients who call back for additional appointments get in more easily. There's increased cooperation between technical and front-desk staff because of the easier flow of clients. The front-desk staff doesn't end up having to make excuses for tardy technicians or listen to complaints as clients are forced to wait.

Is there such a thing as too many clients or too-high productivity in a salon/spa/medspa? Yes! It's not wise to ask staff to operate at higher than 80% productivity. (This is a suggestion; the actual rate may need to be tweaked depending on the type of services your company offers.) Asking staff to produce at a super-high rate will cause burnout. When that happens, the quality of work will plummet.

It's a necessity for your business success – client retention must be tracked, tabulated, analyzed and acted upon to improve performance and offer the best customer experience.

The following client-retention report shows all the key data, including first-time client retention and return rates for existing clients:

MA040

Client-Retention Summary

Harms Sample Salon

Millennium spasalon

December 2011

with return visits before 4/1/2012

	New Clients	Returned to Emp	Returned Other	Total Retained	% Retained
Overall Retention	79	15	5	20	25.32%
	Repeat Clients	Returned to Emp	Returned Other	Total Retained	% Retained
	697	353	110	463	66.43%

New Client Retention Summary

Employee	New Clients	Returned to Emp.	Returned Other	Total Retained	%
Charles, Anthony	10	3	1	4	40.00%
Cunningham, Angie	9	0	1	1	11.11%
Hans, Jen	2	1	0	1	50.00%
Klum, Allie	5	1	1	2	40.00%
Lancer, Stephany	10	2	1	3	30.00%
Manista, Ben	13	3	0	3	23.08%
Other Employees	5	0	1	1	20.00%
Owen, Jessica	4	1	0	1	25.00%
Selander, Shannda	4	0	0	0	0.00%
Semon, Pauline	14	4	0	4	28.57%
Smith, Jerome	0	0	0	0	0.00%
York, Rosa	4	0	0	0	0.00%

Repeat Client Retention Summary

Employee	Repeat Clients	Returned to Emp.	Returned Other	Total Retained	%
Charles, Anthony	104	54	6	60	57.69%
Cunningham, Angie	60	26	8	34	56.67%
Hans, Jen	89	64	6	70	78.65%
Klum, Allie	21	3	6	9	42.86%
Lancer, Stephany	24	7	6	13	54.17%
Manista, Ben	101	60	10	70	69.31%
Other Employees	81	4	49	53	65.43%
Owen, Jessica	84	44	9	53	63.10%
Selander, Shannda	57	43	4	47	82.46%
Semon, Pauline	64	27	14	41	64.06%
Smith, Jerome	0	0	0	0	0.00%
York, Rosa	59	47	1	48	81.36%

Note how the chart reflects rates for both the business as a whole and for individual service providers. The report also shows if a client returned to the business, but not to the original service provider. Accurate retention calculations require that a certain window of time – usually ninety days – lapses from the conclusion of the period being measured to the present.

Putting retention report data to work

The client-retention report can be as detailed as you like, but must at least contain all first-time client names, first visit dates and returned-by dates, if applicable. *NOTE: To analyze client retention data for December 1 through December 31, an accurate report cannot be generated until April 1, because that is the end of the 90-day period.*

In the sample report, of the seventy-nine new clients who visited the salon in December, only twenty returned. That means that fifty-nine were lost, for an overall first-time client-retention rate of 25.32 percent for the month of December.

The report data also shows that of the twenty retained clients, fifteen returned to the original stylist and five returned to others in the salon.

The retention rate for repeat clients is 66.43 percent for the month of December.

With the individual service provider's data, it's easy to see if one or two employees are pulling down the overall client-retention score. (Assigning new clients to technicians with low retention rates will decrease the company's revenue potential.) It will also be evident which service providers encourage clients to utilize the skills of the entire staff, and which are more concerned with building a personal following.

When a service provider loses a lot of new clients, it's important to examine why. Look for patterns among the clients who didn't return and check to see if additional training might be needed. Or, it may be a company-wide challenge. Find where the holes are and get everyone on board to improving retention rates.

Individual retention reports must also become a major performance factor in determining raises and possibilities of advancement. If team members don't retain clients, it is financially impossible to increase their compensation.

Here's how it affects your profitability.

Take a look at sample projections when your client-retention stays the same across five years, at 35% in this example:

RETENTION CHART
Base Year Projections

	2012	2013	2014	2015	2016
Number of retained clients	1500	1590	1667	1732	1787
Average ticket	$50	$50	$50	$50	$50
Visits per year	6	6	6	6	6
New clients per month	75	75	75	75	75
New retention rate	35%	35%	35%	35%	35%
Attrition rate	15%	15%	15%	15%	15%
TOTAL SALES	**$477,000**	**$499,950**	**$519,458**	**$536,039**	**$550,133**

Total increase after four years of growth =	**$73,133**
Percent increase after four years of growth =	**15.33%**

The business has small, incremental growth.

Now, look what happens when you increase the client-retention rate:

Increase retention to 60%

	2012	2013	2014	2015	2016
Number of retained clients	1,500	1,590	1892	2148	2366
Average ticket	$50	$50	$50	$50	$50
Visits per year	6	6	6	6	6
New clients per month	75	75	75	75	75
New retention rate	35%	60%	60%	60%	60%
Attrition rate	15%	15%	15%	15%	15%
TOTAL SALES	**$477,000**	**$567,450**	**$644,333**	**$709,683**	**$765,230**

Total increase after four years of growth = **$288,230**

Percent increase after four years of growth = **60.43%**

In this example, client retention starts at 35%. Then, it soars to 60%, where it is maintained. As you can see, growth is far greater, just by changing this one variable. If you lose a client for every new client you gain, you'll never get ahead. When you start to retain clients at a higher rate, your growth takes off.

Where to start your retention program

Understand your software's retention reports and the way the program calculates retention. If you don't understand the reports, call your software company's support line. If your software program doesn't track client retention, request that the company develop a retention report or switch to a company that has complete reports, such as Millennium from Harms

Ten Keys to Client-Retention Success:

1. Track client retention – not request rates.
Request rates have nothing to do with client retention.

2. Base technician's compensation on their ability to retain clients.
Reward high/improved retention rates with a raise, bonus, prize, etc. Address poor/declining retention rates promptly. Coach, train and mentor until they improve. Release the employee if there's no improvement. Since retention affects the entire business, post rates monthly.

3. Assemble marketing promotions to support retention.
Develop programs aimed at first-time clients, such as thank-you cards, second-visit discounts, haircut/facial/perm/massage clubs, and other simple programs. Use callbacks to find out why first-time clients do not return.

4. Profile and guide new client traffic.
Match new clients to the technician best suited to retain them, based on skill level, personality and personal profile.

5. Develop a marketing program to introduce clients to other qualified techs.
Print and mail an announcement card introducing your staff and what makes your business special. Place the skills of the entire business at the disposal of each client.

6. Perfect the team service concept.
Make sure everyone is responsible for pulling sales and performance in the right direction. Set up team projects, retention-evaluation committees, first-time client programs and other team-based efforts.

7. Assemble a target list of your salon/spa/medspa's real and potential retention obstacles.
It's in the details: parking, music, cleanliness, displays, telephone techniques, signs. Evaluate each person in each service category. If necessary, train and certify him or her.

8. Develop a referral program that encourages retained clients to recommend your business to friends, family and associates.
For example: Send three, get one free.

9. Make a commitment to develop your retention program – and stick with it.
Don't try to move too quickly. Fine-tune the program as you master retention skills. Don't leave retention to chance.

10. Ask, "Is it good for the customer?"
Everything you do in the business must be justified by this question.

Software (www.harms-software.com), which has options for medical spas, resort spas, etc.

Educate your staff on the importance of client retention and what it means to the company's (and their own) future.

Develop a program to increase client retention. It can rejuvenate your salon/spa/medspa and bring virtually unlimited success.

1. If you are not tracking client retention – start tracking it!

2. Post retention numbers and discuss them with your staff.

3. Work as a team to bring up both individual and company-wide numbers.

- How do you welcome new clients? Do you have a welcome kit? What does it include? Think about a letter from the owners, a card from the staff, a coupon for a future service, an overview of the business, etc. Do you offer a tour of your facility, identifying bathrooms and treatment rooms?

- How do you follow up with new clients? Make phone calls, invite them to join your e-mail list or Facebook page, etc.

- How do you engage clients between visits? Look to businesses that you enjoy visiting and "borrow" some of their methods, such as a newsletter or e-mail blast.

- How do you remind clients about upcoming appointments? Ask if they'd prefer a text, phone call or e-mail.

- How do you reconnect with clients who have stopped coming to your business? Call them, send an e-mail, mail a special offer.

Are your methods hurting retention?

Some salons, spas and medspas experience poor retention because their scheduling, tracking and reward systems are actually working against it. Client retention requires many elements working together to make it successful. Are you doing everything you can to make it work? Who gets the new clients? If it's the new technician, this may be detrimental to client retention rates.

New stylists are often ill-equipped to guarantee successful client experiences, especially for first-time customers. They may lack the seasoning and skill certification necessary to create a memorable initial visit. Owners are placing the future of their business (the new client) in the hands of the staff who are the least likely to guarantee success.

GOOD TO KNOW!

1. Staff members at every level have responsibility for client retention.

2. Periodically review what's involved in making client experiences special. Tweak your program, as needed.

3. Follow up, follow up, follow up. Even long-term clients want to know they're valued. Don't just offer promotions to new clients.

There are many examples of traditional systems that may not be conducive to retention and growth. Consider these questions. If you answer "no" to any of them, then your systems are inhibiting your salon/spa/medspa's growth:

☐ Do I send new clients to veteran technicians?

☐ Do I accurately and diligently track the percentage of new clients who return for subsequent visits within ninety days?

☐ Does my compensation system specifically reward superior client retention?

☐ Do I hold technicians accountable for their client-retention rates as part of their jobs?

☐ Does the front-desk coordinator meticulously profile new clients to select the service provider who is best suited to retain them?

☐ Does my team realize the importance of customer service and professionalism (not just technical ability) to the retention rate?

☐ Do we offer first-time client orientations?

☐ Do we offer consultations for new clients?

☐ Do we send thank-you notes, e-blasts, telemarketing and other promotional messages?

☐ Do we make follow-up phone calls to check on client satisfaction?

☐ Do we have a detailed pre-booking system?

☐ Do we send reminders via text message or e-mail?

Challenge your staff to come up with ways to enhance the client experience. It goes far beyond the technical skills. Look for better ways to book appointments, greet clients, promote special services and more. Everyone on the team has a hand in whether clients come back.

Client retention is a team sport!

The goal is to improve retention, not to increase stress for you and your staff.

Here are six steps to make sure you're on the right track:

Step One

Get comfortable with retention terms and variables. Make two charts: One to show where you are now, the other to show your goals. The charts will be helpful for your initial staff meeting on retention.

Step Two

Have a staff meeting devoted entirely to client retention. Discuss the charts from step one and how all staff members will benefit from the program. It should be a relaxed meeting. Once your staff understands the reports, consistently make those numbers a part of your regular meetings.

Step Three

This is a four-parter:

☐ If you don't already have retention promotions in place, get them done.

☐ Make sure your tracking program is up and running.

☐ Complete your list of retention hot spots; find ways to eliminate them.

☐ Begin a marketing program that encourages clients to try other team members.

Step Four

Begin monthly retention performance evaluations with all staff members. This includes the receptionist and any others who have contact with clients.

Step Five

Review your compensation program. Start including retention performance as the basis for raises (commission or salary), bonuses and prizes. Owners who pay high commissions will find difficulty with this step, as there is often no room for increases.

Step Six

Fine-tune your program as you go. Be consistent. Have patience with the process.

Target goal: A 10% increase in retention over the first six months.

Remember: First-time client retention will start to level off as you approach 60%.

My personal goals for
Client Retention:

_____

_____

_____

_____

_____

_____

_____

_____

_____

_____

_____

_____

_____

_____

_____

_____

_____

_____

CHAPTER SEVEN

Front Desk/ Guest Services

Everybody plays full on.

Everybody plays full on.

CHAPTER 7 Guest Services

I t's trite, but true: You never get a second chance to make a first impression. If a client's first impression is not a good one, the odds of a return visit to your business are severely curtailed. Even a less-than-ideal initial phone conversation has a great impact on whether a potential client ever walks through your doors.

Guest services must be everybody's responsibility. In the first part of this chapter, we'll be referring to the staff members who comprise your front-desk team. Later in the chapter, we'll address guest services from a company-wide stance.

So let's start with your front-desk staff members. There are many terms used to describe these positions: front-desk employee, guest-care specialist, guest-services staff, call-center employees, guest-services coordinator, etc. You might have managers and/or supervisors in this area, as well.

There is no one right term for these positions. We'll use these titles interchangeably. What is absolute is that these employees should be a crucial part of your team. When you train them and treat them right, you'll see a positive impact on your bottom line. It's worth the time and effort. (Strategies has an entire seminar based around your guest-services team which can be brought to your business, in addition to the options at the Strategies Business Academy. These programs are valuable for every member of your team to help them understand the challenges of the front desk, and to work together for the benefit of the client and the company.)

When clients cross the threshold to your business, your front-desk staff should make them feel comfortable and ease their transition from a hectic "outside world" to the calming atmosphere of your salon, spa or medspa. Every time that staff person answers the phone or greets a customer, the client is grading them. It's a lot of pressure! And yet, many owners and managers think of this position almost as an afterthought.

Your guest-services team must consist of competent, enthusiastic, service-savvy employees who know how to be efficient and productive in an ever-changing environment. Think of a service provider who is in the middle of a service. Imagine that person is constantly interrupted by phone calls, questions and people waiting for attention. It would be nearly impossible for that person to complete the service. This is what your front-desk staff is faced with every day. It takes a special kind of person to excel in that environment.

The front-desk culture must always revolve around a single objective: total client satisfaction. There is more to the client's guest-services experience than being greeted with a smile or having their phone calls answered by the second ring.

Every aspect of the customer experience must be controlled and consistent. To achieve this, responsibility must be assigned. There must be someone to say, "This is my job." A truly exceptional employee will say, "This is my job. How can I do it better to further serve the customer?"

As your salon, spa or medspa grows and/or adds services, it's especially important to clarify roles at the front desk. Whose primary responsibility are the phones, appointment bookings, client greetings, new customer tours, monetary transactions, balancing the cash drawer, inventory handling, taking clients to treatment rooms, retail displays?

Is there one person who can do everything? Probably not, especially if the business is large. Chances are, to achieve the efficiency level at which the company must operate, it's time to divide and delegate. Depending on the size of your business, you may have one or more employees in this department. A manager or coordinator will supervise others who work at the front desk or in a guest-services position.

Establishing responsibilities

Salon/Spa/Medspa Coordinator

Whichever title you prefer, a manager or coordinator bears tremendous responsibility for smooth operations. This is the person to whom front-desk personnel reports. While it varies business to business, a manager or coordinator is often largely responsible for some of the fundamental operations of the company, such as payroll, inventory ordering and maintenance, and interviewing new employees.

Let's look at some of the responsibilities that owners and general managers may assign to the guest-services manager:

- **Interviewing, hiring and dismissing:** Often, the coordinator will engage applicants in an initial interview and offer feedback to the owner. He or she may also be responsible for deciding where to advertise for a position and placing the ads. This requires a full understanding of the company's culture, knowledge of the tasks required by each staff member, a strong sense of intuition and excellent interpersonal skills. (Find detailed information on this process in the Employee Relations chapter.) Beyond the hiring process, the coordinator must be able to deal with negative situations, such as personality conflicts, and reprimanding, up to and including dismissal.

- **Inventory maintenance and ordering:** How much inventory to carry? Which lines? How often to reorder? What are the hot sellers? How frequently does inventory turn? You may wish to have your guest-services manager be the lead on this area, as he or she is often the closest to the retail section and sees first-hand how the retail operation is running.

- **Accounting and finance, including payroll:** There are many facets to maintaining a company's fiscal security: accurate and prompt bank deposits and credit card authorizations, evaluation and budgeting of overhead costs, efficient and timely tax reporting, etc. You may wish for your front-desk coordinator to assist your bookkeeper in these tasks

- **Client interaction:** Customer service can easily go unrecognized and unappreciated until a glitch occurs. It's up to the coordinator to help make sure that problems are few in number and nonrecurring. He or she should be responsible for training new employees (in every department) on guest-services procedures. Look to your coordinator for ideas about improving guest services, including scheduling and communication issues.

Receptionist

Often underrated and undervalued, the receptionist (or front-desk or guest-services) position is critical to the company. The receptionist is on the front lines, and is frequently the first voice heard or face seen by clients. Whether or not the responsibility is adequately acknowledged, the people in this position command a lot of power. The position requires an outgoing personality; a professional demeanor and presentation; excellent communication skills; and the ability to improvise when unexpected situations arise (as they often do). He or she must be excellent at multi-tasking and not easily flustered. There will always be demanding clients with inflexible schedules and situations to deal with, such as when a client becomes ill or gets stuck in traffic.

Call-center personnel

When clients wish to book or reschedule an appointment; inquire about a price, service or product; get directions or purchase a gift certificate, the response must be courteous and accurate. Especially in busy salons/spas/medspas, it is almost impossible

1. Hire the right people for your front-desk area.
2. View the front-desk area as a profit driver and train staff accordingly.
3. Make guest services everyone's responsibility.

for an overwhelmed front-desk staff to offer each client the attention he or she deserves.

Out of this need to better serve clients, the call center or booking center was born.

Today's call-center staff members work almost exclusively on the telephone and computer, handling calls and scheduling appointments. The sole purpose of the booker and the booking room is to remove the telephones from the front desk and allow a little more tranquility in the reception area. Some businesses have retained lines at the front desk to handle excessive call volume; others have removed them completely.

Caution: The addition of a call center does not automatically create a need for additional staff. A serious problem for many salons, spas and medspas is a lack of organization at the front desk. Organization, in whatever form it takes, is the first step to discovering whether your front desk is truly understaffed, or if better systems would help the situation.

- **Create specific, detailed job descriptions for each team member who works at the front desk.** Everyone must know his or her responsibilities, and accountabilities must be written into each position.

- **Review your systems.** Ask staff for input. Make sure that all appropriate staff are skill certified. Hiring to fill a position at the front desk requires more than a dawning awareness of an ill-defined need. Once the need is recognized, specific guidelines for its resolution must be developed. For example: If your desk is suddenly "more hectic" than usual, might it be due to a higher number of new clients and walk-ins, or increased retail traffic due to the introduction of a new product line? Many front desk problems have geographic solutions: Moving the register, shifting retail displays, changing seating and so on.

- **Streamline operations; make your systems foolproof.** The less guesswork that's involved, the more efficiently your front-desk area will run.

- **If everyone is working within well-defined parameters with top-notch systems, and the workload is still too great, check the cash flow to see if adding new staff if feasible.** However, redirecting workflow and streamlining existing operations is often all that is necessary to regain control of the front desk.

On-site or off-site?

Smaller businesses may find that call-center operations are simply more convenient when kept in-house. A single team member may be all that's needed to keep things running smoothly.

Larger operations usually need to have dedicated personnel just to handle those phone requests. Businesses with multiple locations also are often well-served by a dedicated call center.

With all that great software available (Strategies is especially a fan of Millennium by Harms Software, www.harms-software. com.), it's much easier to track appointments, preferences, etc. All that information is available in an instant with a call center.

There are a number of advantages to having a call center or booking room:

- **Less noise:** When the reception area is near the service floor or a treatment room, it can be distracting and irritating to both staff and clients to hear constantly ringing phones. A booking room can add a measure of serenity and peace for clients. The sound of a ringing phone prevents relaxation and takes away from the client experience. It's also calmer for service providers.

- **Improved traffic flow:** Clients shouldn't have to be "put on hold" when checking in or out. The benefits of moving the phones away from the desk can be enormous. Daunting check-in and checkout lines are frequently eliminated when the desk team is no longer tied to the phones. They can move into the retail area, walk clients to treatment rooms, and so on, without the concern of missing a call or having a caller have to wait for assistance.

- **Client care can shift into high gear:** With a call center, receptionists and coordinators can focus fully on providing guests with a higher level of service. Check-in and checkout become easier and more personal.

- **Increased sales opportunities:** The front desk is a sales and customer-service department. Adding a call center provides the desk team a greater opportunity to create new opportunities for overall salon/spa/medspa growth. Up-selling, cross-selling, offering gift cards, explaining promotions, etc. can all receive more of the time and attention they deserve.

When to consider adding a call center

Despite the many advantages, having a dedicated call center is not for every business. A call center should be added to better serve customer needs while also serving the needs of the business. You may wish to add a call center when:

- A high volume of calls routinely interferes with the desk staff's ability to offer maximum client service.

- Bottlenecks at the desk occur, revolving around which team member has the time to check clients in or out.

- Clients comment about an inability to easily "reach a person" when trying to make an appointment or get other information over the phone; or complain about feeling rushed when trying to get information over the phone.

The right fit for your guest-services department

You've streamlined your check-in and checkout procedures. Volume at your salon, spa or medspa is increasing by the day. Or maybe your long-term receptionist is moving across the country. Sooner or later, no matter how you divide the responsibilities of guest services, you're going to need to hire. Whatever the reason, you don't want to cut corners when staffing these crucial positions.

While recruitment is covered in the chapter on human resources, this is a position that is often viewed as a throwaway, so it's worthwhile to talk about hiring effectively. Clients won't make it to a service provider if they're not treated right when they are on the phone; or they won't come back if they're not treated well when they come in for their first appointment.

Your first step is to write a comprehensive job description for the position. Your current front-desk coordinator will be invaluable in putting one together. List duties, computer skills, attitudes, etc. Also make a list of the benefits of the position, and nuts and bolts stuff, such as hours.

The right fit

Where and how to find your perfect guest-services employee will depend largely on your market and resources. Cooperative partnerships, outreach programs, community and charity involvement, and referrals from current clients and staff are all excellent starting places. Don't be afraid to put the word out! The more potential employees know about your business, the more applications you will receive for available positions. And the more potential staff members know about your business, the more qualified applications you'll receive.

Don't feel as though you must hire from within the industry. Customer-service excellence is what you're after, and you may find qualified candidates in restaurants, tourism, retail and other industries.

Perhaps the most important qualification for guest-services staff is that they fit into your company's culture and show the initiative to be a true team player and contributor to your company's bottom line and growth plan. This is true whether you're looking for a behind-the-scenes person to answer the phone or someone who will be front and center at the desk every day.

Spend more, get more

Competent, dependable management and desk personnel are crucial to the success of a salon, spa or medspa. The skills and dependability of people in these positions must be adequately rewarded. Don't try to get away as inexpensively as possible. You (should) expect a lot from your guest-services team. Reward them fairly:

• Offer a good hourly rate. Be competitive not just with others in the industry, but with similar positions in other industries, such as the tourism, restaurant or retail industries.

• Include them in bonus programs. Rewarding these staffers when goals are met or exceeded will help keep morale up and motivate top performance. These team members are often besieged from all sides; this makes it even more important to show concrete appreciation for their hard work.

• Make continuing education opportunities available. (We naturally recommend Strategies' Front Desk/Guest Services seminar, available at our headquarters in Centerbrook, Conn., or on-site at your business.)

• Give your front-desk staff a plan for advancement.

• Offer benefits, including health insurance, vacation, sick time and/or a retirement plan.

There is often high turnover in this position simply because owners lack the commitment to integrate these players fully into the team. People don't job-hop when they feel part of the team. If you experience a lot of turnover at the front desk, look at your own policies. Hold formal exit interviews and be open to what you'll hear. Look around and see if you favor your technical staff. There's no reason why your guest-services staff shouldn't be looking at the position as a career.

While you want to pay your guest-services team fairly, you also must abide by your cash flow. Don't hire people at salaries you can't sustain; don't give raises that aren't supported by your cash-flow plan.

Training is essential

Once you've hired, you have a one-time-only opportunity to maximize what you're hoping to accomplish with a dedicated guest-services staffer. When you have your systems locked in, training your new guest-services employees will be much simpler. Beyond specifics, such as phone scripts or procedures for booking appointments, you must ensure that your guest-services team members share your passion for exceptional customer experiences. You can always teach someone a new computer program, but if the employee isn't focused on enhancing each client's visit, it will be difficult for that employee to fit in to your culture.

It starts with the most basic of philosophies: Clients must be treated as honored guests. While your requirements may vary, here are some basic requirements that you may wish to adopt:

- Clients should not be allowed to enter your business without a proper greeting from the front-desk staff member.

- Clients should not be allowed to sit in the reception area without being offered a beverage and other amenities.

- Every new client must receive a tour of your business, including introductions to other staff members and an overview of services.

- Clients should be booked for their next appointments, if possible, before they leave your business.

- Clients should receive retail recommendations on each visit.

Your guest-services staff employees must have exceptional people skills. This cannot be emphasized enough. In every aspect of the position, these team members must display grace and confidence. In fact, when the right person is in that position, the whole mood of the business can be elevated!

Here are some key ways your guest-services staff makes a difference to the way a client perceives your salon, spa or medspa:

- **It starts with hello:** Every customer wants to feel valued, and that starts right when the client walks through the door (or even before, if the customer has mobility issues and needs a bit of help just to enter the business). Every client should be immediately acknowledged with a greeting and a smile. Getting out from behind the desk to offer a handshake takes it one step further, as does greeting a client by name. Front-desk staff members should always speak first and not wait for a client to initiate conversation. Even in the busiest times when the client will have to wait a moment to receive full attention, a greeting should be offered.

- **Offer assistance:** The front-desk staffer must be aware of opportunities to help enhance the client experience. This includes tours for new clients, and offering beverages, snacks, magazines, etc., to a client who is waiting.

- **Respect the relationship:** Let's face it; people can be difficult. Clients and fellow staff members are only human. When a client comes late or on the wrong day, wants a special price or is just rude, the front-desk staff must maintain a pleasant demeanor and work neutrally for resolution. Similarly, there is often conflict between front-desk and technical staff. Train your staff to respect one another and to work together to solve conflict.

- **Wrap it up:** The front-desk staff has great responsibility in offering clients the opportunity to purchase products and pre-book. This is the last encounter that the client has with your business. It should be easy, pleasant and positive.

- **Keep it confidential:** Front-desk staff may have "insider information" about clients. All information about clients should be kept confidential. No gossiping allowed!

Scripting for success

Your front-desk staff deals with dozens of different situations every day. Knowing what to say and how to say it will ensure that clients and potential clients are getting the right message in the right way about your business.

When things get crazy at the front desk, it's good to know that inquiries will be handled in a consistent, professional way. If there's a standard answer or certain way for the phone to be answered, you must have a script. It's not just enough to have words on a page; work with your front-desk staff to make sure that the delivery is as good as the words. You don't want responses to sound forced or artificial, so work with your front-desk staff to make sure that the information provided is accurate and reflects real-life speech.

Every area should be covered with scripts. Here are a few ideas to get you started:

- How to answer the phone.

- What to say when a service provider is no longer with the company.

- What to say when a service provider is unable to serve a specific client.

- Price requests.

- Product return policies.

- When a client calls to cancel an appointment.

- How to deal with clients who are unhappy.

Further, it's important that front-desk staff truly understand the strengths of each service provider, as they will often be called upon to make the appropriate recommendation. They must also know the length of time each service requires, especially if this varies between service providers. The more information your front-desk staff has, the easier it will be for clients to have positive experiences, which leads to improved client-retention rates.

Additionally, educate your front-desk staff about what each service involves, whether any special preparations are needed, and what the client can expect on the day of the visit and afterwards, if appropriate. Clients don't appreciate having to speak to three different people to get answers! A knowledgeable front-desk staff inspires confidence in your company as a whole and the services you offer.

Myth: Front desk is a non-productive department

Fact: The front desk can be a huge growth driver.

Often, front desk is viewed as a department that doesn't produce revenue. If that's how you view it, there's a reason for it: you!

Your front-desk staff can and should be valuable, revenue-producing members of your team.

It all starts with booking appointments. Let's look at an example. You may believe that your front-desk or call-center staffer simply books appointment that a client requests. Here's how that works in a forward-thinking business.

Say there's an empty hour on the books for Wednesday at 10 a.m. Here it is Tuesday and that hour is wide open for the next day. Your front-desk coordinator calls the client (who is currently booked for the following week at 10 a.m.), and says, "We have an appointment open for tomorrow at 10. I know you like to come in on Wednesday mornings. Would you like me to put you down for tomorrow?"

The client may agree to the appointment change or not. If she doesn't, fine; she'll come in next week. If she does, then an appointment is now open for the following week and there's no wasted time the next day. Always think: "This morning before the afternoon; today before tomorrow; this week before next week." Imagine how your sales could increase if this behavior was applied every day, especially during slow periods! Make your front-desk staff a full partner in your team, and you'll see extraordinary results.

Here's another example.

You may look at your receptionist as someone who just rings up products. What if your front-desk staff used the products themselves and had full knowledge of the benefits of each? Then, when a client comes to the desk with the prescription, she can say, "I see you're purchasing the moisturizer that Katie recommended. I use both the moisturizer and the serum, and my skin has never felt better! Would you like me to get you the serum, as well?" See the difference? Do you think your sales would improve if you allowed your front-desk staff to be active members of your team? (And if you need more information about prescribing products, check out the chapter on Retailing.)

Building average ticket

Let's build on the previous example. Small increases to average ticket sales add up to major profit. Your front-desk staff are key players. Their time spent with clients is precious, and clients often share tidbits about their lives when they check in and check out. When front-desk staff have excellent relationships with technical staff, they can work as a team to benefit the client.

Here are some ways that front-desk staff can boost average ticket sales:

• **Knowing the client.** As we just mentioned, front-desk staff have special insight into what's going on in a client's life. Did the customer run in stressed out? Did she mention children? Or an upcoming vacation? Not only should this information be passed on to service providers, it should be recorded in the client's record. The more information that is possessed, the more that appropriate items and treatments can be recommended.

- **Create the sizzle.** No one wants a manicure. They want a total experience. Front-desk staff must know each service inside and out and be able to provide detailed information to clients, including how it will make them feel.

- **Offer one more step.** Guest-services staff have the opportunity to help clients want to add on to their services. A great time to do this is when the client is making the appointment. Educate your guest-services staff as to what procedures match up well, and how to phrase the request, building on the client's own language. Again, it's about building the relationship with the client.

- **Show it.** Your guest-services staff are closest to your retail displays. Ask for their input on how to best showcase products and how clients interact with displays.

- **Take it home.** Make sure your staff understands the importantance of home maintenance. Again, retail doesn't get sold without the participation of your guest-services staff!

- **Offer a freebie.** In theory, no client should ever be waiting for an appointment. Reality is a different story. Service providers run late for a variety of reasons. The client will not look favorably upon being kept waiting. Give the front-desk staff latitude to offer a free service if a client is to be kept waiting. Clients will be less unhappy with the wait and will be introduced to a new service that they may decide to add to their beauty routine, such as a manicure, brow wax or conditioning treatment.

• **Talk it up.** Whatever your company is promoting, whether services or products, your guest-services staff should be talking them up, both on the phone and in person. When clients trust your guest-services staff, they will more likely listen to what's being recommended.

Hitting goal

As in every other area of your business, regular communication with front-desk staff members is crucial. These staff members should be included in daily huddles. If you have a larger guest-services team, you may also want to hold daily huddles for the department.

Guest-services staff members should be familiar with the company's goals for any given period.

Here are some goals you may want to scoreboard:

• **Retail product sold:** It is up to the front-desk associate to ensure that each client has the opportunity to purchase the products recommended by the technicians. The guest-services team has a huge responsibility when it comes to selling retail. It's also important that displays be kept organized and dust-free to maximize their appeal.

- **Gift cards/certificates sold:** Especially around holidays such as Valentine's Day and Mother's Day, you'll want to scoreboard gift cards. Every client should be pitched on purchasing gift cards, both on the phone and in person. Guest-services staff should recommend purchasing the gift cards for family, friends, co-workers and so on. It's not about buying a haircut or massage; it's about the experience.

- **Percent of appointments pre-booked:** If you're not making pre-booking a team sport, it's time to start. All clients must have the opportunity to book their next appointment in advance. Pre-booking should start before the service is completed. The pre-book should be recommended as a way to keep the experience going. Don't ask if the client wants to make an appointment. Suggest one!

- **Up-selling and cross-promotion:** Tracking these numbers both for individuals and as a team will show who's really savvy about products. Just small increases here will tally up fast. Your front-desk team should be major players in these efforts.

- **Productivity:** Are there a lot of fifteen-minute gaps in technicians' schedules, which, if strung continuously, would allow time to see more clients? Do lunch hours run long? Do technicians' schedules begin late or end early? Are some service providers overbooked, while others have several hours free? Productivity will soar when appointments are scheduled wisely, when alternative technicians are recommended, and when time standards are adhered to. Pay heed to this; your

FRONT DESK/GUEST SERVICES 273

guest-services team may be feeling pressure from certain service providers. The goal must be what is best for the business. Let the standards be known, and let your staff know that you will back your front-desk team when issues come up.

Take a look at this sample of how productivity can be influenced by your front-desk staff. In the first example, a couple of service providers are booked to the max with waiting lists, while other service providers have large chunks of unproductive time.

Just by booking differently and suggesting other service providers, see how much more balanced the workload is in the second example. That's the power of a front-desk employee who understands how productivity works!

Evaluating your guest-services team

Like any other position, front-desk staff should be evaluated on both concrete results and "soft skills," such as communication and customer interactions. Be sure your expectations are clear in all areas, such as:

- How effective is the front-desk team at filling vacant hours on the book, no matter which technician's column they occupy?

- How good are they at cross-selling or up-selling product and services?

- How do they deal with difficult clients?

- Do they maintain control of the reception area, even during busy times?

- Do they make clients feel comfortable?

Pre-book: Before

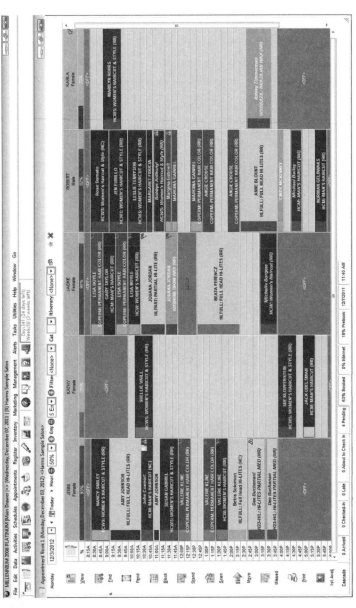

Pre-book: After

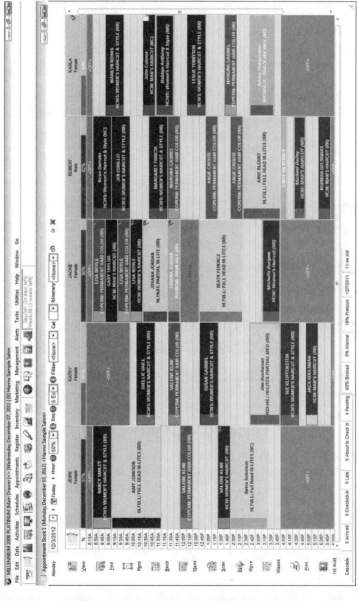

Use your software programs to track tangibles, to help you when conducting evaluations, keeping in mind the following:

- Track the average total of daily transactions for the entire month. Divide this number by the number of team members working the desk at any given hour. This calculation yields the number of transactions-per-hour per employee, and will tell you when your business is under-staffed or over-staffed.

- Check the volume: If the desk is handling a lot of transactions per hour, the team may not be able to provide the level of customer service that's optimal. If the number of transactions for any given hour is low, the team may need other work to occupy their time. These other tasks might include updating displays, contacting clients who haven't been in for a while, working on marketing projects, etc.

Making the grade

Every employee obviously needs to add value to your business. On page 277 there's a simple test that can help you evaluate your front-desk employees. Remember, you need to allow your front-desk staffer to be a full member of your team. This is a test for your actions, as well. If a front-desk staffer doesn't know this week's goals, is that her fault or yours? This test will help you benchmark your performance, as well as that of each front-desk staff member.

The Guest Services Acid Test

Employees add value or they add cost

Using a scale of 1 for "never" and 5 for "always," ask:
"Does my front-desk team member ..."

NEVER.......ALWAYS

1) ... operate based on clearly defined performance goals?	1 2 3 4 5
2) ... keep productivity as a top priority, working with specified guidelines?	1 2 3 4 5
3) ... take responsibility for client satisfaction?	1 2 3 4 5
4) ... put the needs and concerns of clients first?	1 2 3 4 5
5) ... recommend the services of the entire company?	1 2 3 4 5
6) ...understand the talents and skills of each technical provider?	1 2 3 4 5
7) ... regularly participate in leadership team meetings?	1 2 3 4 5
8) ... know the company's weekly/monthly sales objectives?	1 2 3 4 5
9) ... assist in planning work schedules to ensure maximum coverage?	1 2 3 4 5
10) ... contribute to increasing average ticket?	1 2 3 4 5
11) ... recommend retail, following up on recommendations from the service provider?	1 2 3 4 5
12) ... follow all systems?	1 2 3 4 5
13) ... present a professional personal appearance?	1 2 3 4 5
14) ... use good judgment when addressing challenges, with both team members and clients?	1 2 3 4 5
15) ... maintain high levels of respect for clients and staff?	1 2 3 4 5
16) ... deliver value-added service?	1 2 3 4 5

TOTAL SCORE: _____

Total your responses. The highest possible score is 80; the lowest 16. Compare your score with the chart below to see how your front-desk contributes to your company. If the score was less than 4 on any question, target that area for improvement. A 3 or less indicates an area that must receive immediate attention.

16 - 25 Little or No Contribution to Company Growth You must make major changes stat. If the score is this low, leadership must change immediately, before asking front-desk team members to make changes.

26 - 45 Minimal Contribution Your front-desk systems and policies need a major overhaul.

46 - 60 Average Contribution Some systems are most likely in place. Additional structure and training need to be instituted.

61 - 70 Strong Contribution Your front desk is on the right track. Look at weak areas to clearly define objectives. Small improvements will provide big results.

71 - 80 First-rate Contribution You and your front-desk staff should be proud! Your front desk is well-structured, with high performance. Keep it there with bigger objectives and incentive programs.

Priorities 101

Strategies finds that the top concerns are sometimes different from the leaders' viewpoint as from the perspective of the people on the frontlines. Look at these lists as a starting point for ongoing discussions. Front-desk staff are often told to "Just do it," without regard for their expertise and unique perspective. To maximize the front desk and ensure your front-desk team are able to provide optimum service, revisit these lists often.

The Top 10 aspects of customer service – as seen by front-desk team members:

1. Help clients to feel "at home."

2. Be a friendly, knowledgeable voice on the phone.

3. Offer a smiling face at the desk.

4. Place clients with appropriate service providers.

5. Maintain efficient scheduling.

6. Ensure there's a clean, welcoming environment.

7. Put customer needs first.

8. Make a good first impression and last impression.

9. Send out promotional materials, such as birthday and miss-you cards or e-mails.

10. Know retail and service preferences, and use this information to help the client.

What owners and managers want in a front-desk team member:

- Someone who can multi-task
- Excellent customer-service skills
- A positive attitude
- A friendly personality
- Accuracy and consistency
- Desire to grow the business
- Great telephone skills
- Terrific attendance
- A fashionable and professional appearance
- Career-minded
- Respect

What front-desk team members want:

- Technical and professional education
- Support from leadership
- Better communication among staff
- Updated computer system
- Effective physical setup
- A clear idea of goals and expectations
- Feeling as though they're an important member of the team

Ten steps to excellent customer service

Share these steps with your front-desk staff, explaining that they're an important part of the job. The details will be up to you as every culture is different. They are a good jumping-off point for discussion. You may wish to include these criteria in your job descriptions.

1. **Dress to impress.** What you wear communicates what you think of yourself and others. Wear clothes that mirror the culture. Be clean and neat; don't forget to keep your make-up and jewelry in line with the dress code.

2. **Wear a smile.** As they sang in "Annie," you're never fully dressed without a smile. Customers and fellow staff members deserve the best you can offer. Your upbeat attitude can change the mood of the entire business. Leave your baggage at the door, and come to work upbeat and ready to face the day. Don't forget to smile as you're answering the phone. It may seem corny, but people can hear the difference.

3. **Be confident.** When you meet new customers, introduce yourself. Let them know you are there to help. When repeat customers come in, greet them by name. Your confidence will help them trust your recommendations.

4. **Listen.** Listening is more than just hearing words. Show a genuine interest in your clients. Make appropriate recommendations based on the information you've gained through listening carefully.

5. **Promote the business.** Talk up your company. Know what's going on and make sure that customers are aware of current promotions. Use your social media connections to spread the word.

6. **Use the phone to touch base with clients.** E-mail is great, but nothing beats the personal touch. Try calling on clients' birthdays, to check on a client who hasn't been in for a while, to see how a client liked a recent service, etc. When you have extra time at the desk, use the phone and let clients know how much you appreciate their business. Personal notes are also greatly appreciated.

7. **Show respect.** Every client deserves your respect. That doesn't mean that you want each one as a close friend. The same is true for co-workers. Whether you hang with them outside of work is beside the point. Show respect to all, even when they're behaving badly. Be the better person. Be kind. Be professional. Always. No exceptions.

8. **Give thanks.** Remember to thank every customer. Add a "please" to every request. Don't take anyone for granted.

9. **Set the tone.** Everyone has personal problems. Everyone has bad days. The important thing is not to let it interfere with courtesy and service. Don't let your bad mood infect the entire business. Leave your baggage at the door, and look at each day as a fresh start. Clients deserve sunny skies when they walk into your business. Your mood can quickly spread through the entire company. Attitudes are conta-

gious. Work to make sure you're spreading sunshine, not dark clouds.

10. **Think like a customer.** Especially at the front desk, get in the habit of seeing things from a client's point of view. Hold to policy when appropriate; bend the rules when necessary. The bottom line is customer satisfaction.

Guest services – a full-court press

We've been focusing on your front-desk staff. Guest services, however, requires the commitment of your entire team. Your guest-services goal is probably simple: Make visits easy and pleasing experiences. This means that everyone who works in your salon, spa or medspa, everything the company does, everything you create, should help create an enjoyable and comfortable visit for your clients.

Have you ever been to a business and been annoyed by how long you sat in the reception area? Ever run across an employee who was rude, rushed, and unsympathetic or did not respect you? Ever not get the results you were promised?

Did you return to that company?

Competition is fierce. It doesn't take much for a client to decide to try a new place. Yes, sometimes it's price related. Most of the time, though, it's because of an interaction that could have been avoided.

Let's look at some areas where a client experience can turn sour.

- **On the phone.** The person who answers the phone must sound as though she appreciates that client's call. It doesn't matter who answers the phone or how busy she is. She should sound pleasant and go out of her way to help, connecting clients to the solutions and information they need.

- **In the reception area.** Clients should feel welcome, comfortable and valued. Wait time should be minimal. The reception area itself should be maximized for client relaxation. Think cushy chairs, refreshments, etc. Any staff member who walks into the area should greet clients who are waiting there.

- **During the service.** The technician delivering a service must meet and exceed expectations. She should explain what is happening as she goes along, highlighting products and techniques used. She should focus her entire attention on the client's needs.

- **After the visit.** New clients should receive follow-up calls. Ask if they are happy with new services and technicians, whether they received product recommendations and at-home care tips, etc. If they didn't pre-book their next appointment, ask them to do so now. Even if you get a lot of voicemail, this extra step shows that your company cares. Be sure to follow up on any critiques they offer. Once a client comes in regularly, it still is important to make these calls every few visits.

No-Compromise Excellence

When it comes to customer service, good just isn't good enough. Achieving "No-Compromise Excellence" means that your entire team is on their "A" game every day. It means that no shortcuts are tolerated and that every system is regularly evaluated for flaws. It means bringing heart and soul, as well as efficiency, to every action.

It's easy to be average. It's easy to provide "enough." Excellence requires an ongoing commitment. Excellence means never resting on your laurels. Excellence is the only way to survive in challenging times. Excellence is enjoyable and profitable. Why would you want to achieve anything else?

To achieve and maintain a standard of excellence, there must be systems for everything in your business. You must know your critical numbers, such as client-retention rates, and be able to communicate those numbers (and your goals for those numbers) to your staff.

Consistency counts. If some of your service providers are committed to No-Compromise Excellence and others aren't, then your business is falling short. No-Compromise Excellence means a consistent, quality experience every time throughout every area of your salon, spa or medspa.

Are you up to the challenge?

We spent the first part of this chapter zooming in to the staff on the front lines. Now let's talk about technical staff and providing service excellence.

There's a system for that

When you systematize every process in your business, it becomes second-nature to deliver world-class service. This means scripts and step-by-step procedures (and training) on everything your business offers.

There is a direct correlation between client-retention rates and the quality and detail of customer-service systems.

How would you rank your customer-service systems? Are they wowing your clients, or merely meeting their expectations? Take a look at this chart. Where would you put the majority of your customers? How would your staff rank them? (Don't guess; use the chart on page 286 in a staff meeting!)

Knowledge is power

The more information you have about a client, the more you can target her experience. Develop a complete file on every customer.

Guest profiles may include:

- Personal information, such as name, nickname, address, phone, e-mail, etc.

- Types of services used.

- Specific of those services, such as color information or type of massage.

- Preferred days/times for services.

- Recommended frequency of visits.

- Products that were recommended and whether they were purchased.

- Additional products purchased.

- Preferences, such as whether a customer wants to be contacted by phone, text or e-mail.

- Other information, such as birthday, anniversary, pets, occupation, etc.

- Guest comments on the service, technician, reception area, etc.

How happy are your clients?

Five levels can be used to define your clients.

Where are your clients now?
At what level do you want them to be?

IS THE CLIENT...	IF SO, THE CLIENT IS...
1. Dissatisfied?	Probably departed forever
2. Marginally satisfied?	A casual customer; will consider any business
3. Basically satisfied?	Neutral, although will likely give you another try
4. Happy?	Retained, a return client
5. Truly wowed?	Loyal, loves your business and tells others

To have most of your clients at Level 4 or 5, you must have a customer-service system in place. This will ensure that few customers are at Level 1, 2 or 3, and if they are, there is a system in place to convert them to wildly happy, loyal guests.

It's important to define who enters all this information into the system. If it's not delineated, information will fall through the cracks. The more specific the information on file, the more chances your guest will receive the world-class service she deserves, the kind that will keep her coming back and recommending your business to others.

Set the standard

If you want to have more Level 5 clients (and who doesn't?), you must identify the core competencies to do so, including skills, attitudes and knowledge. Keep these attributes in mind when hiring and promoting.

Provide training for your staff on your company's mission, value, vision and goals. Help them understand how their jobs fit in with bringing these to life. This is where skill certification will be valuable as you seek to train on both technical skills and skills such as communication and client interaction.

Everything that your company does must feed into this goal of customer satisfaction and offering world-class service. This includes all forms of communication, from advertisements, to how things are phrased verbally, to body language and dress code. Don't leave anything to chance! Make sure that your staff know the standards for everything they do.

When a client is unhappy

Sometimes clients are legitimately unhappy with a service. Have a detailed policy on how to deal with these clients. When handled properly, they can move from angry to singing your praises.

Make sure notes are taken on why the customer is not fully satisfied. Include those notes in the client's profile, in order to avoid future issues.

Do everything to make the client happy, such as re-doing the service or offering a discount. Have a written explanation of what occurred and how it was resolved.

Some customers are dissatisfied as a result of long wait times, noise or the temperature of the room, while they're essentially happy with the service they received. Be on the lookout for patterns and add steps into your skill-certification program to ensure that customer comfort is always top priority.

Develop a system for dealing with customer complaints, including who has the authority to resolve the complaint. It's all about making clients happy. Remember, an unhappy customer will tell far more people about the negative experience. With social media, it's even easier to spew about negative (or even perceived negative) experiences. Of course, it's easier for customers to rave about your business as well. Detailed notes about likes, dislikes and preferences will help ensure the world-class service that everyone desires.

Some businesses offer an unconditional guarantee. The very offer implies excellence! Don't offer it unless you are willing to stand behind it – no matter what. If you and your staff are truly committed to creating an ideal experience each time, it shouldn't be an issue.

There is no "I" in team

To truly provide the type of service that all but ensures loyal customers, a shift must occur. The goal is that the client is no longer attached to one service provider; rather, the customer "belongs" to the salon, spa or medspa. As such, it is everyone's responsibility to keep that client happy and coming back. This involves a culture shift.

GOOD TO KNOW!

1. Keep your team-service contracts in a prominent place for both staff and guests.

2. Keep detailed records of customer services and experiences.

3. Periodically review how many of your customers are Level 4 and 5 and look for ways to increase those numbers.

When the guest belongs to the business, you'll never lose a customer because her preferred technician is too busy or on vacation; customers don't jump ship because a service provider leaves; and service isn't held up when a technician is running late. That guest forms her opinion based on the business as a whole, and how everyone pitches in to ensure a top-notch experience.

Again, your client-retention numbers will be invaluable as you move through the process of changing thinking from "me/my" to "our."

You probably know that it takes more money to get a new customer, rather than keeping a current customer. The chart on page 290 is a striking example of just how much just one customer can be worth to your business.

Calculating a client's lifetime value

Average client ticket $42

Visits per year 7.5

Client life cycle . . . . 6 years

Cost to retain client during life cycle $120

(based on $20 per client per year)

Total individual lifetime value **$1,770**

Average new clients from referrals 5

(family members, friends, co-workers, acquaintenances)

Total lifetime value of referrals $8,850

Total client lifetime value **$10,620**

Worth their weight in gold

Now let's focus on your best customers. Do you really know how much service and product your best clients will buy? It's worth knowing this information.

Run a few reports and find out:

• **Who your most valuable customers are.** It might not be the ones who come in most often. Do you have a program in place to reward your best customers? Businesses often offer perks and discounts to new customers when the focus should be on retaining your top clients.

- **Who is spreading the word about your business.** Client referrals can be a huge source of revenue. Make sure you're tracking how new customers hear about your business and what motivates them to purchase specific services/products. Consider a thank-you program for client referrals.

- **Which customers aren't worth the extra time.** We're not suggesting that you not give every client top-notch experiences. However, it's reality that some clients are high maintenance. All clients are not created equally. Know how much time and expense you're willing to expend on any given client. Be clear and firm in your parameters. Sometimes you just have to say no.

Check out the chart on page 292 for an eye-opening look at the value of new customers compared to retained customers. (Of course, this is just an example. We don't mean to suggest that acquiring new clients isn't important. However, offering "wow" experiences to existing clients can increase your bottom line, at less expense. It's just another example of why offering world-class service is a necessity.)

Not yours, not mine – ours

In the beauty industry, disputes often seem to come down to whose client is it. There is a sense of possessiveness that you don't find in other fields. For example, every driver in the Indy 500 has a pit crew. Auto races are won (and lost) based on the skills of the pit crew.

Focus on new clients

Bring in 50 new $2,250

Retain 10 existing clients $200

Total marketing cost $2,450

Total customers 60

Annual sales projection $8,190

(based on annual per client sales of $315 with a 32% first-time client retention rate)

Focus on client retention

Bring in 10 new $450

Retain 100 existing clients $2,000

Total cost $2,450

Total customers 110

Annual sales projection $31,500

(based on annual per client sales of $315 with a 55% first-time client retention rate)

Not a racing fan? Think of the last time you went to the symphony. Yes, there may have been a violin solo. There was also an entire orchestra backing up that person. Further, there were people handling lights and sound. To go deeper, even the person handling the box office had a hand in how the symphony experience was.

This idea of "it takes a village" can be practiced in your business with the concept of "team service." With team service, everyone takes responsibility for selling hours and making sure that each customer is more than satisfied. That may be a radical concept in a world where "It's not my job," and "I don't have time for that" are commonplace.

It starts with the concept that each customer "belongs" to every employee in the business. Next, there must come the realization that every action (or lack thereof) affects the client experience. Finally, it means that even if I don't personally encounter a customer, there is a good chance that something I did will reflect the clients' overall impression of the business. Team service doesn't release anyone of responsibility; rather, it enhances each employee's responsibility to every customer, every interaction.

Additionally, your team members in every department should know the goals of the company, both short-term and long-range, and be working to meet and exceed them. Yes, within each interaction an employee may have more or less influence on the customer's satisfaction. When everyone is playing their best game, bumps in the road are few. There's the opportunity for everyone to pitch in to help the customer, improve client retention, increase retail sales and so on. Growth is so much easier when everyone is pointed in the same direction!

This type of thinking often represents a sea change in a company, especially for a service-oriented business. It's not going to happen all at once. Stay committed and help your team understand the why and how of team service.

Try these steps to ensure a successful shift to team thinking:

• **Know why it's important and have a plan to implement this change within your company.** If you're wishy-washy, your staff will feel as though you're not serious about this. Make sure you have both the broad strokes and fine detail.

• **Get the word out.** The communication piece is crucial to introducing the concept of team service. It's not just about a client going to Meg if Jen is on vacation. Everything from client retention to profitability to career growth is affected. You won't get everyone on board with one meeting. Be prepared to talk about it constantly, every day at huddle, at every meeting, in individual conversations. Have a grand kick-off to get your staff excited about the concept. You will never be "done" educating your team about this.

• **Signature required.** Your entire team must buy into the concept. One or two grumbles can cause the whole commitment to go sour. Have written "team service contracts," and have every staff member sign them. (More on suggested wording later in this chapter.) If someone is a holdout or just giving lip service to the concept, hold private conversations to bring that person on board. Expect it to take time for the concept to sink in and be assimilated.

• **Provide praise.** See the team concept in practice? Praise your team members in the moment. Compile a list to review in a staff meeting. Too often, we only catch people doing something wrong. Especially with a new program, it's important to provide positive feedback. Keep the excitement going.

- **Make the skills of the entire staff available.** Again, it comes back to education. Having one staff member with a waiting list while another has open time does not serve the customer well. Customers should be booked to maximize productivity. It's about what best serves the client. Don't be so eager, though, that a client is booked for a technician who is not skill certified in a particular service. It's all about exceeding customer expectations. Make it convenient; make it a great experience.

- **Put systems in place.** It's not enough to just say, "We're going to team service." This will only work if there are systems for everything that will affect the customer experience: answering the phone, booking hours, greeting clients, dealing with upset customers, etc.

- **Let the clients know.** At the end of the day, the reason for implementing team service is to take better care of your clients. Let them know about the change and how it benefits them. Post a sign, send a letter or e-mail, call them, whatever it takes. Clearly explain what this change means for them. Make sure your staff is prepared to answer questions about the new system. This should also be part of orientation for new clients. The concept can be emphasized during the tour of your facility.

- **Use the consult.** During a consultation with a client, be sure to have the concept of team service explained. This is a good time to introduce a client to another service provider, someone with similar skills or a staff member who offers another service. The more people your client meets, the more willing she'll be to use the services of someone other than her "regular" technician. Those face-to-face encounters will also be helpful in your up-selling efforts.

- **Have a goal.** Know what you want to achieve through team service. Include your staff in developing goals, such as improving new client retention. Post a scoreboard to keep track of the results. Review them daily. Don't forget to celebrate successes!

- **Skill certification is key.** Skill certification (fully explained in the Employee Relations chapter) must be part of your team-service program. This will ensure consistent services.

- **Try again.** A major shift won't come about instantly. Change can be difficult; old habits are hard to shed. Your staff needs encouragement, direction and feedback. Don't be adversarial. Step back to understand why the concept didn't work in a situation. Clarify your expectations, coach the employee, and move forward. Keep the vision clear and the focus positive. The last thing you want is for employee negativity and fear to impact the client experience.

Team-service contracts

A team-service contract cements the concept of growth through teamwork, for both staff and clients. It's a written commitment to the process.

Make developing the contract a team effort: Staff will more likely adhere to a contract they helped develop. When it is written, print out a big copy, hang it in the dispensary or staff break room. Have everyone sign it. Review it often.

The client contract informs clients about the benefits of team service. It should explain what the goal is: exceeding customer expectations every time. It's an invitation to experience the options and conveniences that team service creates. Again, gather staff input for the development of the contract. When it is completed, make sure every client learns about it. Frame it for the reception area, include it in your service menu, etc. Every client must be exposed to it and understand it. And then your team must live up to the promise!

Use these templates to develop your own team-service contracts.

Team-service contract – for your staff

Our goal is to provide the best quality service to our customers. This means we must continually look for ways to improve, efficiently using resources and always seeking better ways to grow our company.

Going halfway simply doesn't make the grade.

Unlike many other salons, spas and medspas, the skills of our entire staff are available to all clients. We regard waiting lists as a sign of inefficiency and lack of teamwork. Each team member takes responsibility for every hour on the appointment book. Our clients' schedules are more important than our own. As long as there is time on the schedule and the skill is available, we will accommodate our clients' needs without inconvenience or delay.

We do not allow personal egos or clienteles to interfere with the service and satisfaction of our clients. Without exception, we regard and service every client as a customer of our company.

Client retention is our report card. Our productivity rate is our efficiency score. Our commitment to team service is the centerpiece of everything we do, individually and as a company.

Team service contract – for your clients

Unlike many other salons, spa and medspas, we practice the highest form of team service. This means that the skills of our entire team are available to you. We don't lock you into one technician. We don't keep you on a waiting list.

Meeting your needs and busy schedule is our top priority. Not every technician is a master of all skills. Each has areas of expertise that, in combination, offer you a variety of options that is truly unrivaled.

To ensure consistent service quality and technical skill, each staff member goes through a detailed skill-certification program. This means you can always have confidence and peace of mind, knowing that you are in the talented hands of a skill-certified team member. You'll receive the highest quality experience, every visit – guaranteed.

Team service: A primer for clients

Beyond posting the team-service contract, you need a plan for educating clients on the program. After all, you are most likely trying to change years of thinking. Unless clients understand what team service is and why it benefits them, it is unlikely that they will embrace it.

Your entire staff should be prepared to answer questions about the program. You may need two paths: one for educating existing clients and one to explain the program to new clients. You may find new clients more receptive to the concept as they are starting fresh with your salon, spa or medspa.

New clients

Let's first talk about new clients. New clients start with a relatively blank slate. They probably know a little bit about your business, and may have been referred to you by a friend or family member, or come across your marketing.

Educating new clients about team service is sometimes easier, as they are learning a lot of new information about your business.

Here are some ways to help them understand the team-service concept:

- New client tours. Your guest-services coordinator should welcome the new client and give her a tour, introducing her to staff members and who does what and how each contributes to her experience. You may want to offer a gift bag, including samples, menu of services and the team-service contract.

- Technicians should conduct a consultation, inviting other staff members to assist. This encourages client/team interaction and helps the client see that everyone is working together on her behalf.

- During the service itself, make sure that staff references the team-service contract and how each service provider fits into that promise. Role play this in staff meetings so it sounds natural. Obviously, it needs to be timed right so that you're not interrupting someone mid-massage or just as you're about to inject Botox! Still, it's important for the client to have this information. Here's a sample: "Let me tell you a little about our business. We are dedicated to making sure you are completely satisfied with everything we do. We practice team service, so we can better assist you. We keep detailed records so that a variety of staff members may provide the service you desire. Plus, our in-house training program ensures that you'll receive a great service every time." You may want to end by asking if the client has any questions.

- Recommend future enhancements or services – or if someone has time on the books, ask if they'd like a complementary service.

- Remind clients that they can schedule their next appointment with any technician. Suggest one or more by name.

Existing clients

Existing clients are different. They may be comfortable with the status quo and may not immediately be interested in hearing about these changes. Communication is key. Throughout the entire client experience, the benefits of team service should be reviewed.

• Make sure the team-service contract for clients is prominently displayed. This may invite questions and will open up the conversation.

• During the consultation and service, technicians should explain team service. Be prepared for questions. Just as with new clients, including one or more staff members in the conversation may help the customer feel more comfortable going to another service provider in the future.

• After the service, encourage clients to take advantage of team service. Some clients will "get it" right away and be open to seeing other service providers. Other clients will be more "old school" and will only want to see one stylist. Remember, it's about customer choice and convenience.

• Give existing clients a reason to try another technician. Don't forget to up-sell or offer an incentive for trying a new technician and/or service. Remember, it's all about giving the client the most excellent service possible.

Happiness project

Maybe money can't buy happiness, but you can all but guarantee it with the right systems. Here's a seven-step system that Strategies Founder/CEO Neil Ducoff developed to help businesses achieve happiness for their clients. It does not address the specific services/products you might offer; rather it touches upon a system that ensures that clients are offered the right recommendations, every visit.

Here's how it works:

1. The purpose of The Happiness System is to create seamless accountability and follow-through from service providers and guest-services staff at checkout. In essence, it is a simple tracking system to ensure accurate and complete service tickets, verbal and written pre-book and series recommendations, and verbal and written retail recommendations. Every customer deserves "happiness." It is a disservice both to the client and to the company when "happiness" is not provided. Even if a customer is from out of town, redeeming a gift card, etc., the procedures should be followed.

2. All service providers and guest services staff must be trained on The Happiness System and its three components:

    a. Accurate service tickets to ensure all services received are charged for and priced correctly.

    b. A verbal and written pre-book recommendation from the service provider. It should sound like: "Here's when this service needs to be done again. Guest services will schedule your next visit at checkout." Or, "I suggest we schedule you for the following series beginning on (date). Guest services will schedule these at checkout." Pre-book ratio gains are the direct result of a system that links recommendations with checkout. Otherwise, clients simply check out and the opportunity is lost.

    c. A verbal and written retail recommendation from the service provider: It should sound something like: "Here's what I used on you today and what I recommend for continued at-home use. I'm writing them down for you, and guest services will assist you at checkout."

4. Guest-services staff at checkout should check that every service provider completed the steps outlined above. Then, your guest-services staff needs to complete the system. "Susan recommended that _____ services be done on (date). Do you prefer the same day of the week and time, or something different?" Never say, "Do you want to book your next appointment?" It's the same procedure for retail: "Susan recommended these products for your home use between visits; shall I get them for you?"

5. When it is clear that the service provider completed steps 1 -3 and that pre-book and retail recommendations were verbal and written, guest services simply rings through "happiness." If a step was incomplete, there's no "happiness." Guest-services staff should alert a manager when a service provider fails to complete the steps three times on any one day or if another trend is noticed (such as not recommending retail when a specific service was completed).

6. The more "happiness" there is, the higher the company's pre-book rate and retail sales, not to mention higher average tickets because all services rendered are charged for at the correct price.

7. Inspect and acknowledge; inspect and correct. Acknowledge service providers who earn high scores on "happiness." Applaud them in daily huddles. Coach and counsel service providers who earn inconsistent "happiness."

For those service providers who are bucking the system, hold beginning-of-day, midday and end-of-day conversations. Try, "Sarah, you sent five clients to checkout and only one 'happiness.' This is not how we service clients at our company. Where are you stuck and how can we help you master the system?"

The Happiness System has two-fold benefits:

• It ensures that systems are followed to ensure that product/ service recommendations are made. This will lead to higher pre-book and retail numbers.

• Clients are given the appropriate options to maintain their services. This leads to greater customer satisfaction. Of course, the recommendations must be framed in a way that makes customer satisfaction the primary focus.

My personal goals for
Guest Services:

CHAPTER
EIGHT
Marketing

Hear ye, hear ye:
Getting the word out about your business
through effective marketing.

Hear ye, hear ye: Getting the word out about your business through effective marketing.

CHAPTER 8 Marketing

Marketing is one of the most rapidly changing and integral aspects of your business. After all, few businesses survive by the Field of Dreams philosophy: "If you build it, they will come."

Even regular clients can be fickle, trying out the new guy down the street if you haven't managed to remain top of mind. While word of mouth is important, your marketing efforts will reach many more potential clients.

Forget buying one telephone book ad a year and waiting for the calls to come in. You need a multi-pronged ongoing marketing plan. What's more, marketing today is so closely tied to technology that it can seem as though your efforts are out-of-date just as soon as you can get them done. But that's no excuse to slack off.

Don't let more than a few days go by without some kind of marketing effort.

That might sound overwhelming and expensive, but one of the big advantages about technology is that many of today's key marketing strategies are low-cost or even free. So, no more huge outlays of cash on a one-time newspaper ad that you just hope will work.

What hasn't changed is that you must designate a percentage of your budget to marketing – the average is 4-8% for an established company; start-ups should plan a higher percentage – and you must have a plan. One of the easiest ways to develop your plan is by the calendar. Tie promotional efforts into seasons, holidays and special days, such as graduations.

Some marketing tasks you'll probably want to handle yourself. Others can easily be assigned to staff members. Once you have a plan in place, it becomes much less daunting to consider the continuous marketing that is necessary to be competitive. Even with a plan, there may be unexpected opportunities that pop up. Have some undesignated marketing funds available, so that when an opportunity comes up that truly serves your market, you'll be able to jump on it.

First a few general marketing rules:

1. Have a marketing budget.

2. Create an annual marketing calendar. This doesn't mean that other opportunities won't come up during the year, but it will give you an overall plan.

3. Know the goal of each marketing effort.

4. Just because someone is selling it, doesn't mean it's the right marketing vehicle for your business.

5. Just because it's cool and exciting, doesn't mean it's the right marketing vehicle for your business.

6. Marketing is a continual process.

7. Don't put all your eggs in one basket. Marketing must be a multi-pronged effort to reach the greatest number of potential clients.

8. Remember, there are no guarantees. Even if a marketing effort seems like a sure thing, it isn't. No one can promise you results. There are too many variables.

9. Clients must continually be reminded of your business and what it offers. It's often the cumulative result of various marketing efforts that get a client to pick up the phone.

10. Know why you're marketing. Promoting your business should feed your productivity, profitability and growth. Even "image advertising" that doesn't promote a specific item or service should be helping to bring in new clients. Look at how marketing ties in with your critical numbers, such as productivity.

11. Marketing efforts should be measured for effectiveness. Bear in mind that not all efforts will have an immediate payback. Marketing often has a cumuluative effect.

Now, let's look at some of the specific ways you can promote your business.

Website

Your website is your face on the Internet. Many people do their research online. Don't underestimate the importance of a clean, easy-to-navigate website.

Your home page should reflect what your business is about. The graphics should instantly convey a message about who you are: Trendy, for example, for a salon, or relaxing for a day spa.

If you don't already have your domain name (such as, www.strategies.com), try typing in what you want. It will show you if the domain name is available or if another company already has it. Keep your domain name simple and easy to remember. You can try .net or .biz, if the .com version of your name isn't available, which is usually a better choice than shortening your business name. Don't make it difficult to guess your website name.

Here are some basics to include on your website:

- Contact information, including address and phone number. It's amazing how many websites "bury" that information. If a customer has to search, they just might call someplace else.

- Your hours of operation

- Services you offer. Be descriptive; have photos. Some salons/spas/medspas list their prices; others don't. There are advantages and disadvantages to both. If you're not trying to compete on price, you may just want to list the services. You then have a greater opportunity to offer a personalized plan when the potential client calls.

- Your mission. This should describe your philosophy of doing business and give a flavor of what your company is about.

- Who you are. You may want to list all employees or just the principles of the company. Photos are a great addition. Some companies offer straightforward bios; others have fun questionnaires that tell an employee's favorite fruit or first concert experience. Pick a style that reflects the type of company you are. You may also want to include the history of your company.

- An option to sign-up for your e-mail list (more about e-mailing below).

- Company news, including staff announcements, awards won, new offerings, etc.

- Products. If you offer retail, you may want to allow people to order through your website. This means adding an e-commerce option, which will add costs, but also add sales.

- Just-for-fun contests and surveys.

- A blog (more on that later, too).

- Think beyond words. You can add photos of new looks or even video.

You must decide:

- Who's going to design your website. You can hire someone or go the do-it-yourself route. There are plenty of website-builders available. Just do an online search!

- Whose website you admire. If it's a local business, speak to the owner about who did the design. Most websites list the design company at the bottom of the homepage. Contact the company if you want more information – or simply figure out why you like the site, and strive to incorporate similar elements into your own.

- Who will keep your website updated. Assign the job to a staff member. If your website isn't updated frequently, people won't return.

E-mail lists

Your e-mail list is going to be one of your most valuable marketing tools, so cultivate it and use it carefully so people don't opt out of receiving your messages.

Ask everyone if you can add them to your list – new customers, long-time customers, friends and family, staff members and their friends and families, business associates, neighbors, etc. Plus, have an opt-in option on your website.

- You must ask permission to send promotional e-mails. Anything else is SPAM. You don't want to risk being blocked by individuals nor by your Internet provider.

- Never (ever!) send an e-mail where others can see to whom you've sent the e-mail. It is a total violation of privacy to send a promotional e-mail where the recipient can see the e-mail addresses and/or names of 50 or 500 other recipients. Learn how to create a list of addresses.

- Use an e-mail distribution company to help send out professional e-mails. Constant Contact (www.constantcontact.com) is one that deals with businesses of every size. SpaBoom is another (www.spaboom.com) that deals exclusively with spas. Demandforce is a popular choice, as well (www.demandforce.com).

- Always have an opt-out option. Yes, you want everyone to read your e-mails. Still, you must have an opt-out or unsubscribe option. And make it easy to do so. If people genuinely don't want to receive your e-mails, they'll just delete them and will be upset if they can't figure out how to stop getting them. An "unsubscribe" option that's obvious will keep your company in their good graces. Depending on what system you use, you may have the option of asking a few questions about why they chose to stop getting your e-mails. Often, it's simply that they are trying to get fewer e-mails! If you get feedback about the content or frequency, then you may want to tweak that.

- Have something to say. People will stop opening/reading your e-mails if there's no value. What would be of interest to your clients and prospective clients? How about new treatments, discounts, how-to information, expanded hours, a holiday party, e-coupons, new staff, and last-minute openings?

- Decide how often to send e-mails. Some businesses do this on a regular basis, such as monthly or quarterly. Others do it on an as-needed basis. Find a balance so that you are frequently top-of-mind, but that you don't e-mail so often that people get sick of hearing about your business.

- Remember that not everyone will read your e-mail on the day you send it. So, if you're going to hold a one-day sale, for example, make sure that you promote it ahead of time. Otherwise, expect to hear from some disappointed clients.

- Make sure that every e-mail has your logo, contact information, web address and hours. It sounds basic, but if any of those components are missing and a client has to go search for your phone number, that client might just call someone else instead.

Newsletters

Whether by e-mail or regular mail, newsletters are a great way to keep in touch with your customers. They're easy to design. They must be of value to your clients; otherwise no one will read them. Think quick tips, what's new in your business, special offers, etc. They don't have to be fancy. Sometimes, they can be printed in-house. If you're going to do them, put your schedule on the marketing calendar.

Print mail

It may seem old-fashioned, but sending direct-mail pieces has its place in a marketing plan. With so many technological options – and the ever-rising cost of mailing – it might seem that direct-mail marketing is as extinct as the Tyrannosaurus Rex.

In a way, that's exactly why you should consider sending occasional mail pieces. People receive much less mail than they used to. A well-thought out piece of mail from your business can really stand out.

Here are some ideas:

- **Holiday cards.** First, it sends warm wishes at a notable time of year. Second, it's an opportunity to offer a discount, good in January, when sales tend to drop off for many businesses. Just make sure that the card is a generic winter scene or similar, as not everyone celebrates the same holiday, or even any December holiday, at all. A handwritten note adds a special touch in addition to the printed message, or have your whole staff sign the card. Yes, it's a bit of a chore, but it's one that many businesses don't do.

- **Birthday cards.** If you ask new clients and those who sign up for your e-mails the month and date of their birthdays, you've instantly developed a targeted marketing list. E-cards are great; once again, a card in the mail will really stand out!

Simply offer good wishes (preferably with a hand-written note) or offer a birthday month discount.

- **Brochures.** Here's where costs can really add up. If you have something truly special to promote, a full-color brochure can knock your customers socks off. If you're going to spend the money for printing and mailing, have an awesome design and a spot-on message. A student studying design at a local college might jump at the chance to design your brochure, and that route will cost less than using a design firm. Use a professional to write the copy, as well. And it should go without saying to proof, proof, proof. Nothing like sending out 1,000 brochures, only to realize there's a typo in the headline. Every element counts. Make sure your paper choice, for example, reflects the atmosphere of your salon/spa/medspa, both in color and texture. Imagine that you are going through your mail at home and got a brochure. What would make you open it and read it? It's a great idea to check with your staff, customers and others in the business community to get additional opinions. Your post office can help you with mailing rate options.

- **Oversized postcards.** These are a great idea, and may be an option, if you decide a brochure isn't for you, but that you still want a direct-mail piece. You choose from a variety of sizes, including over-sized postcards that really stand out in the mail. You still have the graphics and writing challenges, but costs will be less because the design is less complicated. Check out a vendor, such as Modern Postcard (www.modernpostcard.com). They can help you with the whole project from A to Z. Look at sending the postcard bulk rate, rather than first class. Your post office staff will be able to guide you, if you decide not to use a mailing house.

- **Don't forget the most basic of direct-mail pieces: the humble letter.** Do you receive a lot of letters these days? Probably not! That's why sending a letter can be so effective. Thank a new client for giving you a try, or thank a long-term client for being loyal. It doesn't have to be elaborate. Or, send a handwritten note on a card. As more of our communications become electronic and rushed, a personal note has that much more meaning.

PR

PR stands for "public relations" and it's a great way to get free publicity for your business. All PR starts with a press release – you'll find the components of a press release below.

Let's first talk about what you might want to publicize and who you might want to contact.

One reason that more businesses don't go after "free" publicity is time. It is very time-consuming to constantly send out press releases and contact media sources. On the other hand, the opportunities are great. We've become a 24/7 society and news outlets have more time to fill than ever before. For example, a local television outlet probably had just two or three news shows at one time: at 6 p.m., 11 p.m. and maybe a noon news. Now, they may have two or more hours to fill, early morning, mid-day, dinnertime and late night. It's not uncommon for a station to have news at 5, 5:30 and 6 p.m. All that time has to be filled, no matter what's going on (or not) in your state and the world!

Here's how to begin:

• Make a list of all the media outlets in your area, including newspapers (both local and regional), magazines, television and radio stations, cable access outlets, and online publications (such as AOL's www.patch.com, which offers hyper-local news and events). Do an online search for "newspapers Cleveland," for example. Then, go to each publication's or station's website. Look for wording, such as "submit a press release," or "contact us." Your media list should include the name of the media outlet, editor's name (if applicable), the outlet's website and the e-mail address where to submit news items. Also, make a note of the deadline for submissions. With a monthly publication, that might be two or more months out. Respect the deadline!

• Arrange a calendar with times when you know you'll have a press release to send, for example, your annual holiday party or anniversary celebration.

• Make a list of other types of press releases you can send: new employees, new products, community events, educational seminars that you and your staff have attended, donations the business makes, etc.

• When writing your press release, keep in mind the readers or viewers. Tie your news into how it benefits them.

• Regularly check the media's websites and look for ways to integrate your products and services into their promotions. Think beyond the Mother's Day makeovers. Consider new looks for back-to-school, trends for grooms, environmentally friendly products your business has started using, etc.

Additional tips:

• Whenever possible, submit your press releases via e-mail. You will stand a much greater chance of being published and having more of your information used. Don't make extra work for the media outlet! This is especially true for print media.

• When sending e-mail press releases, never send to a group of reporters where everybody's e-mail is showing. Send them separately or use "BCC." Include a note that explains what is attached and why the information is useful.

• Both attach the press release and paste the copy in the e-mail. Many newsrooms don't have the latest computers and can't open documents in the latest formats. If you paste the document in the e-mail itself, you eliminate the possibility that a reporter won't read your release because he can't open it.

• Be proactive. If a TV station does an interview with a competitor, don't call them and say, "We do that, too." Instead, think about another opportunity where you can offer your expertise. Timing is also important. A newspaper won't write two back-to-back articles about trends in medspas. So, save your "pitch" for a later date.

GOOD TO KNOW!

1. Take advantage of technology for free and almost free marketing options.

2. There's no one right way to do marketing. What works for a friend's business might not work for yours.

3. It's often a cumulative effect that brings in a new customer. Don't be discouraged if a specific effort doesn't immediately show results.

- If a reporter calls or e-mails, he or she is on deadline. Respond quickly. Often, reporters call multiple sources to get a quote for an article or segment. Whoever responds first gets in the piece. If you are serious about getting press, drop everything to answer a reporter inquiry. Tell your staff that this is important, so they know not to just add the message to the pile. If a reporter calls and you're not available, let staff know who else is authorized to speak to the press.

- Many TV stations have local style and fashion programs, and news segments. Make contact with those hosts, so that you'll be top of mind if they have a need. A personal note will separate you from the crowd.

- Don't forget cable access. It might not have the cache that network television has, but people watch those shows and they are hyper-local. Check out your local listings and think about how you and your business could fit in. There may be a weekly about town show, for example. Contact them to see if you can be a guest to promote a big event or remodel.

- Think beyond beauty. As a business owner, you are an expert on many things beyond the latest styles and trends. Be a resource for business topics, such as staff retention, profitability and amazing customer service.

- Be grateful. When a publication profiles your business or you're interviewed on a radio show, always write a note of thanks. For publications that regularly publish your news and notes (such as in their events calendar), send a holiday card and note. Few people do, and it means a lot to the reporter.

At right are the basic components of a press release, which should be on your letterhead, using an easy-to-read 12-point type (such as Arial).

Facebook

A Facebook page serves in a similar fashion as your website. It's a great place to promote new services, share your hours and contact information, and keep in touch with your customers ("fans").

It's easy and free to open an account. Just go to www.facebook.com to get started.

Click on "create a page for a celebrity, band or business." This will enable people to become "fans" of your page. You personally might also want to have a Facebook page. You'll have "friends" on that page.

Technology is changing so quickly that in a few years, Facebook might be passé, as MySpace is now, despite the fact that it was flourishing a few years ago. Google+ is just coming to the

Anatomy of a Press Release

This lets the editor or reporter know that it's OK to use this information immediately. If you don't want the information to become public for a few days, write EMBARGOED UNTIL JUNE 4, 9 A.M. This lets the reporter/editor know when it is OK to publish the information. It goes on the LEFT side of the page.

UPPER-CASE or Initial Caps: Make your headline as compelling as possible – an editor should know what the "meat" of the press release is just by reading the headline/subhead. It is centered on the page.

This is the dateline. It lets the editor know where the company is that's sending the news. Add a hyphen after your state to let the reader know the press release is beginning. It goes on the left side of the page, at the start of the first paragraph.

The second paragraph should give more information, for example, what kind of experience your new staff member has or what exactly your Happy Hour Houston will feature.

The final paragraphs should add any more facts and should give basic information about your company, such as your areas of specialty and a little history. This is where you can add in details, such as your address and phone number, if they weren't given in the first paragraph.

The contact section is strictly for the editor/reporter. This information will not be released to the public. Most of the time, you will not be contacted. But you want to be easy to reach in case there are questions, an interview is desired or a reporter wants an additional photo. This goes on the left side, under the release date.

The first paragraph should tell the who, what, when, where, why of the press release. Even if the editor does not read any further, this should be enough news to promote an event, say, or introduce a new staff member. The information should be interesting enough, however, that an editor wants more detail, which you will give in the next paragraph..

The third and fourth paragraphs should add more of a feel for the event or announcement. Add in a few quotes, from the owner, other employees and/or customers. If the first two paragraphs are the score; this is the "color commentary."

Three hash marks, centered, signals the end of the press release. Another way to do this is: -30-

FOR IMMEDIATE RELEASE

For further information, contact:
Mary Smith, Owner
XXX-XXX-XXXX
marysmith@salonx.com

HEADLINE GOES HERE, BOLD
Subhead goes here, if needed

Centerbrook, Conn.-

First Paragraph

Second Paragraph

Third and Fourth Paragraphs

Final Paragraphs

###

PHOTO

After the text of the press release, you should write complete captions for any photos that are included. Don't just say "Mary Smith." Say, "Mary Smith, the newest staff member of Salon X, has 15 years of experience and loves to do dramatic makeovers." Make sure that it's clear who's who in any photos – always identify people from left to right, and indicate that in the caption – and which photo is which. When you're e-mailing photos, have the caption name be the same as the name of the attached photos. Photos should be high quality; 300-DPI jpegs are standard. No photos from your phone! Another word for caption is cutline.

forefront. Whatever the name of your preferred social media platform, keep these tips in mind.

• Keep your site updated. Post regularly and encourage your staff to post on your site, as well. No one will return to your site if it's stale.

• Be positive. Make sure your tone is upbeat and inviting.

• Facebook is the perfect place to advertise last-minute promotions and openings. People who are Facebook enthusiasts check multiple times each day.

• Give people a reason to be a "fan" of your page, such as special offers, only available to Facebook fans.

• Make sure you invite people to interact and post. Try surveys, questions and quotes.

• Post lots of photos. People love photos! Be sure to ask for permission to post, say if you're posting photos from an event you hosted.

• Respond to other people's posts on your page. You want this to be an interactive site.

Twitter

Just a few years ago, "tweeting" was something birds did! Today, it seems as though everyone has a Twitter account. It's easy to open an account (www.twitter.com); the challenge is figuring out what to "tweet" and how to condense it to just 140 characters.

To get an idea of what other people are tweeting, pick a variety of people to "follow," both local businesspeople and people such as celebrities and politicians. (And don't forget to follow @nducoff and @strategies4biz to keep up with the latest from Strategies and Neil Ducoff.)

Make sure that your tweets are worthwhile. Refer people to things on your website. Remind them of the final days of a sale. Or, ask that they make their holiday appointments.

If you want to see if your tweets are effective, check out www.tweeteffect.com to see, tweet by tweet, when you gained or lost followers, or www.klout.com, to review your sphere of influence. Want to do better? Tweak your tweets!

Blogs

A "blog" is simply an online column. Visit www.wordpress.com to view some and to set up your own. If you're going to blog (and you can do this on your website), make sure you update it regularly. Make sure you're blogging about something your clients are interested in, not just what you want to promote. Blogging is certainly not an essential part of a marketing plan; it's just another tool available to you. Check out www.strategies.com/blog for inspiration.

Events

Events may not seem as though they're part of marketing, but they are. Events promote your business, and include ones that you host, such as a birthday celebration, and events that others organize, such as a Chamber of Commerce networking night.

There are a few keys to successful event planning:

- Pick your date carefully. Check for religious and secular holidays, as well as other community happenings in town. You want to pick the date with the fewest (if any) conflicts.

- While you want to avoid conflicts, you might want to piggyback on to already planned events. For example, if your town has an annual holiday stroll, that might be the perfect time to host an open house.

- Make sure the event is something that people will want to attend. Don't just plan something to promote the business; offer reasons that potential clients will want to give up valuable free time to stop by. This might include demonstrations, discounts, games, giveaways, special guests, refreshments, etc.

- Choose a catchy theme. When kids have birthday parties, they pick themes, such as dinosaurs, cowboys, popular movies or toys. Think in terms of themes, beyond an anniversary celebration.

- Publicize your event. Use every means possible to bring attention to your event. Ask your mayor to cut the ribbon. Ask a local celebrity to lead the carol sing. Talk to a local sports team about having players at your treasure hunt. Don't forget to involve schools. Children always bring their parents, so if you want music, think high school band instead of your iPod.

Donations

When the Jaycees ask you to give them a gift certificate for their charity auction, that's a donation. It's also a form of marketing as it gets your name in front of those folks who attend the auction. When you're asked to place an ad in the program of the midget football yearbook, it's advertising, yes, but it may also be more of a donation. Have a policy as to how you plan to handle these requests.

Some companies have a set monthly budget for these types of donations. Others designate a few charities to support each year and don't deviate from that list. Still others support the charities that are important to their employees.

It's hard to say no to the local Girl Scout Troop or Little League. A certain number of these types of donations are important for good community relations. And, you certainly might get a good response. Just don't expect a direct payoff. Keep good records of actual donations for tax purposes.

Paid Advertising

Not too long ago, paid advertising was the main way that small businesses put out the word about what they offer. Newspapers, radio, Yellow Pages and TV ads all cost big bucks and often offered little return on investment.

Marketing that uses technology has put a big crimp in paid advertising revenue. That means that deals can be had.

- Make sure you're reaching your potential market. Your big-city newspaper might have greater reach, but if you're advertising cuts and styles for the prom, you might be better advertising in the high school newspaper.

• Join forces with other businesses. If you're in a shopping mall with other, non-competing, businesses, think about advertising as a group. It's a great way to get more exposure at a reduced expense.

• Consider your market. If most of your customers come from a certain town, you're better off advertising in the local publication, even though it reaches fewer people than a regional paper. On the other hand, if your customers come from a wide area or if you're trying to reach a new customer base, advertising in a bigger publication might make sense.

• If an advertising rep has been calling on you, ask to be contacted when there's remnant space available. Often there are last-minute opportunities for quick (and cheaper) sales when publications are trying to get in a few extra ads. It never hurts to ask.

• Think outside the box. Each community has its own flavor for advertising. Whether it's an ad at a sports event or bus side, if you want to make a splash, think about your audience and message and the best way to connect.

Offering coupons or discounts through such companies as Groupon may seem like a great opportunity to bring in new clients. Keep in mind the following if you're considering a Groupon or other coupon promotion:

• Know what the service you are discounting actually costs.

- Be prepared for a flood of responses. Many business owners who have used Groupon (or similar services) have been overwhelmed by the response. It may seem like a positive thing. However, you could be flooded with customers who just want a deal. Be sure you have the staff to handle a large response, and know that you might be turning away regular clients to serve these new clients.

- Know what your fees are or what percentage of sales you'll be giving to the coupon vendor. If you offer a coupon in a local newspaper, the upfront charge is black and white. Make sure you fully understand how your Groupon deal works, so that you're not surprised. Be certain that all the costs involved fit into your marketing plan.

- Have a detailed strategy for how to turn "coupon clients" into regular customers. Also, have a plan for how to up-sell them or sell retail. The point isn't to get them into your business once. It's to increase your base of customers. Make sure your staff is fully trained in how to implement the plan.

Do I need to hire an advertising agency or PR firm?

The short answer is, "It depends." If you are a large, multi-million dollar business with several locations, it might make sense. If you're a small, single location business, you probably can handle everything in-house, using freelance writers or designers, if needed, for special projects.

A few things to consider:

- If you hire a company to help with your advertising, make sure you understand all the fees involved. Will you be paying a retainer fee? Will you be charged per project? What if you want to make changes to an ad? How will those charges work? Can the ad agency negotiate better rates for ads? Will you have a team that's devoted just to your account, or will whoever's available work on your projects? Do you have to spend a minimum per year? Have they worked in your industry before? Are they currently working with clients who are competitors? Take the time for due diligence. Advertising and public relations firms can be expensive propositions – and that's before your media fees enter the picture. Sometimes, it makes perfect sense to hire a firm. Just do your homework.

- You may want to hire a marketing person to handle your advertising and PR. Depending on your needs that could be a part-time or a full-position. That person can also hire a freelancer to round out what is required.

- If you do it on your own, use all your in-house resources. Check with your staff to see if they're interested in designing brochures or doing a weekly blog. There may be undiscovered talent.

My personal goals for
Marketing:

_____

_____

_____

_____

_____

_____

_____

_____

_____

_____

_____

_____

_____

_____

_____

_____

_____

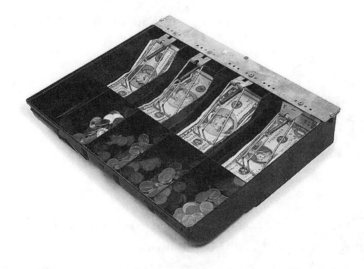

CHAPTER NINE
Retail

Everybody sells:
The secrets to successful retailing.

*Everybody sells: The secret to
successful retailing.*

CHAPTER 9 Retail

Retailing is nothing like it used to be! With more choices than ever before (both of brands and where to buy them), clients need expert guidance (that's you and your staff!) to help them maintain the looks that they desire and have at-home experiences that keep them coming back to your salon, spa or medspa.

Competition is indeed intense, both from the vast variety of brands available (and choices within those lines) and the dizzying number of places to shop, both at retail locations and online.

The first key point to remember is: Everybody sells. Period. End of story. No one should be allowed to get away with saying, "It's not my job." Or, "I don't like to sell." If you offer retail, sales becomes everyone's responsibility. (And, if you're not selling retail, why not?)

Before we discuss how to get your whole team aboard the retail bandwagon, let's go over some of the "technical" details.

"Percent of sales" or "percent of service"?

To avoid confusion, it is important to establish a frame of reference for discussing the financial aspects of retail sales in the salon/spa/medspa environment. Some in the industry have created a standard based on retail sales as a percentage of service revenue. This is an interesting calculation that, on the surface, appears to offer a clear picture of where retail sales fit in the company's overall revenue picture. Some owners and managers use this calculation as a performance goal for individual staff members. For example: "Your retail sales must represent 15% of your service sales in order to qualify for a commission."

What does this calculation really tell you? The truth is, not much. In fact, it yields a distorted and incomplete picture of retail sales in relation to overall performance. Since the formula only shows the ratio of retail to service sales, it naturally shows a higher percentage than when retail is calculated as a percentage of total sales.

In the example below, retail is 24% of service sales ($4,453 ÷ $18,578 = 24%).

RETAIL AS A PERCENT OF SERVICE

Service Sales	$18,578	
Retails Sales	4,453	24%
Total Sales	$23,031	

There is an inherent downside to this calculation. First, it is a ratio of only two revenue categories. It overlooks any relationship to other revenue categories, such gift-card sales. Second, and most importantly, the ratio has no connection to the total combined sales of the salon, spa or medspa, the most important ratio to know.

It is much more beneficial to know, in dollars and percentages, the contribution of every revenue leg to total sales. The ratio between two revenue legs (e.g., retail to service) is immaterial. The ratio of retail sales to total sales is important. In the example below, we calculate service sales as a percentage of total sales ($18,578 ÷ $23,031 = 80.7%). Next, we calculate retail as a percentage of total sales ($4,453 ÷ $23,031 = 19.3%).

RETAIL AS A PERCENT OF TOTAL SALES

Service Sales	$18,578	80.7%
Retails Sales	4,453	19.3%
Total Sales	$23,031	100%

In this calculation, retail sales account for only 19.3% of total sales. This is the actual, no smoke-and-mirrors contribution of retail to total sales. It is almost 5% less than the ratio of retail-to-service sales. It may be impressive to use the 24% of service figure, but it can be misleading and inaccurate.

Whether you are examining expense or revenue categories, the percentage they represent of total sales is the one you want to know and track. That's true whether it's rent or payroll or retail.

When discussing retail sales percentages, clarify that you calculate retail sales as a percentage of total sales. If other people have a higher ratio, ask how they calculate their retail sales percentage. Remember, if they use a ratio of retail-to-service sales, that percentage will always be higher and misleading. More importantly, it fails to show retail's true contribution to total sales.

Determining your retail potential

Retail has become a significant sales contributor at many salons, spas and medspas. Having a successful retail business goes much further than simply putting a bottle of shampoo or lotion on a shelf. Retailing is a process that involves an array of management decisions: space allocation, financial investment, product analysis, creative displays and promotions. Of course, it's all for naught if you don't train your staff in how to recommend and sell products.

Your retail merchandising is greatly influenced by the high-speed pace of change in the consumer market. Professional manufacturers and distributors are driven by stiff competition. Your success is their success. Knowing your customers is one key to a profitable retail department. Later in this chapter, we'll explore the benefits/pitfalls of offering a single line of products vs. multiple lines. Retail is an ever-evolving field, and has the potential to add significantly to your bottom line.

What's realistic?

The industry average for retail sales currently resides between 12%-15% in hair salons, and about 30%-35% in spas that offer no hair services, or in which hair plays "second fiddle" to skin and body services. (Spas that perform a lot of massage services may see slightly lower totals.)

A reasonable target for most hair salons is 20%-25% and, for spas, anything greater than 35%. Medspas should be somewhere in the middle.

Always remember two cautions when setting retail goals:

- **Make goals realistic.** If your salon is currently at 7% retail, don't expect an immediate jump to 15%. Fifteen percent may not sound like a lot, but it's more than twice as much as 7%.

- **Calculate retail sales (and every revenue category) as a percent of total sales, not of service sales.** This will provide a clear view of the role retail plays in your business.

Key ratios to measure retail performance

As with any other performance data, the power of the following ratios will not be realized if not clearly communicated to staff. Successful retailers feed performance objectives and data to staff. They play the retailing game every day to win – and to win, the team must know the score. In this regard, monthly meetings and quarterly reviews just aren't enough. Goals must be communicated and reviewed daily.

Use the following key ratio calculations to set retail goals and monitor performance for individuals and for the salon, spa or medspa:

Retail as a percent of total revenues

Formula: Retail sales ÷ total revenues

Average retail ticket

Formula: Total retail sales ÷ number of retail tickets

Retail tickets as a percent of total tickets

Formula: Retail tickets ÷ total tickets

Retail customers as a percent of total customers

Formula: Retail customers ÷ total customers

Turn, turn, turn

To succeed in retail sales, you must manage inventory costs and inventory turns. If inventory costs are allowed to "free-float" as the result of uncontrolled buying practices, inventory will become bloated and the number of turns will decrease. Additions to retail inventory must be planned carefully and budgeted. Stick to your budgets to avoid overstocking. Even if you're buying the right products, too many will just sit on the shelf, collecting dust. Similarly, discontinue or keep minimal stock on any slow-moving items. Don't be afraid to update your stock. It's your job to control your costs and to educate the consumer on what products work best for their needs.

Inventory turns, or stock turnover, are a fundamental principle of retailing. It measures the number of times during a given period – usually a year – that the average amount of retail stock on hand is sold. Though usually computed on a yearly basis, it may be calculated for any period desired. Make monitoring inventory "stock turn" a must.

Strive to turn your inventory four or more times per year. When you do, watch your retail profits grow.

The rate of stock turn is commonly determined by dividing the average inventory purchase cost into the cost of sales for the merchandise sold. Quite frequently, however, it is computed by dividing the average inventory at retail price into the net sales figure.

When computing inventory turns, observe two cautions:

1. Sales and average stock figures must be comparable (i.e., both should cover the same operating period, and be stated either in terms of cost or retail prices).

2. The average stock must be representative (i.e., it should accurately reflect the average size of the inventory for the period it covers).

Let's look at three different formulas to calculate inventory turn. Each example assumes the following: A salon begins the year with 100 bottles of shampoo costing $5 each, and retailing for $10 each. During the year, more bottles of shampoo are purchased; 60 bottles remain in stock at the end of the year. During the year, 600 bottles of shampoo were sold for net sales of $6,000 and a cost of $3,000. The annual rate of stock turn may now be calculated as follows:

Three Formulas To Calculate Inventory Turns

1. Opening inventory at COST (100 x $5) $500
   Closing inventory at COST (60 x $5) . . . . <u>300</u>
                                            800
   Average inventory at cost (800 ÷ 2) 400
   Cost of goods sold (600 x $5) $3,000
   STOCK TURN RATE . . . . $3,000 ÷ $400 = 7.5

2. Opening inventory at RETAIL PRICE (100 x $10)$1,000
   Closing inventory at RETAIL (60 x $10) . . . . <u>600</u>
                                          1,600
   Average inventory at RETAIL (1,600 ÷ 2) 800
   Net sales $6,000
   STOCK TURN RATE . . . . $6,000 ÷ $800 = 7.5

3. Opening inventory in UNITS 100
   Closing inventory in UNITS. . . . . <u>60</u>
                                          160
   Average inventory in UNITS 80
   Net sales in UNITS 600
   STOCK TURN RATE . . . . 600 ÷ 80 = 7.5

Advantages of rapid stock turns

Satisfactory inventory turnover is the result of good merchandising.

The advantages of a rapid rate of stock turns are clear. By limiting the investment in inventory, expenses such as interest, taxes, insurance on merchandise, and display and storage space are all reduced. Return on inventory investment improves exponentially.

Caution: Many believe there is a direct relationship between stock turnover and profit, and that a retailer can boost profit by increasing the turnover rate. And sometimes, this is true. However, whether profits increase with stock turnover depends entirely upon the methods used. For example: You may increase stock turnover by reducing inventory while maintaining the same sales volume. This may be achieved by eliminating slow-moving items or by dropping entire product lines. Increased profits are not sure to result from reducing stock, even if sales volume holds steady. Purchasing in smaller quantities may result in increased handling and shipping costs, as well as eliminating opportunities for quantity discounts. If slow-moving lines are sold at a discounted price, the profit margin is eroded.

An increase in stock turnover is not always the best strategy to increase profits. Profits are the end result of a collection of sound retailing practices. Concentrate on careful buying, judicious pricing, a well-balanced stock, effective sales promotions and properly trained staff. Higher inventory turns – and profits – will then follow.

There's a thin line between minimizing inventory costs, and actually running out of a product (sometimes called a "stock-out"). The other side of this coin is the large buy-in required by some manufacturers, where you end up with too much merchandise.

Somewhere between too little and too much, are the "Four Rs": the right product, in the right quantity, in the right place, at the right time.

To find your best inventory plan, you'll need accurate forecasts and a proactive attitude:

- You must focus on the products that impact your business the most. For example: Is there one line that clients particularly like? Is there a new hot product that clients are requesting?

- Compare and contrast various plans and strategies (e.g., vary stock levels or re-ordering procedures).

- As each new or modified strategy is implemented, you must track the outcome.

These results should be integrated into the next new strategy.

As you work to create a viable inventory strategy, a number of factors will affect the process, some of which are out of your control.

Here are just a few to keep in mind:

- **Forecast error.** It can happen to anyone, especially someone new to the process. Regularly updating projected figures when actuals become available (e.g., weekly or monthly) will make each forecast more accurate than the one before.

- **Desired service level.** Will you place special orders for clients, or sell only what's on the shelves? What level of service do you want from your distributor or manufacturer?

- **Lead time for restocking.** How long does the process take, from start to finish? Can you get same-day or next-day delivery?

- **Costs.** Are you responsible for shipping and freight charges? What is the administrative cost of the time spent monitoring, ordering and stocking inventory? (This can be greatly reduced by a good point-of-sale software program.)

Predicting the future

Forecasting is an important activity for business owners because it dovetails with the planning process. Objective forecasts rely on data and figures, and mathematically extrapolate future performance based on the past. This is why accurate record keeping is a must! Especially for start-ups, your sales rep can help in this process.

Seasonality is the tendency of sales to move up and down according to the season or time of year. Salons, spas and medspas that are located in resort areas, or locales subject to extreme variations in weather, are all too familiar with this issue. Holidays are another big factor in forecasting.

Accurate forecasts can help blunt the edges of your company's seasonality. If you've ever plummeted from the high of overwhelming gift certificate sales to the low of redemption time, you know the value of mapping out the space between. This is where a good forecasting model can be invaluable: It will project expected fluctuations in client traffic and sales, enabling you to anticipate inflows and outflows of cash, and set appropriate sales goals.

Anticipating cash inflows and outflows is integral to the budgeting process. When you know what to expect at any given time of year, you can adjust sales goals to ensure liquidity.

Single line vs. multiple lines

Before we start talking about selling merchandise, let's take a few moments to discuss carrying a single line vs. carrying multiple lines. Naturally, there are pros and cons to both.

Multiple Lines

Pros

- You're not putting all your eggs in one basket.
- Customers have greater choice.
- It's easier to special order a product that you don't carry.
- More lines mean more of a chance that a client is already familiar with one or more brands of product prior to visiting your business.
- You always have products in stock, even if one company is having supply issues.

Cons

- Clients can become confused about what to buy.
- It may be more challenging to recommend specific products.
- Products end up competing with each other.

- It can be challenging to decide which brands to feature. Clients may question why a certain brand is "better" than another one.

- Manufacturers may not be as supportive of businesses that only carry small quantities of their products.

- Inventory is more difficult to manage, so you may end up with overstocks.

Single Line

Pros

- Staff can focus on learning one product line in-depth.

- Competition between multiple brands is eliminated.

- Manufacturer is committed to your success. This may mean additional education, merchandising and display assistance, samples, etc.

- Your brand isn't diluted as it might be with multiple lines.

Cons

- You may have limited options if you're unhappy with the relationship.

- You are making an all-or-nothing investment.

- You may be making a long-term commitment that will be difficult to break.

- Clients may request types of items that aren't carried within the line.

Selling systems

The key to bringing in more money from retail is (obviously) the actual selling of products. Great inventory management will only take you so far. If you don't have a black-and-white system in place to sell those carefully selected products, you'll never raise your retail numbers. Clients will usually buy what technicians recommend. They want expert advice.

GOOD TO KNOW!

1. Creative displays are the perfect way to draw customers in to browse your retail section.

2. Tie special promotions into holidays, birthdays and other special times.

3. Try a survey of your customers to learn valuable information, which will help you, plan your retail program.

If your retail sales percentages are lackluster, it is most likely due to the lack of a systematized approach to retailing. Some staff members may be choosing not to sell. The product recommendation must be an inseparable part of the salon/spa/medspa experience. Failure to recommend professional products for home maintenance shortchanges the customer.

Design your retailing system to achieve consistency in the selling process, and watch retail performance improve dramatically. Just think of what it would do to your company's profitability if 90% (or more) of clients received product recommendations. How much more would you do in retail sales? It all comes back to having a system in place where selling retail is required, not optional.

Without a system to guide the process, the fear of rejection often associated with retail selling is difficult for most individuals to overcome. Service providers might feel as though they're intruding on the customer's time or simply don't know how to approach selling. Fearing failure, they just don't try. Other employees, seeing that their colleagues aren't selling, decide that they're no longer going to make the effort either, leaving your retail numbers in the cellar, with no way of rising.

When you have a system in place, it helps defuse those fears. When selling is mandatory, it eliminates the "Why am I the only one who's selling?" mindset. Most clients will appreciate the product recommendations for what they are: a way to continue their salon/spa/medspa experience at home.

Fear of selling: Just say no

The business of sales is a unique beast. While you'll seldom hear an employee say, "I just can't do injectables," or "It's not my style to do a chocolate facial," people will often fall back on, "I'm not a salesperson."

If you hear such comments from you're staff, memorize these words: "That's great! We're not selling products; we're helping our clients."

Sales is all about education. First, you're educating your team. Second, your team educates individual clients on how the products will help them. You provide solutions to your clients. While products must be recommended on a personalized basis, the system of connecting people to products must remain constant.

Here's the simple formula that Strategies has been recommending for years:

Every client receives a "prescription" of three product recommendations. These products must be discussed with the client, as well as written on a piece of paper, just as a doctor writes a prescription for medicine.

Of course, it's not quite that easy. Even with the absolute of writing down three product recommendations, you're dealing with people. Some staff members will love the idea of this formula, working hard to ensure that each client receives the right recommendations. Others will mumble something to the client, or even worse, hand off the prescription without explanation. While people's personalities certainly come into play, you cannot waiver on the dictum that everybody sells. So, let's explore some ways to get team members on board with retail.

Repositioning selling

Suppose you explain to your staff that they are to focus on determining each client's needs, and reviewing the appropriate services and products to satisfy those needs. To achieve this, the salon/spa/medspa will provide the staff with a system, tools to efficiently discover the client's needs in order to prescribe services and products. That doesn't sound too daunting, does it?

Once again, it's a matter of semantics. Whether you call it selling, educating or prescribing, the objective is the same – to create a sale that will enhance the client's experience.

1. Make sure all staff has the training and tools to recommend appropriate products. Every client receives a prescription for home care: three products written down. Everybody is responsible for sales.

2. Inventory control will make or break your retail program. Get a system in place so that you won't be running out of products or having too much stock on hand.

3. Start a bonus program that includes all staff.

Staff members often react negatively to selling because they are uncomfortable with the process. It's a new behavior that requires a certain level of proficiency. It also requires a certain level of self-esteem and self-confidence. Whether or not someone considers herself a natural salesperson, everyone on your staff can follow the procedures you establish. It's not selling ice at the North Pole; it's all about helping the customer. Once employees understand the selling process, they can reap the personal, professional and financial rewards it can deliver.

It's a darn good feeling when a customer takes your personal recommendation for home care, especially when you know that it will bring a customer greater satisfaction following the service. When recommendations are given with an open heart and the client's needs in mind, your guidance will be appreciated, whether or not it results in a direct purchase.

Sell the experience; prescribe the product

With sales of any kind, a significant emotional experience must occur for consumers. Whether it is how good a facial makes their skin feel, how beautiful a great hairstyle brings on confidence, or how relaxed a massage makes them feel, it always comes back to emotion. Salon/spa/medspa technicians need to produce these positive emotions in order to establish trust in a sales relationship. Clients most often buy the products used during services in order to duplicate how they feel.

Trust begins with an incredible service that firmly establishes the customer's confidence in a technician's ability. Only after this trust is established will he or she take a professional recommendation seriously.

It's an educational process, and this must begin at the consultation and continue throughout the service. Recommendations shouldn't come out of the blue.

The recommendation should come in the form of a prescription. Prescribing products is simply the process of writing the suggested products on a piece of paper for the client to take home. This may be the actual products used in the service or products needed to maintain the look and feel of a treatment, or they may be products especially formulated for home use. Not only should product names be written down, but also how and when to use them. This individualized prescription then becomes a vital reference for clients, rather than a sales pitch.

Questions that lead to "yes"

Sometimes it will be clear-cut what a client needs to take home. Or there may be one product that is a standout recommendation. Rather than only recommend that one product, each staff member must become an expert at defining and filling customer needs. The way to do this is through conversation with the client. Without asking questions, it's impossible to learn what a client really needs. Role-play until your staff feels comfortable with these discussions and understands when to have them.

Staff should ask questions:

• On a broad range of possible client problems which you can help solve.

• That narrow the focus until you discover specific needs.

• That continue to produce "yes" answers. Think of the process as a flow chart, with different alternatives depending on the customer's responses.

• To isolate client objections, and prevent random objections from getting out of control. It's your job to direct the course of a conversation on product recommendations. While it's easy to get off-topic, gently guide the conversation back to the product recommendations.

• That help you use client information to make a sale. Repeat words and phrases that the client uses. Show your understanding.

Service providers should:

• Talk about products as they're using them. Relate the information to the treatment that's being given, focusing on the benefits to the client.

• Display the products being used, if appropriate.

• Allow the client to touch the packaging and product, if appropriate.

• Not be fixated on closing a sale. Rather, they should focus on
the service being given and how specific products will help
the customer once he or she returns home.

Skill certifying the sales process

Think the need for skill certification applies only to technical
skills? Think again. Any area in which you want consistency, or
consistent improvement, should be skill certified. This includes
retail sales. Skill certification ensures that your sales systems
are being followed consistently. The result? Increased sales.

There are four primary areas in which skills should be certified for retail: product knowledge, inventory, displays, and sales.

Here are some ideas to get you started:

• **Product knowledge**
Product knowledge enables team members to hold intelli-
gent, informed sales conversations with clients. This section
of your program must address the ability to open a dialogue
with clients, present information effectively, and respond to
questions confidently.

• **Inventory**
Explain to your staff the importance of keeping an eye on
inventory and make sure that everyone understands how
inventory turns can drive the bottom line.

• **Displays**
Displays should give customers a feeling and not just be
a stack of merchandise. All staff must be trained in an

established procedure for keeping retail shelves adequately stocked, clean and appealing to clients. Merchandising is all about presentation.

• **Sales**

This training section must provide the tools, procedures and scripts for staff to master your selling system as a whole, including add-ons and closing sales, as well as dealing with clients who say "no."

Six steps to successful product recommendations

As we've been discussing, the ability to communicate with clients, understand their needs and make appropriate recommendations is crucial to the selling process.

Here are six steps employees can follow that all but guarantee retail success:

1. **Know the product:** Anyone in a position to field client questions about product should be able to respond correctly. This includes technicians, managers, front-desk staff, everyone!

2. **Talk to clients before the service begins:** Although some information might seem evident, it is a sign of respect to ask questions and allow the client to voice his or her concerns and needs. With a new client, this will be a longer process; however, every client should be evaluated prior to the start of the service. It's similar to a doctor asking questions about your symptoms prior to offering a diagnosis.

3. **Keep the conversation going throughout the service:** You may find that once you're underway with a service or treatment that something else is necessary. If you believe the client will be better off by adding or deleting elements of services, or by using another retail line, explain why. Then, respect the customer's decision.

4. **Provide a commentary:** As you work, inform clients of what you are doing and the products used. Always ask if they have questions, and answer them completely. If you don't know the answer, be honest – and then find out.

5. **Use your own words:** Don't sound as though you're reading the copy off the side of the box or quoting a commercial. Be yourself. Offer information based on personal experience or others you know who use the products.

6. **Write it down:** It always comes back to this. Write down the prescription for products. You can even go as far as writing directions, such as "Use a dime-sized amount daily," or, "Twice a week during the winter months." This also helps the front-desk staff person to use the right language in closing the sale.

Special considerations for the guest-care/front-desk staff

We've spent a good deal of time on how the service providers can influence a sale. As we've talked about, everybody sells. In the training process, don't ignore your guest-services or front-desk staff. They can have a major impact on how much retail is sold.

Here are some tips to help maximize the potential that's at your front desk:

• It is up to the guest-care staff, those who operate the cash register, to ensure that each client has the opportunity to purchase the products recommended by the technicians. Technicians usually open the door; the guest-care team closes the deal. They are also responsible for the complete experience when a client just stops in to purchase product.

• Retailing to clients lets them take the salon/spa/medspa feeling home with them. Recommending retail is another form of the services being provided.

• The guest-services staff must know products inside and out.

• Your front-desk staff has a great responsibility for reducing theft. One of the easiest (and most customer friendly) ways is to simply offer assistance when a customer is browsing.

• Staff should suggest a companion product in addition to those that have been chosen or recommended. Every product has a feature and a benefit. Talk with clients to determine their needs. A stylist, for example, may have suggested three hair products. Perhaps there is a skin-care item that would also be appropriate.

• The front-desk staff is often situated closest to the retail displays. That means there are multiple opportunities throughout the day to straighten the displayed merchandise. Count on your guest-services staff for having "insider information" about how customers interact with the displays, as well as getting a heads up on hot sellers.

Fine-tuning retail merchandising

Retailing is an ongoing process. New products and lines are continually introduced. Customer needs and attitudes change. Don't become complacent and believe that what worked last year will continue to produce the same results. Understand that retail is a creature all its own.

To better understand what your clients are looking for, you may wish to conduct a "needs assessment." This will help guide you in choosing lines and adding products based on your customers' habits, preferences and perceptions. After all, the best way to determine what's on the minds of your clients is to ask them!

How A Needs Assessment Works

1. **Plan ahead:** Remember that retail works well ahead of where you are now, so leave enough time to conduct this process.

2. **Determine what information you already have:** Use your database to check on client preferences, buying habits, demographics, etc.

3. **Develop the questions for the assessment:** Be sure to ask your staff and leadership team for their input. Make sure that the final questions are focused.

4. Assign a project leader so that the assessment stays on task and reaches its goals

5. Figure out the process: Will you conduct a survey, hold focus groups, or conduct personal interviews? What will clients be most open to? Will you offer an incentive for completing the survey or attending the focus group?

- A survey should be designed with the end goal in mind. Don't come up with the questions until you determine what information you really want to find out. If you want to know whether to discontinue a particular product, for example, ask clients about the benefits they derive from it. That way you know why a client uses a product. There may be other products that do the same thing, either better or at a different price point. Be sure to include demographic questions, as well, to help you pin down your target audiences for various products. In addition to asking customers to complete a survey when they come in for a treatment or through the mail, surveys can be also be conducted online. Check out www.surveymonkey.com, www.constantcontact.com or www.zoomerang.com to learn more.

- Focus groups can be held at a special time to a pre-screened group of clients; you may also conduct one as part of an open house or other special event. Follow the guidelines for the survey to ensure that you get the information that you can use. This gives you the advantage of having people get into a discussion about the products with plenty of give and take. You also have the advantage of seeing facial expressions and body language.

- Personal interviews. Staff should be doing this every day in the form of consultations with their clients. Have a system for accurately and promptly cataloging responses. You may wish to give your employees specific questions to ask to make sure you're getting the information you need. You may also wish to call a group of clients to solicit their opinions.

6. **Analyze results:** When the project manager filters all of the information clients offer, you will be left with knowledge that can help refine your retail program.

Retail marketing strategy

The core that you should develop your retail marketing strategy around should focus on the "Five Ps."

They are:

1. **Product:** This includes what you carry and how much you carry of it.

2. **People:** This is all about ensuring that your staff is thoroughly trained on product use, and that they understand how to convey that information to customers.

3. **Place:** This includes where you have your retail and how you display it. (More on this later in the chapter.)

4. **Price:** This obviously has an impact on profits. Price impacts buying decisions and the perception of value. Don't

try to hide prices; help clients understand why a product is important to them, and price becomes less of an issue.

5. **Promotion:** Promotion consists of getting the products front and center. It may include advertising, signage, contests, special pricing, even how your staff talks about the products. Make sure the message is consistent throughout your business.

Working with your sales representative

Some distributor representatives are merely order takers. They come in, see what you're running low on and are out the door. This is not what you want! The best time to learn about what services your distributor will offer is while you're selecting what lines to carry. This relationship is especially critical when you are carrying a single line, but each distributor representative should bring something to the table beyond order taking.

Here are some of the roles that your sales consultant or representative might play:

Confidante

A good sales consultant will both listen to what you're saying and know how to interpret so that you're ordering the right mix of products in the right quantities. There's a sense of trust; you feel comfortable saying what's really on your mind about the products, sales, the market, your customers, even your company's financials.

Advisor

Your consultant or rep should see the bigger picture, recognize trends, and be able to offer guidance on what to order and where the market is going. Again, it's not just about taking an order; it's a partnership.

Strategist

Your rep should be able to see the products from the client's point of view. He or she should strive to build a competitive advantage for your business, working with you, not against you.

Marketer

Your rep should be brimming with ideas on how to best promote the products, both individually and as a complete line. You're under no obligation to use those ideas. However, your rep should always be looking for ways to help you sell. That's a win-win-win.

Trainer

You should be able to look to your rep to provide you and your staff with ongoing educational opportunities. Not every opportunity will be a fit, but you should be able to count on your product company to help you continue learning.

Getting the most from your relationship with your consultant

1. **Ask questions before you commit:** Learn what his or her areas of expertise and interest are. This relationship should help make your business stronger.

2. **Get your plan in place:** Work with your consultant to come up with a plan. Make sure both sides know the objectives and their roles in achieving them.

3. **Make time for it:** Schedule regular meetings in order to advance the partnership. Begin with a problem-solving session to discuss your most pressing business needs. Follow up with strategic planning, implementation ideas, and how to measure and assess results. Make sure your consultant knows that you expect this to be a partnership.

Beyond the product

The percent of clients sold is also sometimes referred to as the closing ratio. Obviously, the higher this number, the better. Certain times of year present greater opportunities to push this number upward, including:

• Valentine's Day

• Mother's Day

• The December holiday season.

Many companies also have plans in place to recognize clients' birthdays, anniversaries, and other special events. In fact, any day can be made special; all it takes is a certificate or invitation from the salon/spa/medspa. New product and service launches may be of particular interest to longstanding clients.

Retail purchases are often impulsive, so the goal is to make it as easy as possible for your clients to have access to merchandise. Even beyond the prescriptions for products, people enjoy browsing. You want to enhance the experience and make it easy to buy products beyond the original prescription or shopping list.

There are many ways to catch clients' eyes: through color, motion or position. However you decide to arrange things, always remember that accessibility is key. In order to buy, clients must be able to see, touch and smell products.

- Choose the focal point of the display area – a central fixture, unique piece of furniture or an unusual composition (e.g., a new product line placed at strategic purchase points). Build your display outward from or around this focal point.

- Know your products; make certain they are grouped appropriately into displays that make sense.

- Pay attention to lighting. You may choose use lighting to highlight particular items. Your lighting should create ambiance – soothing, funky, etc. You may want special lighting for various holidays and promotions. Make sure your lighting adds to (rather than competes with) your displays.

- Use color wisely. Color should help draw a client to the display as part of an integrated look.

- Shop your local party store. You'll find lots of inexpensive touches for your displays, plus merchandising ideas.

- Talk to your sales rep for sales ideas. Ask what other salons/spas/medspas are doing with their displays and what worked well for other businesses the previous year. You don't always have to reinvent the wheel.

- Change displays regularly. This includes window displays, as well as in-store displays.

- Talk to your staff members and see if any have an interest in design. Or help a local student get experience by designing your displays.

- Get feedback from friends or family. Have them walk through your retail area, trying to see it from a customer's point of view.

- Keep it moving. This may mean creating special packages, offering slow-selling products as a gift with purchase, or simply giving it away through contests. Sometimes just moving the product to a different location makes a huge difference. Again, your sales rep may have some ideas.

- Make it easy to reach. Don't make your customers twist, turn and reach just to get at your products. Keep products facing forward. Have room between items, so that customers can easily remove them from the shelves. Have a product open for "testing."

- Use sales promotion materials, such as flyers, shelf talkers, hanging signs, etc. Help your potential client understand the products and what they can do.

Leadership rules for retailing

Whether your company excels at retailing is firmly on the shoulders of its leadership team.

Before you blame your staff for low retail numbers, read these rules of engagement:

Retailing Rule Number 1:

Leadership and culture are the powers behind retail sales. How is it that one can be stuck at 10%–15% retail to total sales, while others don't even break a sweat at 25%–35% or higher? Answer: One has a retailing (i.e., selling) culture and the non-performer does not. When leadership creates and maintains a retail culture, the process of selling retail (and services) is planned and expected. Systems are created to drive retail, ensuring that recommendations are made and sales are closed at the front desk. When retailing is part of the culture, it's the only acceptable behavior; anything less is a compromise.

Retailing Rule Number 2:

Reward the right behavior. Retail commissions do not work in salons, spas and medspas. Why? Because retail commissions give employees a choice of whether to sell. If you don't believe that, answer these three questions:

1. How many of your employees have elected not to participate in retailing professional products?

2. How many of these employees continue to be paid handsomely, simply because they generate service sales?

3. How many of your front-desk staff opt out of selling retail because the commissions go to technicians, or they're tired of technicians whining about not getting credit?

So, how do you get everybody on board? Once your team is trained in how to sell, convert your retail commission program to a team bonus program. Here are the easy steps:

1. Set a retail goal for each month. The entire team must hit this goal to activate the bonus pool. Make sure that everybody knows what the goal is. Make sure everybody knows what the reward is. Some ideas for goal-setting:

   - Percentage of clients buying
   - Retail Per Client Ticket (RPCT)
   - Percentage of retail to service sales/total sales
   - Pieces Per Client (PPC)

2. Use daily scoreboards and huddles to drive and communicate progress.

3. When you hit goal (and you usually will), distribute the bonus pool to all team members, including front-desk staff. You may wish to tie this to hours worked or other criteria.

My personal goals for
Retail:

CHAPTER TEN
Exit Strategy

*Your legacy starts
with a plan.*

*Your legacy starts
with a plan.*

CHAPTER 10 Exit Strategy

You probably didn't look at it this way, but you've been preparing to leave your company since before you even opened your doors. Ignore this reality and you place your business legacy at risk. The smoothest transitions, the sales that bring in the greatest amount for the owner, the tradition of excellence that is continued after the sale, all of these start with a well thought-out succession plan or exit strategy.

Still not convinced that you need to start thinking about your exit? Consider these reasons to create a succession plan as soon as possible:

- **Sudden death of the owner.** There, we said it. Let's get that out of the way. No one likes to contemplate his or her own demise, much less plan for it. The fact is that it happens, frequently without warning. Instantly, the company leader is gone. It's like dying without leaving a will that communicates your last wishes and instructions. (You do have a will, don't you?)

- **Illness and health issues.** Again, this is reality. People get into accidents; they develop serious illnesses. Your succession plan will allow for a smooth transition if illness or disability occurs. Preparing a succession plan under the pressure of the pending long-term or permanent absence of the leader hinders the thorough evaluation of options and invites conflicts.

- **Assuming a family member will want to take over.** Your successor should be the best person to lead the company. Family and blood relations hold no guarantee of effective leadership. Moreover, they may not even want your job. Better to plan than to be surprised.

- **You grew your company to the limits of your leadership capabilities.** This is a tough one to contemplate because it means that you need to admit that you don't have all the answers and can't do it all. When you continue to hang on even when you're not the best person for the job, you will damage your company, and that means harming the reputation that you've worked so hard to develop. Have a plan for hiring or promoting someone with the right skills to take over before things start to fall through the cracks.

- **Falling out of love with your job.** It may be a dirty, little secret, but it occurs. And why should your company suffer because of it? Get over it. Your exit strategy will allow you to redefine your role and allow new leadership to continue to grow the business. You may still own the company, but now you're having fun again. Alternatively, you could get out all together and reap the benefits of having sold a well-run company. Or maybe you've fallen out of love with the entire industry. Again, better to get a plan in place than to destroy what was formerly a labor of love.

• **Time to retire.** Retirement doesn't necessarily translate into "sell the company." Why sell the business if it's successful and continuing to create wealth for you? Retirement and selling the business can, of course, can go hand in hand. Make it a conscious choice and not a default.

Succession planning and exit strategies demand that you be honest about your skills, talents, leadership abilities and passions. It's impossible to plan when you are not candid about what you are capable of doing, and more importantly, what you love doing and want to be doing. Even if you are truly leading the business of your dreams, ask yourself for how long you want to be doing it.

Most owners – even those who are totally obsessed with their work – eventually want to hang up their hats and concentrate their days on fishing, stamp collecting or cupcake making. It's a decision that not only affects your daily routine, but your financial future, and, perhaps, the financial stability of your family.

Succession planning can help ensure a company's survival through an ownership transition. Two important steps in succession planning are devising an exit strategy and developing long-range financial goals.

The earlier you begin the planning process, the better. Do not assume that getting out of the business will be easier than breaking in. Goals that are set early are more easily met.

Professional advice is imperative. Start by:

- **Consulting a financial planner.** Too many business owners feel an aversion to planning of any kind. Factor in the numbers aspect and it's no surprise that this is something many people avoid. Yet there are instances in which procrastination quite literally does not pay. Financial planning is one of them. You cannot reach non-existent goals. A financial planner will help you devise personal and business goals, including an exit strategy. Remember that your plans will affect your taxes and/or your estate. If you are transferring business ownership to a family member, don't forget about estate and gift taxes.

- **Consulting an attorney.** A reliable attorney, working in tandem with a knowledgeable financial planner, can ensure that everything is properly funded, and all the tools necessary to ensure a smooth ownership transition are in place.

Wherever you are in the process of planning your exit strategy, there are a few factors that must be kept in mind:

- **Consider your existing business plan.** Does it tie into your personal objectives? An exit strategy must exist within the reality of what the business can accomplish.

- **Realize that getting out can be challenging.** You cannot assume your children, for example, will recognize the true value of the business or that you will get as much as you want for the business in a sale. Assumptions can leave you out in left field.

- **Decide what you want to do after you leave.** If, on your final day, you want to drive directly to the airport and hop a plane for the Caribbean, you'll need to invest time now in hiring and training key personnel. If you want to sell to employees or family, make certain the business is in a good cash position, so the transaction will go smoothly. Again, this is why it's so important to identify a good financial planner and business attorney with whom you can start to form relationships.

As a business evolves beyond the exhilarating start-up phase and matures, it's natural for business owners to want to stay in control and lead the company they built. Isn't that what the entrepreneurial dream is about?

There are two fundamental flaws in this thinking. First, when the leader and the company become indistinguishable from one another, the viability and value of the business are compromised. The business can falter because of the owner's actions. The value of the company is diminished because the owner is the business. The second flaw is a no-brainer that people may forget about: The lifespan of a business can and should far exceed the working life of the owner.

The necessity of succession

For a business to thrive and endure beyond its current leader, there must be a succession plan in place. One basic reason to do so is because the livelihoods and security of your employees and their families must be protected. In addition to that, after all the work of building a successful company, the last thing owners want to see is their companies in distress because they are no longer in charge.

A succession plan creates a personal exit strategy from your company. Even if selling is a distant thought, you must define the process that will allow new leaders or a new owner to take over the company in a smooth and orderly fashion. The search for a buyer willing to pay a premium for your company can be enhanced when a succession plan is already in play.

It's not about you; it's about the business you've created. When the line that separates you from your business becomes indistinguishable, it's unlikely that you will find value in creating a succession plan.

At that point you are your business. It doesn't work without you. You will hold on to control until you or something else breaks. Then it's too late. Get over yourself. This is not about you, it's about the enduring success of your business. Celebrate, honor, respect and protect what you have worked so hard to build. Create your succession plan to give your business life after you.

You create a business plan to start a company. You create a succession plan to ensure its future. Both are non-negotiables.

Creating an ownership attitude

One interesting possibility for succession is employee ownership. This certainly isn't for every company, but employee stock ownership plans (ESOPs) can both reward employees now and set the foundation for future sale.

You cannot start this type of arrangement simply by handing over stock in the company. You must lay the groundwork for employee ownership.

To do so, you must help your employees to recognize their impact on the business, to feel a sense of ownership in it. You can start by creating a culture of respect and openness. This might involve sharing information, such as goal-setting procedures and initiatives, some revenue and expense figures, and even long-term expansion plans.

The goal is to create team-based objectives that call upon the creativity and ambition of everyone on staff; and running the business with honesty and integrity. Teamwork, communication and participatory meetings can go a long way toward making this happen, sometimes even further than money or stock certificates.

But not always. What happens when you want to do something "special" for employees who display all the characteristics of ownership except the financial tie-in that stock offers? Deciding if offering stock to employees is the most desirable course of action requires research and footwork.

The decision to assign employee stock should proceed from an existing pattern of positive, professional and growth-oriented behavior – it's not something you do as an attempt to change behavior. The best candidates for stock ownership are usually the employees who have already proven that they want to grow the company. Cultivation of an ownership attitude and culture must begin long before you start thinking about giving away pieces of the business.

Considerations of distributing stock

Most business owners are jealously possessive of their companies – from the financial inner workings to the color of the curtains. So the prospect of shared responsibility and accountability can be frightening. There is a great deal of trust involved. Aside from the emotional impact of the decision, there are a number of logistical items to consider:

• How much of your company are you willing to give away?

• Would you rather do a one-time offering, or set up a defined contribution plan?

• Stock ownership comes with fiscal responsibilities. What happens if you want to approach a lender for a future business loan? Will other stockholders be willing to assume that risk?

• What if an employee or group of employees who hold a considerable amount of stock decide to leave the company?

• What if, due to unforeseen circumstances, you just want the stock back? What is involved in reclaiming shares?

• Do you need to incorporate the company before assigning stock to employees?

- Will you be able to deal objectively with minority partners? How much is their opinion worth, both legally and ethically?

- Does the company have a significant growth opportunity in the coming years? Will all stockholders derive value from this growth?

- Who will manage the process (if it's a one-time assignment) or the program (if you set up a defined contribution plan)?

- What are the Internal Revenue Service (IRS) reporting requirements for maintaining your stock distribution program?

As you can see, there is a lot of due diligence involved in setting up an employee ownership plan, and a certain amount of oversight is necessary to maintain it. The ultimate measure of whether to pursue such a program will be how well you have planned (or are willing to plan) for the future.

An ownership state of mind

Training employees for ownership may be one of the best things you can do for them and for your business. A vision of what ownership is really like will probably create a greater sense of respect for the position in the minds of employees.

There are major advantages in communicating business information to key staff. The amount and kind of information you share is a matter of individual choice, but shared information must focus employees on the promise of the business, and their potential as an integral part of it.

You needn't fully open the financials to employees, or involve them in all decisions – but they will need more than a rudimentary idea of how the business works. Otherwise, they will fill in the blanks with their own ideas, which may not coincide with yours. Further, the most effective input comes from people who know what they're talking about.

What can sharing information do for your company?

- **It helps employees contribute effectively to fiscal (and other) growth.** If employees don't know how a profit-and-loss statement works, or what a cash-flow plan looks like, they have no concept of how expenses impact the bottom line. If they don't know how much time and effort goes into developing a marketing agenda, they have no idea of the wastefulness of not following it.

- **It instills accountability for actions and habits.** Squelching inappropriate behavior becomes as easy as asking, "Would you do that if it were your business?" (Team members will certainly hold one another accountable when the business belongs to everyone!)

- **It enables the business to function without you (and that's your ultimate goal).** Once employees are clued in to its operations, they can, in effect, take ownership of the company. This may translate into a new respect for resources, improved customer care, higher productivity and/or an increased focus on education.

GOOD TO KNOW!

1. Start training key employees to help carry the torch.

2. Consider an Employee Stock Ownership Plan (ESOP).

3. Goodwill will only take you so far; proven systems and a vibrant culture are what make a business attractive to buyers.

ESOP options

Employee ownership programs can be broadly categorized according to three basic approaches. Each offers benefits and operates according to different rules, so it makes sense to explore them all before making any decisions. The choice you make should be based on a combination of factors such as the company's key objectives and goals; business and employee characteristics; and what employees want in long-term and short-term incentives. Additionally, there are, of course, always issues of time, effort and funding.

The three categories listed here require varying degrees of management, and levels of initial fiscal investment. The three program approaches to consider are:

• Performance-based plans

• Broad-based plans

• Leveraged employee stock ownership plans (ESOPs)

Performance-based plans live up to their name by offering managerial discretion over how, to whom, and in what amounts stock awards will be distributed. Performance-based plans include stock bonus awards (both restrictive and non-restrictive); direct stock purchase offers; stock options; and simulated equity (including "phantom stock" and stock-appreciation rights). These plans can be customized for individual team members or the team as a whole. You may wish to have a vesting schedule, so that an award's full value is not realized for several years. Non-restrictive stock bonus awards, in particular, can play an important supplementary role in your bonus system.

Broad-based plans are designed for distributing equity across a wide cross-section of employees. They include Section 423 Stock Purchase Plans; broad-based employee stock option plans; and non-leveraged employee stock ownership plans. Broad-based ownership plans are governed by fairly strict guidelines, and they may not be performance-based or customized for individual team members. Usually, if you implement one of these plans, all employees must be included.

Leveraged employee stock ownership plans may be used to help the business meet certain financial goals through employee ownership. Through a leveraged ESOP, a business can finance company stock purchases on behalf of employees and repay the debt with future earnings. As the loan is repaid, stock is gradually released to employee accounts according to a pre-determined formula, usually based on earnings. Employees may take distributions from their accounts when they leave the business.

No matter which program you feel best fits your company, there will be certain common-sense considerations, such as vesting schedules, restrictions and allocation formulas.

The driving forces behind a solid majority of employee ownership plans are employee- and owner-focused: About half are used to provide a "market" for departing owners of profitable, closely held businesses; most of the other half function as supplemental employee benefit plans. Both of these uses are important, because they can help resolve two specific key issues:

- finding creative, relatively inexpensive ways of restructuring (or instituting) employee retention and benefit options.

- enabling owners to assess the value of a business – as well as find a market, secure a buyer and know the business is in good hands. You could call it "business succession planning."

For many, selling to employees gradually is more appealing than trying to put a price tag on fixtures, equipment and square footage, and then attracting a lump-sum buyer. In addition to other tangible benefits such as increased productivity and tax benefits, employee ownership plans bring intrinsic value to the table in the form of increased loyalty and a culture of improved teamwork. The theory is that everyone with an ownership stake in a business will help it succeed. But you have to get started right.

Early stage items to be aware of

No matter how long or how well you plan, experience is always the best teacher. There are many nuances and little-known facts that will only become apparent once your program is in place. Here are a few things to be aware of at the outset:

- **Financial consequences are unavoidable.** Transactions between shareholders and employees must be reflected in the financial statements.

- **Reacquiring stock when an employee leaves can be a hassle.** It's considered a distribution, and you can't have a distribution unless you have retained earnings. Does your company have retained earnings? While it's definitely a good idea to incorporate a buy-out clause in any stock award or program, the business must be able to honor it when the time comes.

- **Price (value) determinations on stock are important.** But they are often difficult to ascertain in small, private companies.

- **You may need to authorize preferred stock.** This will come in handy if you need to raise capital later. Preferred stock commands a higher price than common stock, which can be reserved for employee distributions.

- **Employee distributions should match their positions in the business.** Many enthusiastic owners offer large grants to employees early, which restricts their ability to further award them later, or to adequately award newer employees.

Many owners are understandably reluctant to issue stock to employees at all. But it can be an effective method of raising outside cash and motivating employees – as long as it's done judiciously.

Here is a glossary of terms you need to know about employee ownership:

- **Broad-based stock option plans:** enable a broad base of employees to acquire shares on option.

- **Direct stock purchase offer/plan:** an offer made to employees to purchase a stated number of shares of stock.

- **Employee stock ownership plan (ESOP):** A non-leveraged ESOP is similar to a deferred profit-sharing plan, in that a company makes contributions to the ESOP trust each year on behalf of employees. These contributions are invested primarily in company stock and then allocated to employee accounts. A leveraged ESOP can borrow money to purchase employer securities (stock) for ESOP participants. While funds can be borrowed directly from the sponsoring corporation, usually a bank or other qualified lender loans money to the ESOP.

- **Exercise:** purchase of stock pursuant to an option.

- **Exercise price:** price stated in option for purchase of shares.

- **Fair market value (FMV):** the price a buyer would be willing to pay for a share of stock.

- **Non-restrictive stock bonus:** usually given to key employees for achieving financial or strategic goals; similar to a cash bonus, except it's in stock rather than cash.

- **Phantom stock:** units of value corresponding to an equivalent number of shares of stock granted to an employee for a specified period of time. At maturity, the employee is generally compensated in cash in an amount based on the increased value of the phantom stock. (Also see "simulated equity.")

- **Restrictive stock award:** subject to conditions (e.g., vesting or specific performance requirements) before realizing its full benefit.

- **Section 423 Stock Purchase Plan:** gives employees the chance to purchase company stock through payroll deductions at a discount from fair market value.

- **Simulated equity:** deferred compensation/incentives compensation tool that provides employees the economic benefits of stock ownership without the employee having to purchase stock or the corporation having to transfer actual ownership of the stock.

- **Stock appreciation right (SAR):** the right to receive the appreciation value of a certain number of shares of company stock over a specified period of time, typically paid in cash. (Also see "simulated equity.")

- **Stock option:** a right to buy a stated number of shares of stock, for a stated period of time, at a stated price.

- **Transferable stock option (TSO):** an option that may be transferred from an employee to a non-employee third party.

What's the value?

A commonly asked question from business owners is: What is my business worth? It usually arises when they are ready to sell, and need an easily determined asking price. But it will also arise when you want to introduce a stock-ownership program. An ESOP requires an impartial, professional value assessment. Business owners are well-advised to get one at the outset of any stock-compensation program. Otherwise, employees don't know what they're getting and you don't know what you're giving. It's a crucial point to consider no matter what your exit strategy.

Business appraisers usually rely upon the concept of fair market value (FMV) when assessing what a business is worth. This is generally the price a willing buyer would pay a willing seller for an asset when both buyer and seller are knowledgeable about the asset and the market for such assets, and neither buyer nor seller is under compulsion to transact.

FMV is determined using a number of indicators, including physical assets, goodwill, and the ability to generate revenue, earnings and cash flow. (Goodwill is an important intangible asset, but should not be overstated.)

There are a number of ways to value a company, such as the "asset approach" and "discounted cash flow approach." One of the most common ways is a formula approach based on a multiple of revenues (usually a ratio of 1.5). This is simple to calculate, but you must make certain that the quirks of the market and any one-time gains or losses are accounted for in the calculation.

Prepping your company for sale

The purpose of business, as most entrepreneurs and their employees know, is to make money. The prospect of a nice paycheck, and the autonomy to determine how it's built, are two of the greatest ownership temptations – for both current and potential owners.

You should be running your business so that it will retain its value after you leave. This means the business must be able to stand on its own, that the systems are strong enough to survive without you. Systemic, repeatable service and growth procedures will ensure that you have more to bargain with than used fixtures and equipment.

So, it's time. You want to sell your business and have decided that an outright sale is the way to go. You have an idea for what you think it's worth. Just as you'd have to hire an appraiser when selling your home, you need to have an independent opinion of what your business is worth. Remember, your business ultimately is only worth what someone is willing to pay. That is influenced by many factors. Just as in the house-buying market, everything from location to the economic climate factors in.

There are many valuation models; we'll consider four of the most common here:

• **Market-based valuation:** The asking price is based on the sales prices of similar businesses in the area and/or industry (usually using industry-average sales figures as a multiplier). This isn't the most comprehensive method – but it's fast, simple and relatively inexpensive. Plus, it clicks with buyers.

• **Asset-based valuation:** This process takes into account the "book" value and the "liquidation" value of a business, though they usually are not the only factors that determine an asking price. This type of valuation appraises the value of a company's assets as the sum of all fixed assets and equipment; improvements in the physical location; inventory; and the owner's discretionary cash for one year.

• **Capitalization of income:** This method focuses on cash flow and return on investment (ROI). It also takes into account important intangibles such as the workforce, industry trends, sales projections, market position, and the business's maturity. This method yields a company value based on multiples of earnings. If earnings and sales figures are stable, it's a pretty good technique. However, it doesn't indicate specific areas that may need improvement.

• **Earnings-based valuation:** This process takes into account the business's historical finances, including debt payments, cash flows (past, present and projected), and revenues.

An appraiser or broker will often combine an earnings-based valuation with an asset-based valuation in order to complete a more accurate appraisal. For many small businesses, 3 to 4 times their annual net profit is close to their market worth.

1. Get your exit strategy on paper now.
2. Consult an attorney and financial planner for assistance.
3. Work to create a strong company that can survive without your involvement.

So, for example, if your business generated $1.5 million in revenues with a 10% net profit, it could feasibly hit the market at $450,000-$600,000. But there's a caveat:

The multiple you can realistically ask for varies according to its history, the state of the industry, the market, your management structure, proprietary products, your niche position, growth rate and size, and so on.

Additionally, a new owner may be more passively involved than you have been.

Let's continue our example: If the business generates $1.5 million per year, but you have always managed it, a new owner may then have to hire a manager. Assuming the manager is compensated $50,000 per year, the new base for your 3 to 4 multiple is reduced.

You may want to be able to show that your involvement in the business as a service provider is not being overstated or understated. To help you determine this, you may wish to use an "owner's benefits chart," such as the one featured on page 396.

Owner's Benefits	2010	2011	2012
Salon Service Sales			
Owners Service Sales			
Owners % of Total Service			
Owner's W2			
Life Insurance			
Disability Ins.			
Health Ins.			
Internet			
Misc. Phone			
Misc. Office			
IRA Match			
Bonus			
Cell Phones			
Family on Staff			
Payroll Taxes Salon Portion			
Owner Education			
Total Benefits	$	$	$
Net Profit			
Depreciation			
W2			
Fringe Benefits			
Adjusted Net Income	$	$	$

This will help show how much of the business you're personally responsible for. It's a great way to help prospective owners see if "you" are the business or if it can easily and profitably succeed without you.

What about goodwill?

Goodwill is anything above the fair market value (FMV) of a company's tangible assets. It may include rights to intellectual property (such as trademarks and copyrights), customer lists or non-compete agreements.

It also includes the reputation, customer relationships, brand identity and the working environment that a business has built. It is difficult to place a monetary value on goodwill, even for accountants and other professionals.

Goodwill is important when buying or selling a business, so its estimated value must be accurate. Underestimating your company's goodwill position may prevent you from receiving its full value at sale; overestimating it may cause potential buyers to walk away. Utilize an accountant or business appraiser to help you determine what is fair.

Do I really need outside help?

It may be tempting to handle all the details yourself to save money. This can be short-sighted. Business-valuation professionals provide unbiased opinions of a company's value. In other words, they make sure the price is right when an owner is ready to divest himself or herself of all or a portion of the business. An expert appraisal can save time, money and stress by ensuring your goals are realistic from the outset.

Additionally, the objectivity of a third-party valuation will be crucial if others examine the results. For example: An appraisal may be examined by the IRS to determine if gift or estate taxes are due on a transaction, or by a judge if you are dissolving a partnership. No matter the purpose, however, the result should be a comprehensive statement of your company's worth.

You either choose to hire an individual or a full-service firm to conduct a business appraisal. Full-service firms should have access to information on current appraisal and legislative requirements, as well as the resources to properly value all the business's assets.

Individual appraisers should belong to a professional association such as the American Society of Appraisers (www.appraisers.org).

Broker info

The main reason to use a business broker is protection of your bottom line. Fundamentally, they are similar to residential real-estate brokers: Using one will usually result in more potential buyers, which will generate more competition in bidding. A business broker will also know how to identify the right buyer, one who truly understands the value of your business, so you will leave the transaction confident that you got the best price and terms.

Depending on your state, a broker may represent the seller, buyer, both or even the transaction itself. Visit the International Business Brokers' Association website (www.ibba.org) for more information.

What you need to sell

If the purpose of obtaining a business valuation is to determine whether your company is saleable, then you must ask yourself a very important question before you even get started: Why do you want to sell? Believe it or not, your reason may raise red flags with prospective buyers.

Being ready to retire or move on to other things will likely not cause a second thought. If the business is in trouble, however, you need to try to fix the problems before putting it on the block. (For what it's worth, if you fix the problems, you may decide not to sell.)

A business valuation is critical to any exit strategy. Reporting requirements for small businesses have many gray areas, but keeping good records can ensure that the numbers mean what you think they do. It will also ensure that a buyer sees the company's consistency and potential.

A thorough business profile will include the following information:

- a history and nature of the business
- a financial overview (5 years)
- the company's operational structure

- its management and employees
- its competitive situation
- industry and market expectations
- the company's strategies and projections
- financial statements showing the company's performance over the past six months
- Schedule C and related tax forms for the past three years
- a comprehensive list of assets, including equipment, fixtures, office furniture and other tangibles. (Include your original purchase cost, accumulated depreciation, and any repairs or upgrades that have increased their value.)
- an inventory of supplies and their cost
- a list of all contracts, and their terms and expiration dates
- a list of all notes payable and their outstanding balances
- a list of accounts receivable
- a comprehensive list of intangible assets such as trademarks, copyrights, the business name

It can take awhile

Most professionals agree that a business cannot be prepared for sale overnight. In fact, it can take up to two years to optimally position the business. Very little of that time is required to gather and organize existing documents, so what takes so long?

The most important part of positioning a business for sale is extricating the owner from its day-to-day operations. This situation is prevalent throughout the small business world – yet obtaining the best selling price for the business usually requires the owner's "ouster."

Why? The business needs to run smoothly without the owner's presence. A buyer doesn't want to feel that the company will fall apart within a few months of the owner's departure.

The actual sales transaction may be the easy end of the deal. The systems that drive the business are some of its most valuable intangible assets. You will need to codify any company policies and procedures that exist only as unwritten rules. (This is a good idea even if you aren't considering selling the business.)

For example: If your customer service mandate is to treat clients "like royalty" – it's time to define royalty, because it could mean something different to every employee. These newly written policies become an addition to your existing employee handbook, position statements and operations manual.

The final sales price of a business will ultimately depend on how badly the buyer wants to buy and how badly the seller wants to sell. A broker can help you meet in the middle, but the buyer and seller must both be willing and excited about the transaction.

There is no cookie-cutter approach to determining a company's value. Each valuation is specific to the business being examined. If you want an accurate, fair appraisal, you'll need two things: complete honesty and a business broker or appraiser. A business appraisal requires accurate, complete financial statements – preferably five years' worth – including balance sheets, income statements, and sources and uses of funds.

An appraiser may also evaluate real estate and equipment holdings, and analyze local and national conditions that may affect the business. (e.g., Are local market conditions favorable for growth? Will the current national recession impact demand for luxury services? Will a recovery increase demand?) The entire process may take a few months.

The buyer does have the final word on whether a sale takes place. The benefit of hiring a business broker to evaluate a company's fiscal fitness is that he or she can determine a fair market value for the business – without the emotional baggage that a lot of owners who have invested time, energy and resources in a small business feel. They won't let you over- or under-value the business.

Only when you know what you have can you decide what to do with it. Otherwise, business owners run the risk of having others make the decision for them, which puts them at a serious disadvantage during any kind of planning or negotiations.

Constructing your exit plan

Remember, the earlier you have an exit plan in place, the better. And despite the way it may feel, developing an exit strategy is not a capitulation to, or an acknowledgement of, impending doom or failure; it's a wise business move.

An exit strategy affects how you grow the business. In fact, it should affect every decision you make, and impact everything you do. Think of it this way: Devising an exit strategy is about maximizing its value at the time (whenever it is) that you plan to get out.

For example: Businesses are commonly sold to employees, partners or competitors. Chances are, the buyer already has a good idea of how they want the business to run, whether it stays where it is or is incorporated into another existing business. Either way, a primary focus for the seller is to build value into the company by growing and securing the client list. You will also need to shore up your systems.

An exit strategy should help an owner bring his or her tenure with a business to a satisfying end. Be proactive and ensure that your strategy best serves you and your company.

- Consider your existing business plan. Does it tie into your personal objectives? An exit strategy must exist within the reality of what the business can accomplish.

- Realize that getting out is usually more difficult than getting in. You cannot assume there will be a buyer, that you will be offered a reasonable price, or that your children will recognize the true value of the company. These assumptions are the ones that will leave you "stuck" – at a time when your energy and enthusiasm for the business may already be waning.

Are you ready to go?

Here's a possibly sobering question: Would you buy your company as it stands today? If not, why not? What can you do to make it better?

Start with your business model. Make sure it covers every aspect of your company and is easily replicated without your involvement. Then, fill in these areas, as needed:

- Strong financials are key, as are high rates of productivity and profitability. Debt should be minimal, if at all.
- Staff and guest retention – how high are your numbers?
- Business structure and leadership team should be in place so that a new owner can come in and work within the existing structure.
- There should be a strong company brand with both your culture and marketing supporting the same message.
- Community involvement should be significant and the company should be recognized as an ethical business.
- Current owner should be a leader and not a needed service provider.
- Staff is educated on how to reach company goals and feel as though they can flourish without your involvement in the business.
- Multiple layers of leaders are developed within the company, including leadership with each key area of the business.

- A solid training program should be in place, with clear growth paths.
- Guest services should be top-notch.
- The business shouldn't appear as though it's up for sale. No-compromise excellence should be practiced throughout the company, every day.
- Take action now!

My personal goals for
Exit Strategy:

Index